LF

D0893609

CHINA EYES JAPAN

CHINA EYES JAPAN

Allen S. Whiting

University of California Press
Berkeley • Los Angeles • London

ALBRIGHT COLLEGE LIBRARY

University of California Press
Berkeley and Los Angeles, California

University of California Press, Ltd.
London, England

© 1989 by
The Regents of the University of California

Library of Congress Cataloging-in-Publication Data

Whiting, Allen Suess, 1926–
  China eyes Japan / Allen S. Whiting.
    p.   cm.
  Bibliography: p.
  Includes index.
  ISBN 0-520-06511-5 (alk. paper)
    1. China—Foreign relations—Japan. 2. Japan—Foreign
relations—China. 3. China—Foreign relations—1976–
I. Title.
DS740.5.J3W48   1989
327.51052—dc19   88-38067
                                                       CIP

Printed in the United States of America

1   2   3   4   5   6   7   8   9

327.51052
W 598c

226140

32.50

To David

Contents

Acknowledgments

According to the agreed rules of our discussions and interviews, my indebtedness to several dozen Chinese and Japanese officials, scholars, journalists, business persons, and students must be unspecified. The notes, however, provide ample testimony to their invaluable contribution, without which this study would be a shadow of its present self.

I am grateful for the generous support rendered by the University of Arizona, which awarded me a Research Professorship for the fall semester in 1985, and by the Committee on Scholarly Communication with the People's Republic of China, which funded my two-month research trip there in July–August 1986. The Contemporary China Center at the Research School of Pacific Studies, Australian National University, provided office facilities and research assistance during the summer of 1985.

The Chinese Academy of Social Sciences kindly sponsored my research in China and gave special help in arranging travel and contacts in various cities. Its Institute of Japanese Studies in Beijing acted as official host. Members of the Institute of World Economics and Politics, the Institute of Soviet and East European Studies, the Institute of International Relations, the China Institute of Contemporary International Relations, the Beijing Institute of International Strategic Studies, the Ministry of Foreign Affairs, and the Ministry of Foreign Economic Relations and Trade gave generously of their time and knowledge.

The editors of *Renmin Ribao*, *Liaowang*, *Shijie Zhishi*, and *Zhongguo Qingnian Bao* in Beijing, *Wen Wei Bao* and *Jiefang Ribao* in Shanghai, and *Nanfang Ribao* in Guangzhou were all most cooperative and patient with my questions.

Discussions were also kindly arranged by the Siberian Research Institute of the Heilongjiang Academy of Social Sciences in Harbin, the Jilin Academy of Social Sciences and the Institute of Korean Studies in Changchun, the Dalian Institute of International Relations and the International Relations and Social Science Association of Dalian, the Institute of Japanese Studies in the Tianjin Academy of Social Sciences and Nankai University in Tianjin, the Shanghai Institute for International Studies and the World Economy Institute in the Shanghai Academy of Social Science, Fudan University, the World Economy Research Institute in the Jiangsu Academy of Social Sciences, Wuhan University, and Hubei Teachers College in Wuhan, and the Guangdong Academy of Social Sciences.

In Japan I was fortunate during June and October 1986 to have full cooperation from the Ministry of Foreign Affairs, the Japanese Defense Agency, the National Defense College, the Japan External Trade Organization, members of the Commission for Sino-Japanese Friendship in the Twenty-first Century, the Research Institute for Peace and Security, Kazan Kai, Keio University, and correspondents from Kyodo, *Mainichi, Nikkei Business*, and Xinhua. Specialists in Marubeni Corporation and Japan-China Oil Development Corporation were also helpful.

I cannot stress too greatly the absence of any responsibility of the foregoing institutes and the individuals therein for whatever errors and misconceptions follow. Although I conscientiously tried to record their words and interpret their feelings, misperception and miscommunication are inevitable in human discourse, especially when it occurs across cultures and languages. The use of paraphrase, summary, and generalization can compound the chance of error. Where such instances arise in the book, I apologize to my sources and look forward to their corrective comments.

Charles Hedtke provided a critical review of the early chapters and Ju-yen Teng offered very insightful comments on a first draft that greatly improved the revision. My research assistants, Shih-kuang Chien and Kristina Sie Mao, went beyond the call of duty in offering substantive suggestions as well as help in locating and translating various materials.

I would like to express my appreciation for the speed, support, and spirit exemplified by the University of California Press staff, including Sheila Levine, Betsey Scheiner, Jay Plano, and Kate Gross.

The standard acknowledgment to one's spouse cannot do justice in this case. Alice C. Whiting not only broke through my resistance to the word processor. She also broke through the many obstacles, most of which I inadvertently created, in its utilization over the months of drafting and revising. Her patient ability to cope with my tension as well as the machine's obstructionism quite literally made this book possible.

1

Introduction

THE PROBLEM DEFINED

In 1984 Tokyo and Beijing announced the formation of the Commission for Sino-Japanese Friendship in the Twenty-first Century. Hu Yaobang, general secretary of the Chinese Communist party, and Nakasone Yasuhiro, prime minister of Japan, lent their prestige to this commission and their personal interactions were symbolic of its goals. Developments seemed promising for the prognosis of Chae-jin Lee, one of the foremost specialists on this relationship:

> As long as the Chinese can sustain a stable domestic political basis for their four modernizations policy and can improve their bureaucratic and managerial performance, the normalization of economic and diplomatic relations between China and Japan suggests that both will be able to learn from their past achievements and mistakes and to work out a mature and viable system of mutually beneficial economic cooperation in the years to come. It is also conceivable that the experiences of both countries will move them closer together in terms of their economic and political policies in Asia and elsewhere.[1]

This positive prognosis, together with high-level support for Sino-Japanese "friendship," challenged the dominant Chinese image of its smaller neighbor that had been derived from fifty years of Japanese military aggression and territorial annexation, beginning with China's defeat in 1895 and ending with Japan's surrender in 1945.

Japan's rapid modernization in the latter half of the nineteenth century had been a model for many Chinese reformers and revolutionaries, some of whom studied in Japan before and after World War I. But Tokyo's seizure of the northeast (Manchuria) in 1931–32 and its brutal invasion of 1937–45, with its attendant atrocities, left bitter memories throughout the populace. The establishment of the People's Republic of China (PRC) in 1949 did not win Japanese diplomatic recognition because American policy forced Tokyo's ties to remain with the defeated Chiang Kai-shek regime

1

on Taiwan. This, together with the emergence of American military bases in Japan in support of an American-Japanese mutual security treaty, gave credence to Chinese communist propaganda attacks against "Japanese militarism and monopoly capitalism." For the next twenty years Japanese villains populated novels, films, and plays as the scourge of recent history. In addition, Japan's potential threat loomed large in official Chinese statements. Thus, the Sino-Soviet treaty of February 14, 1950, explicitly committed the signatories to mutual assistance in the event of attack by "Japan or any states allied with her." While this language clearly targeted the United States by implication, subsequent utterances did not neglect to make specific reference to Japan. For example, on August 1, 1971, a top Chinese military commander celebrated Red Army day with a dire warning against the threat of revived Japanese militarism.

Suddenly these themes became muted. In the aftermath of Henry Kissinger's secret trip to Beijing in July 1971, anti-Japanese propaganda declined. Washington's move toward Beijing loosened Tokyo's ties with Taiwan. After President Richard Nixon's historic meeting with Mao Zedong in February 1972, negotiations between Beijing and Tokyo quickly led to the reestablishment of diplomatic relations that September. Trade and travel between the two capitals grew yearly. The Sino-Japanese Treaty of Peace and Friendship in August 1978 further improved relations and made possible Deng Xiaoping's triumphal tour of Japan that fall.

This rapid change in relations caused concern in Soviet analyses and optimism in American thinking at the official level. In both Moscow and Washington, the prospect of a Sino-Japanese-American entente directed against "the polar bear in the north" (to use Deng's colorful allusion) seemed auspicious. Academic specialists, however, remained skeptical. This was exemplified by Chalmers Johnson, who observed that "China and Japan have been interacting with each other and misunderstanding each other for a century. . . . There is little evidence that either country understands the other any better than it did in the past." Although he notes that "well-educated Chinese and Japanese can learn each other's language rather easily," he adds that "it is doubtful whether any two people in the twentieth century have approached each other with more profoundly misleading stereotypes."[2]

Johnson's skepticism raised the basic question underlying this study: Can the Chinese leadership overcome its negative image of Japan, derived from past conflict, in order to pursue a positive relationship based on its national interests? Or will Beijing's perceptions and reactions remain conditioned by, if not captive to, the historical heritage of humiliation and hatred? To what extent do "profoundly misleading stereotypes" continue to determine the Chinese view of Japan?

Hu Yaobang's willingness to commit his political prestige to this relationship challenged me to monitor subsequent developments. Could friendship with Japan be sold to the Chinese people through official campaigns and management of the media? Beijing's ability to reverse policy and, presumably, change popular perceptions was amply demonstrated in moving from alliance to confrontation with the Soviet Union and from confrontation to alignment with the United States. Perhaps Deng's pragmatism, captured in his celebrated aphorism "It makes no difference whether the cat is black or white as long as it catches mice," would lead to a close relationship with the Japanese based on economic complementarity and parallel strategic interests. This in turn could transform Chinese attitudes and behavior toward their former enemy. If so, the implications go far beyond Sino-Japanese relations, potentially affecting the global balance of power in ways that are feared in Moscow and hoped for in Washington.

Several commonplace assumptions support this scenario. Many outside observers take for granted that communist regimes are able to control both policy and public opinion. This is particularly true with respect to China, where the appearance of mass conformity with an official line had been in evidence throughout the various campaigns of the 1950s as well as Mao Zedong's nihilistic Cultural Revolution of the 1960s. Put crudely, these observers assume that whatever the official line is, the population will act accordingly, especially if the subject does not affect their immediate concerns, as is the case with foreign policy. Coupled with this is the assumption that governmental behavior is determined by the rational pursuit of an identifiable national interest. Seen at a distance, the complex, multilayered bureaucracy, which is subject to divergent domestic influences, becomes a monolithic entity subsumed under the convenient national caption of "China" or its capital, "Beijing," a usage that I also employ, but without the attendant implications. This practice is frequently carried to the point of reification in such references as "China said" or, worse, "China believed" or "China perceived." Such references communicate the image of a wholly rational and purposeful policy process. In reality, only in time of extreme crisis, when a country's security is seen as literally endangered, does a common agreement on the national interest and the urgency of the moment impel competing political figures and organizations to unite behind a single goal or policy.

Given these assumptions, it follows that Chinese policy toward Japan during the 1980s should have been fundamentally positive and favorable to a steadily strengthened relationship, both because of the larger Sino-American relationship within which the Washington-Tokyo alliance was a part and because of the Chinese interest in Japan itself. The Chinese interest in Japan includes the acquisition of Japanese capital through investment and loans as well as the acquisition of Japanese technology through trade and investment. Less tangible and explicit, but no less important, is China's strategic interest in Japan's contribution to the military balance in East Asia to offset the rapid and continuing growth of Soviet power throughout the region.

This scenario might not necessarily unfold in a wholly smooth and harmonious fashion. Three obstacles could be expected. The first and foremost obstacle would be residual resentment against Japan as a past predator. Mao Zedong and Zhou Enlai foreswore reparations in 1972, as had Chiang Kai-shek immediately after World War II, so officially there were no scores to be settled. But Chinese sensitivity to Japanese atonement for the past, or the absence thereof, had already raised a brief problem in 1972 and might remain relevant. The second obstacle would be the well-known Chinese proclivity for addressing foreign relations in terms of explicit principles before compromising these in practice. This tendency had been dramatically, if confusingly, manifest in addressing the Taiwan problem and Sino-American relations at various points over the years 1955–72. A third obstacle would be the Chinese tendency to bargain hard by imposing a sense of guilt and the burden of concession on the opposite party. This might have the effect of raising tensions in Sino-Japanese relations where none actually existed. Assuming, however, that basic Chinese interests pointed toward the policy of improving relations with Japan, these obstacles would be overcome in time as both sides learned how to cope with whatever untoward consequences might result from their interaction. This is the prognosis suggested by Chae-jin Lee.

One such learning situation arose in 1982, perhaps in part prompting the formation of the Commission for Friendship in the Twenty-first Century. We will examine the details subsequently. Here it suffices to note that Japanese reporters found that the officially approved Japanese high school textbooks had softened the references to past aggression in Asia in general and China in particular, including the infamous Nanjing Massacre of December 1937. Beijing protested, as did other governments, unleashing a month-long domestic media campaign in China devoted to the suffering caused by the Japanese invasion and the danger of revived Japanese militarism. Tokyo, after initial hesitation, apologized and promised that the textbooks would be corrected and no future provocations permitted. This facilitated Prime Minister Suzuki Zenkō's visit to China that fall, but the virulence of the earlier domestic media campaign suggested that the historical heritage of the wartime experience was a volatile issue. In addition, it raised the question of what images and expectations of Japan lay behind the media reaction. This in turn raised the related question of the likely impact of media coverage on younger generations that lacked any first-hand knowledge of the war except what had been transmitted by family and relatives. In short, how much would the future Chinese view of Japan remain hostage to the past? Beijing "learned" in 1982 that it could pressure Tokyo into compliance, a lesson that became costly in 1985.

This became a major issue again in September 1985 when university students in Beijing and elsewhere staged anti-Japanese demonstrations. Although the details will concern us later, an initial summary is relevant here. August 1985 was the fortieth anniversary of Japan's surrender in World War II. As such the month evoked commemorative meetings worldwide, among both the victors and the vanquished. In Japan, Prime Minister Nakasone marked the event by attending in his official capacity a memorial ceremony at the Yasukuni Shrine in Tokyo, which, among other things, honors all Japanese soldiers killed in war. His predecessors had only gone "unofficially" because of the sensitivity at home and abroad over the fact that the shrine includes the name cards of fourteen Japanese officers sentenced to death by the Tokyo War Crimes Trial after World War II.

The reaction to Nakasone's visit was strong throughout Asia, but nowhere more so than in Beijing, where student posters and shouted slogans attacked Japanese aggression, Nakasone, and "the second invasion" or, more explicitly, "the economic invasion." The last phrase referred to Japan's preeminence in Chinese foreign trade, with one-fourth of total imports. Japan's economic position in China was evident in the huge billboard advertisements in major cities, the ubiquitous Japanese-made taxicabs, and the spread of consumer products, such as television sets, washing machines, and tape recorders. This economic penetration of China was accompanied by the growing presence of Japanese businessmen, who far outnumbered and outdistanced their European and American competitors.

Foreign reporters and observers speculated widely on the causes of these demonstrations, which were without precedent in post-Mao China. Some attributed them to official encouragement aimed at putting pressure on Japan to provide better economic relations by means of improved terms of trade (China's $5 billion foreign trade deficit with Japan was being publicly blamed on unfair obstacles to the Japanese market). Others thought the students used Japan as a safe surrogate target for attacking the government on other matters such as the poor quality of food and housing on campus, the privileged position of officials' sons and daughters, both at the university and afterward in job assignments, bureaucratic obstructionism, and corruption. Still others attributed the demonstrations to the factional manipulation of student grievances designed to embarrass Deng and Hu on the question of Japan in the context of a Central Committee meeting and party conference scheduled at that time in Beijing.

Few observers accepted the contention that the students acted spontaneously on the basis of genuine anti-Japanese sentiments. Skepticism on both points seems logical. It would be impossible for any such event to occur without someone in authority learning of the preparations in advance; therefore, if it had not been prevented, it must have been acquiesced in, if not quietly encouraged. Moreover, because the regime's declared policy was to promote closer economic relations with Japan, leading ultimately to "friendship," the real purpose of the protests must have been something other than what was uttered.

Chinese officials hastened to reassure the Japanese that indeed the students were acting spontaneously and, although understandably angered by Nakasone's visit to the Yasukuni Shrine, that they were "confused." Prominent authorities then visited the campuses to meet with students, ostensibly engaging in a corrective dialogue and forestalling demonstrations that were expected later that fall. These activities, however, did not convince the skeptics in Japan and elsewhere, who saw them as part of a complicated maneuver to gain leverage against Tokyo. But in actuality, as my extensive interviews revealed the following year, the students were acting on their own deeply felt antagonism toward Japan.

This raised the 1982 question anew: what images and expectations of Japan exist among Chinese youth? From where are they derived? How do they relate the wartime past to the economic and political present and with what implications for the future? Perhaps the most intriguing question of all is the extent to which images and expectations extant in the official media shape and reinforce attitudes contrary to official policy. To the extent that this phenomenon exists, does it reflect ambivalence in official attitudes or division within officialdom?

Obviously these questions challenge the commonplace assumptions cited earlier and, in doing so, the optimistic scenario of how Sino-Japanese relations will unfold. Particularly in 1986–87, Beijing's handling of these relations became so querulous as to make these questions of immediate importance. Without attempting to explain or attribute motivation at this point, a brief summary illustrates this querulous behavior. One characteristic Chinese response to corrective action on the Japanese side is either to emphasize how much more remains to be done or to close on a negative note rather than to put a positive gloss on the issue in question. This was evident in 1986, for example, when a second textbook controversy arose and was settled with less furor, but won only weak approval in Beijing. Another recurring Chinese tactic is to repeatedly press an issue that is in abeyance pending later action or that Tokyo has insisted it is powerless to affect. A noteworthy instance of this concerns the disposition of a Chinese student dormitory in Kyoto that had been contested by representatives of Taiwan and Beijing in the Japanese courts for more than fifteen years, but which Beijing raised to major significance in 1987. A third aspect of Chinese behavior concerns official protests over private Japanese actions that are thought to be provocative. One such incident occurred in 1986 with the commemoration of Chiang Kai-shek's one hundredth birthday by a nongovernmental group. A more important variant on this theme is when the Chinese government brings pressure on the Japanese government to change the behavior of private Japanese entrepreneurs so that they increase their investment in long-term productive ventures with a high level of technology transfer, rather than investing in quick-return hotel and office construction enterprises. Needless to say, not only do these pressure tactics fail to accomplish their goals but, as is shown by Japanese public opinion polls and officials, they eventually arouse an irritated response.

Although none of these characteristics of Chinese rhetoric and behavior is of great importance in itself, cumulatively they have a negative effect on the Sino-Japanese relationship. This implicit tilt becomes particularly evident, both in China and in Japan, when it is explicitly associated with allegations of bad faith in observing past treaties and agreements and with express concern over the possible return of Japanese militarism. For Chinese audiences, the implications are ominous and, as we will see, are taken seriously by the younger generation as well as their elders. For the Japanese, the resultant question, although perhaps less central, is also troublesome: Is it possible to work out a solid relationship when the past remains so present in the Chinese consciousness? In short, will the Chinese part of this relationship evolve according to practical interest or preconceived image?

RESEARCH DESIGN

These questions and issues raise several research problems, the most serious of which is the lack of direct evidence on leadership policy making and perceptions in China. Negative themes in official statements and the mass media concerning Sino-Japanese relations might reflect any one of four factors: (1) the inevitable differences that arise between any two states, exacerbated in this case by the fact that these two former enemies are attempting a cooperative, but asymmetrical, relationship in which Japan, despite its defeat in the war, retains its dominant role; (2) simple misperceptions that are being reduced with time and experience on both sides; (3) calculated bargaining postures that target Japanese government and business; and (4) compulsive behavior, derived from basic emotions, responding to perceived provocations within the framework of a basically hostile image. The student demonstrations indicate that a fifth factor, public attitudes, should also be considered. As an additional complication, these factors are neither mutually exclusive nor is their relative importance empirically measurable.

The length and virulence of the 1982 media campaign against Japanese textbook revisionism offers a logical point of departure for examining the Chinese treatment of the past and its implications for the present and future. Authoritative publications, especially those aimed at youth, provide images that presumably cue domestic audiences on how to view Japan, wholly apart from what might be said publicly for the benefit of officials and businessmen in Japan, whether positive or negative. Such publications can prove doubly illuminating, on the one hand reflecting official opinion and on the other hand affecting popular perceptions. Being domestically directed these materials cannot be discounted as a calculated bargaining technique except at the most general level.

With the past record of Japanese aggression against China as reference, the publications and statements of 1982–87 can be compared for the way in which they handle this subject and their express or implied design on domestic attitudes. This five-year span of inquiry includes natural periods of attention to the past, such as the fortieth anniversary of the war's end in 1985 and the fiftieth anniversary of its beginning in 1987, as well as particular events such as the Yasukuni Shrine ceremonies and the textbook controversies. It also includes the removal of the ceiling on Japanese defense expenditures in 1987, a test of the Chinese response to the sensitive question of Japanese rearmament.

Comparing publications and official behavior over time within the context of specific Sino-Japanese economic and political interactions permits a preliminary assessment of the importance of the various factors previously mentioned. It can also illuminate the degree to which misperception, and possibly miscalculation, plagued the relationship. These two phenomena in turn can be evaluated for evidence of a learning curve in the way that the Chinese handle the Japanese relationship. The results should be useful for projecting future trends, depending on future Japanese behavior.

I have already challenged several commonplace assumptions about Chinese foreign policy by noting that publications and official statements do not necessarily reflect the private views of the leadership, that in a country as large as China, the capacity for official control over all media, including daily newspapers, magazines, books, and television, is limited, and that divergent policy factions exist and their differences are recurringly evident in the public press, whether express or implied. Having made these observations, however, it should also be noted that a general line of what is sanctioned and what is not with respect to foreign policy can readily be inferred from an overall conformity in sensitive areas, such as Sino-Soviet relations and press commentary on Japanese rearmament. The existence of this general line was confirmed in my private conversations with magazine and newspaper editors in Beijing, Shanghai, and Guangzhou. Because of this general line, it is necessary to use interviews and discussions to probe behind the public messages in order to determine the degree to which these messages reflect genuine beliefs and attitudes among selected groups that potentially are influential on, or influenced by, official policy.

With this general framework of inquiry, I first acquired and analyzed a wide range of Chinese publications on Japan issued in 1982 and thereafter. The beginning year was selected for several reasons beyond the fact that it was the year in which the textbook controversy occurred. Chae-jin Lee had already meticulously researched the earlier period in the relationship in his two books, *Japan Faces China: Political and Economic Relations in the Postwar Era* (Baltimore: Johns Hopkins University Press, 1976) and *China and Japan: New Economic Diplomacy* (Stanford: Hoover Institution, 1984). I also wanted to allow for an appropriate interval after the 1978 Treaty of Peace and Friendship to see how it had affected Chinese and Japanese images of each other. As Lee noted in his second volume, "It is clear that the emotionally charged Sino-Japanese love affair of the 1970s is over and that the Chinese and Japanese have reached the agonizing phase of groping for a more realistic, balanced, and productive partnership in the future."[3]

The publications selected fell readily into two categories: works of small circulation designed for elite consumption and mass-oriented pamphlets, books, magazines, and newspapers, including small picture-and-text booklets for very young children. The second category of publications had been of special value for my earlier pilot study on images of the United States in the Korean War as depicted in successive editions issued during the 1970s after President Nixon's visit. These two categories, in turn, were subdivided between those works primarily concerned with the past and those that focused mainly on current affairs. All were examined for their express or implied images of Japan as a society and the Japanese as a people, with special attention to any implications for the future that followed from the presentation.

I then spent June 1986 in Tokyo and July and August of that year in nine Chinese cities (Beijing, Harbin, Changchun, Dalian, Tianjin, Shanghai, Nanjing, Wuhan, and Guangzhou), gathering additional publications and, most important, interviewing officials, scholars, journalists, and persons engaged in economic interactions on both sides. The ground rules were the same throughout: I transcribed all the interviews on the spot, but there was no attribution to institutions or individuals in the final manuscript. I would only utilize direct quotations anonymously. Also I assumed that publication was unlikely for two years, by which time the sensitivity of the material would be sharply reduced.

My associations in Japan had grown incrementally over the years through earlier contact during my tenure in the U.S. Department of State (1961–66), as Deputy Principal Officer in the Hong Kong Consulate General (1966–68), and through my research on Siberian development and East Asia (1978–79). Former students also helped me in their professional and personal capacities. China officers in the Japanese foreign service, both retired and active, shared their attitudes and experiences, as did business persons. Their frank self-criticism revealed an awareness of Japanese mistakes and problems in developing the new relationship. One also sensed frustration, and at times, irritation, at the seeming inability to educate Chinese officialdom on the nature of a pluralistic, democratic political system within which diverse views and actions cannot be controlled by the government.

My timing proved fortuitous for tapping tensions and underly-

ing emotions in both countries. A sudden fall in China's foreign exchange reserves in 1985, from roughly $17 billion to $11 billion,
largely because of excessive consumer purchases from Japan, had
prompted Beijing to curtail imports sharply. Many Japanese firms
felt the blow in suspended or canceled contracts; a few went bankrupt in the absence of alternative markets for goods that had already been produced. In addition, a new textbook dispute erupted
in May 1986 when a right-wing group won preliminary approval
for a conservative manuscript that muted the language describing
Japan's aggression and atrocities in the 1930s. Less immediate, but
no less relevant, were the anti-Japanese student demonstrations of
the previous fall, the long-standing Kyoto dormitory case, and a
simmering controversy over the forthcoming commemoration of
Chiang Kai-shek's birthday.

These issues provided a ready agenda for discussion that naturally led to more fundamental questions of reciprocal national images and future expectations. The two months in China proved
most illuminating on several counts. First and foremost was the
near unanimity of view expressed in group discourse, whether by
government analysts or university professors. This unanimity contrasted with the temper of the time. In early 1986, the thirtieth anniversary of Mao Zedong's celebrated admonition to "Let a hundred flowers bloom, let a hundred schools of thought contend,"
had been marked with official encouragement for Chinese artists,
writers, and scholars to express diverse opinions. When I arrived
in late June, various intellectual sectors were responding vigorously to this encouragement, having been assured that the re-
pressive Anti-Rightist Campaign of 1957–58 would not reoccur this
time. But no such diversity of opinion emerged in the foreign policy community; conformity remained, whether self-induced or mandated behind the scenes.

Thus, a standard interview session, consisting of three uninter-
rupted hours of intensive exchange, would with rare exception result in the Chinese echoing and amplifying on the initial speaker,
invariably the senior person present. Moreover, the same stand
emerged in eight of the nine cities regardless of location, wartime
experience, or degree of current contact with Japan (Shanghai,
being uniquely open, was the exception). Second rounds of discussion, sometimes over a lengthy dinner with considerable wine con-

sumed, reiterated previously made points, but with more personal elaboration and emotion.

One obvious inference would be to dismiss the entire two months as an exercise in official posturing and as a product of the moment, designed either for my consumption or for transmission to the Japanese. Allowing for this, however, does not invalidate the cumulative impression of deeply held negative images that were being reinforced by the perceived behavior of the Tokyo government and various Japanese groups. The mixture of suspicion, cynicism, anger, and hostility that characterized most of these discussions went well beyond the current official expression of dissatisfaction with trade, textbooks, and Taiwan-related matters. But as Chinese dissatisfaction mounted in 1987, official views increasingly bordered on these emotions, as will be seen in the closing chapters.

There were two notable exceptions to this uniformity of views on Japan, the chief of which occurred among Chinese economists, both official and academic. They freely acknowledged that the terms of trade were inherently disadvantageous to China in the exchange of raw materials, foodstuffs, and light industrial products for advanced industrial goods, technology, and consumer items. They foresaw that this structural imbalance was likely to persist to some degree for many years. They recognized serious shortcomings in Chinese marketing abilities, including product design, quality control, and adaptation to Japanese demand. They pointed to deterrents against Japanese investment, including bureaucratic obstructionism and inadequate infrastructure. Their factual and objective analysis, however, did not appear in the mass media, nor did it arise in discussions with political and strategic analysts.

A second category of exception encompassed the few junior specialists who had studied in Japan. Privately they spoke frankly and sometimes bitterly about their inability to lecture or write in contradiction to their superiors and the official line. In contrast to the majority of their senior associates, whose superficial and often erroneous observations impeded serious discussion, they showed a thorough knowledge of postwar Japan. When one junior instructor with graduate training in Tokyo declared flatly, "We must study Japan like any foreign country," my older escort remarked later, "He shows a lot of courage!"

Traveling alone facilitated informal conversations, especially with younger Chinese and women specialists, who were inhibited, if not prevented, from speaking in a larger group. This revealed a surprising congruence of attitude, however, as far as antipathy toward Japan was concerned. The one discernible generation gap was between the old guard specialists who had studied in Japan during the 1920s and personally participated in the restoration of relations in the early 1970s and those in middle age and below who lacked this experience. The old guard specialists, now fully or partially retired, retained a softer image than that of their more hard-line cohorts and subordinates. In some instances they seemed visibly embarrassed by extreme forecasts of revived Japanese militarism that would ultimately threaten China "and even the United States." Their demurrers, however, were weak or nonexistent in group discussion.

I left these discussions dismayed at the level of discourse. There is an objective basis for differences of opinion with respect to the importance of rising nationalism in Japan, Nakasone's push for lifting the 1 percent of GNP ceiling on defense expenditure, the role that right-wing groups play in influencing the younger generation through slanted textbooks, and the overall Japanese reluctance to acknowledge the enormity of past aggression in Asia. Public opinion polls, newspaper editorials, official statements, films, plays, and specific events could be cited and debated as causes for greater or lesser concern. But rarely if ever was Chinese analysis based on anything other than selected evidence that "proved" a preordained point. All too often, knowledge of contrary evidence was lacking or, when offered, ignored.

Further reflection on this phenomenon is offered in the closing pages. I recount my research experience at the outset so that what follows may be evaluated accordingly. My Chinese is sufficient to understand the gist of a conversation, but to safeguard against error, I used interpreters in most instances. Nuances may be missed, notes may be abbreviated, but insofar as these interviews permit, I have tried to reflect the Chinese view of Japan as it stands today among the most involved, the most informed, and, in some cases, the most influential specialists.

One final point bears mention here and amplification later. Except for the economists, no Chinese officials during my two months of discussions acknowledged any error or shortcoming on China's part. On the contrary, as publicly asserted the following year by no less a person than Deng Xiaoping, all problems in the relationship were alleged to stem from Japanese behavior and therefore it was up to Japan to correct its mistakes. The strong assertion in private of this belief and its subsequent reiteration by high officials bespoke a highly nationalistic and confident Chinese self-image.

Seldom, however, do all the problems in an international relationship stem from one side alone and this is not the case here. Two instances bear on the point. First, the peremptory suspension and cancellation of contracts by the Chinese, initially in 1979 and more recently in 1986, arbitrarily imposed serious burdens on Japanese entrepreneurs. Second, Chinese officials tend to hold their Japanese counterparts responsible for private Japanese statements and actions, but, in doing so, misplace responsibility in a democratic society. These and other cases of problematic Chinese behavior notwithstanding, the Chinese, both in public and in private, still place all blame on the Japanese side. The resultant irritation finally erupted in an unprecedented official contretemps in mid-1987.

The seeming incongruity between the type and level of Japanese provocation and the Chinese reaction compels attention to the relative role of image versus interest in Beijing. Chinese protestations of friendship between the two peoples "separated only by a narrow strip of water" are ritualistically intoned whenever delegations visit. The Commission for Friendship in the Twenty-first Century meets regularly and is received by high officials on both sides. Yet the recurrent Chinese tone is one of lecturing and hectoring. The Chinese recite a record of Japanese shortcomings that suggests bad faith and warn of trouble ahead if these shortcomings are not corrected. This is not conducive to the expressly desired increase in Japanese investment and technology transfer, much less to moving the two countries "closer together in terms of their economic and political policies in Asia and elsewhere," as projected by Chaejin Lee.

For this reason, Chinese images of Japan's past and present are treated prior to examining Chinese economic and political interests in Japan. These interests in turn are reviewed mainly as they are depicted and perceived by Chinese analysts. In view of the heat generated by Beijing, this approach concentrates on the more uncertain element in the relationship.

THE IMPACT OF IMAGES

It might be appropriate to review the rationale for focusing on images and their impact on perceptions. Given the presumed ascendancy of interest over ideology in Chinese foreign policy in the years since the death of Mao, this rationale takes on a particular importance. My own scholarly bent in this direction began in the first years of the Cold War when most scholars and policy makers assumed that all Soviet decision making could be attributed to Stalin, who acted on the immutable premises of Marxism-Leninism. This pattern of decision making was thought to be a heritage of Lenin, the epitome of the authoritarian communist leader.

I questioned the feasibility of such a decision-making system, which spanned such a large country that faced so many problems in both domestic and foreign policy. To test an alternative hypothesis, namely that policy was the product of competing images and the corresponding flows of information derived from different organizations, I examined all the available Soviet publications and materials dealing with China from 1917 to 1924, submitting them to a content analysis that permitted a quantitative comparison of subject matter and description. Depending on whether I focused on Lenin personally or his associates in the foreign ministry, the international communist apparatus, or the international trade union movement, I found sharply contrasting points of emphasis in the selection of evidence from the then turbulent and confusing developments in China with correspondingly different expectations about the course of the communist movement and the Soviet role therein. Hence, the plural term in my title, *Soviet Policies Toward China, 1917–1924* (New York: Columbia University Press, 1954).

I had planned to carry this inquiry forward to test its relevance to the Stalin period and Sino-Soviet relations, but the immediacy of the Korean War and Sino-American conflict diverted my attention, albeit not my research focus. The conventional wisdom explained Mao's entry into that war as a function of an aggressive and expansionist communism that was in partnership with, if not actually directed by, Stalin. However, a close reading of the key publications and official statements, together with a reconstruction of the military movements using U.S. military intelligence, challenged this explanation. Instead, the decision in Beijing to enter the war emerged as the result of national security concerns that had been aroused by a pattern of American statements and actions that had been perceived within the image of a hostile power. Washington and its agent in Tokyo, General Douglas MacArthur, appeared determined to bring down the new communist regime and replace it with the Nationalist government under Chiang Kai-shek, then in refuge on the island of Taiwan. Although this design was wholly opposite the intentions of President Harry Truman and Secretary of State Dean Acheson, its credibility in Beijing lay in the image of American imperialism held by the leadership. This image was reinforced by selected evidence during the summer and fall of 1950. Washington's refusal to heed explicit Chinese warnings against crossing the thirty-eighth parallel resulted in the fateful decision traced in my study, *China Crosses The Yalu* (New York: Macmillan, 1960).

During the 1950s, the dominant paradigm in international relations was established by Hans Morgenthau in his classic work, *Politics Among Nations* (Knopf, 1948). Morgenthau posited power as the universal goal of states and prescribed realistic statesmanship in pursuit of an identifiable national interest as a desirable and feasible means of formulating foreign policy. An alternative paradigm, however, emerged from early studies of social psychology that focused attention on the possibility that preconceptions and misperceptions influenced the behavior of individuals and groups. Together with Ernst B. Haas, I drew on this discipline for the text, *Dynamics of International Relations* (New York: McGraw-Hill, 1956).

In the 1960s and 1970s, a major literature grew around this alternative paradigm, led by Kenneth E. Boulding, *The Image* (Ann Arbor: University of Michigan Press, 1956) and Robert Jervis, *Perception And Misperception in International Politics* (Princeton: Princeton University Press, 1976). This paradigm in turn was both supplemented and refined by the decision-making school of analysis, which focused on the organizational and bureaucratic interests that shape the perceptions and behavior of governments. This school of thought was pioneered by Graham Allison in *Essence of Decision*

(Boston: Little Brown, 1971). Thus, my initial intuitive approach seemed validated, albeit with considerable added sophistication, by other scholars and their findings.

Unfortunately, social science is unlike natural and physical science in its failure to develop a standard vocabulary that is universally accepted by practitioners in the field. Therefore, the use of such terms as image and perception varies from author to author. Although my own definitions do not vary greatly from the general usage, they deserve to be spelled out here as background for the following study. *Image* refers to the preconceived stereotype of a nation, state, or people that is derived from a selective interpretation of history, experience, and self-image. Operationally, image posits that the opposite party is generally good or bad, strong or weak, and a friend or a foe. *Perception* refers to the selective cognition of statements, actions, or events attributed to the opposite party as framed and defined by the preexisting image. To use a figure of speech widely found in the literature, image provides the frame and the lenses through which the external world is seen or perceived.

Several conceptual and methodological limitations need to be stated at the outset. This approach does not assume that image and perception are the sole determinants of decisions in foreign policy. Also, it does not imply that image and perception necessarily result in misperception or miscalculation or that they are invariably "wrong" as distortions of reality. Finally, it does not follow that an image is so rigid and inflexible that it is insusceptible to change over time in the face of conflicting reality and experience.

This approach does assume that image and perception are powerful organizing concepts in the minds of decision makers and, where relevant, publics for coping with foreign phenomena that are complex and remote, yet relevant to national security. Having said this, however, the problem of empirical proof inevitably arises. This problem may be expressed in the form of several questions. How can images and perceptions in the minds of national leaders be reliably determined if the only evidence is published sources and private interviews? All political figures and authoritative media address various audiences, domestic and foreign, with communication that is instrumental and possibly multipurpose. Deception, conscious or unconscious, is a standard ingredient of politics. Put in layman's terms, how do we know that policy makers "really mean what they say?"

Following up on the Allison model, a second question asks how we can differentiate the images and perceptions of decision makers from the information they are given by the various competing organizational components in complex bureaucracies? Information must be acquired, selected, interpreted and transmitted to higher officials, who have a long agenda, domestic and foreign, of problems and decisions. Their reactions, both private and public, to external phenomena depend on what they receive from below and, in pluralistic systems, from outside the government as well. Often their very statements are drafted by one department or another and in the process they are forced by competing organizations to accept compromise positions that obscure their original intentions.

Without exhausting all the questions and challenges that confront this approach, one final problem confronts the analyst: How can the relative weight of image versus interest be empirically determined? This is the ultimate bottom-line obstacle that critics add to the foregoing list of problems that vitiate the admittedly laborious and indirect effort necessary to constructing images and inferring perceptions.

Honesty and humility compel one to concede the validity of these and related questions without, however, abandoning the effort. The utility of this approach lies in the way it addresses the recurrent phenomenon of foreign policy behavior that is contrary to national interest, most notably in crises that have resulted in a war that neither side sought and that might have been averted. The collision between China and America in the Korean peninsula is a classic case in point.

The present study finds that the Chinese reactions to Japanese words and behavior during 1982–87 jeopardized China's interest in better relations between the two countries. An informal content analysis of Chinese publications, together with my private interviews, reveals that an underlying negative image structured Chinese perceptions of Japan and prompted responses of protest and antipathy disproportionate to events. By mid-1987, the cumulative strain triggered high-level acrimonious exchanges between the two capitals that belied official affirmations of friendship and endangered the basic relationship, at least for the near term. In addition, by propagating this negative image of Japan in the media, a younger generation of Chinese without firsthand experience of wartime suffering and atrocities also acquired negative attitudes toward Japan. This phenomenon could have longer-term implications for the relationship. These events run counter to what might be presumed to be the Chinese national interest, as defined by strategic, political, and economic criteria.

OVERVIEW AND SUMMARY

Chapter 2 briefly surveys the period from 1894–95, the first modern Sino-Japanese conflict, through World War II, and down to 1982. In addition to providing background on the historical relationship, it highlights the duality of Chinese perceptions and experiences, positive and negative, over the past century. As might be expected, the negative aspects prove dominant and are important for understanding why, despite the absence of conflict since 1945, more recent images of Japan have been hostile. This duality of positive and negative images is a recurring theme throughout the period under study, 1982–87. It was reflected in my private interviews and it is evident in official and media images of Japan as a country and the Japanese as a people.

Chapter 3 examines how Sino-Japanese history is presented in recent scholarly monographs in China. One recurring theme admonishes the reader to remember the past as a guide to the future and alerts him or her to guard against a revival of Japanese militarism and aggression. This makes writings on the nineteenth and early twentieth century relevant to the present and therefore to our inquiry. The linkage of past and present is found to be stronger and more explicit during the 1982 textbook controversy. At this time, the national journal *Zhongguo Qingnian Bao* (China Youth Daily) recapitulated the details of the 1937–45 war in text and pictures for over a month. I argue that this provided an important image that would underlay the university student demonstrations three years later. The 1985 commemoration in Tokyo of the war's end is also discussed as the immediate stimulus to these demonstrations and the critical context in which they occurred. The theme of wartime recall reemerged in 1986 during a second textbook dispute. This dispute ended without the rancor of the first dispute and without the earlier media attention. Public objections, however, remained on the Chinese side.

The 1985 anti-Japanese student demonstrations receive separate treatment in Chapter 4, both because of their unprecedented nature and because of their special significance for this study. As already noted, foreign reports at the time differed widely as to the origin and objectives of these demonstrations, but in general they questioned their ostensible anti-Japanese character. However, my interviews the following summer with faculty, students, and knowledgeable foreign as well as Chinese sources provided convincing testimony to the authenticity of the student sentiment against Japan's seeming domination of economic modernization and, in particular, against Nakasone's honoring Japanese war dead at the Yasukuni Shrine. To be sure, there were additional complaints against the practices of the current regime, some student-centered, others concerned with societal tendencies. But these coexisted with a deep-seated emotional antagonism against Japan that seriously embarrassed Chinese officialdom, as evidenced by its behavior in subsequent months when plans for further anti-Japanese demonstrations emerged and were effectively thwarted.

Chapter 5 examines how and where contemporary Japan appears as a positive image, and even as a partial role model, in recent Chinese publications. A positive image of Japan is an important element in serious economic writings and in the popular magazine *Zhongguo Qingnian* (Chinese Youth). These favorable analyses and articles balance off somewhat the predominantly negative images described in chapters 2 and 3 and are interesting for their alternative views of Japanese society. Although such views more properly fall within a broader comparison of the foreign models that the Chinese study for modernization, Japan not being singled out, their existence also serves to challenge the more frequent emphasis on revived Japanese nationalism and its potential for militarism. In the final analysis, however, these alternative views receive less attention in the media.

Chapter 6, the longest chapter, covers economic relations between the two countries. Three factors justify this length. First, this is the most tangible and practical interaction and understandably the one on which there is the most evidence. Second, it is central to Beijing's highest priority goal over the past decade: economic modernization. Third, it is a target of constant Chinese complaints and occasional accusations against Japanese good faith. Therefore, the chapter goes into considerable detail on those aspects that point toward close cooperation and those aspects that remain the subject of recurring contention. This is not a study in the details of trade, investment, and technology transfer and the interested reader should turn to more qualified analysts such as Dwight Perkins, Robert Dernberger, Nicholas Lardy, and Roy Grow. The purpose here is rather to place economic interactions in the political context of Chinese demands and Japanese responses. This politicization of economic interaction drives much of the acrimony between Beijing and Tokyo.

Chapter 7, by comparison, is unfortunately short given its focus on the political-military aspects of the relationship and Japan's future role in Asia. Its brevity results in part from the relative paucity of evidence: foreign policy in general and strategic analysis in particular are sensitive subjects about which relatively little public material pertaining to Japan emerged before 1987. However, Nakasone's success in removing the ceiling on defense expenditures in January 1987 released a widening stream of concerned comment, much of which had been anticipated in my private conversations in China the previous summer. The reactions of the newly available military journals in 1987 provided an additional authoritative basis for analysis.

A second factor curtailing the length and content of this chapter is the unwillingness in both Tokyo and Beijing to move toward any substantive military exchange, much less cooperation. Although personal contact between the two military services has increased slowly but steadily, many obstacles to a Sino-Japanese entente exist. Considerable foreign speculation, critical as well as favorable, has turned on the likelihood of such an entente. But official statements in Beijing insist that the PRC pursues "an independent policy" and "will not align itself with any power." Also, Tokyo's policy prohibits the dispatch of military forces abroad and the sale of military hardware or technology abroad. At a more subtle level, the Chinese pursuit of detente with the Soviet Union conflicts with closer ties to Japan and Japanese concern about possible Soviet reactions inhibits a Chinese military connection. Finally, domestic politics in China preclude any substantive development in the area of political-military ties as long as the emotional antipathy to Japan's rearmament remains a central theme in public and private discourse.

An emerging Chinese interest in Pacific basin analyses and proposals for economic cooperation warrants separate study in itself, both because of the rapidly burgeoning literature and its multifaceted ramifications for political and economic relations throughout the region. I have selected only the most salient Chinese references to Japan's role in this regard. Because of their competing interests in Southeast Asia, the two countries are unlikely to cooperate in any broad venture. In addition, there is a Chinese tendency to see Japanese initiatives and aims in terms of the so-called Greater East Asia Co-Prosperity Sphere, the rubric advanced by Japan to justify its military expansionism in the 1930s and 1940s. Today the Chinese see a Japanese thrust toward economic hegemony, to be followed, if possible, by political and then military hegemony.

Chapter 8 captures the essence of how Chinese views of Japan, as articulated by officials and the media, exacerbate Japanese provocations and, as a result, hinder the relationship, allowing image to prevail over interest. Fortuitously for this study, developments in the course of 1987, the final year of inquiry, became a climactic recapitulation of virtually all the problems previously identified and analyzed. That spring and summer witnessed an unprecedented escalation of Chinese protests and a corresponding deterioration of relations even though no new issue or grievance had occurred. At the official level, acerbic comments on both sides reached unprecedented intensity, resulting in the "early retirement" of a Japanese vice minister of foreign affairs and the later ouster of the minister of education, who jeopardized relations with Seoul as well as Beijing. At the popular level, public opinion polls in Japan showed increased criticism of China amid a rash of vandalism that damaged monuments to Sino-Japanese friendship. These actions were reciprocated in China when some display cases at a Japanese consulate were defaced. Joint ministerial-level meetings failed to conceal the friction, although both sides attempted to put the best face on commemorating the fifteenth anniversary of restored relations.

Chapter 9 distills out of the preceding narrative the main political and economic factors in the relationship, together with the

ALBRIGHT COLLEGE LIBRARY   226140

Chinese images and perceptions of Japan that proved salient during 1982–87. Clearly, any analysis and evaluation of causal factors must be intuitive, inferential, and impressionistic, as well as individually offered. Nevertheless I make the effort as the basis for projecting their likely balance and cumulative impact on Sino-Japanese relations in the 1990s. The forecast is one of qualified optimism.

Several observations are in order concerning the presentation of the material. First, the general reader can omit the notes, which almost exclusively identify sources. Second, the proliferation of notes is necessitated by the central focus on images and perceptions. Only by identifying where these images and perceptions appear and how they are presented can the more specialized reader independently assess their relevance to my analysis. Some of the notes also reveal the feedback effect of statements and actions occurring in one country and reported in the other. Full citation permits the discernment of distortion in such reporting.

Another justification for the many notes is that they identify whether the source cited is a translation provided by an official Chinese source, such as the Xinhua news agency or *Beijing Review*, a Japanese source, usually the Kyodo news service, the U.S. government through the Foreign Broadcast Information Service (FBIS), or research assistants and myself. When the FBIS translation was suspect, it was checked where possible against the original text. Thus, in Chapter 8, page 169, the term *yi li* used in *Renmin Ribao* was given in FBIS as "stand like a giant" for China's future posture in Asia. I found "stand erect" as an alternative translation and chose it as the more conservative and, therefore, safer rendering of the writer's meaning. We do not know what was originally intended, much less how millions of readers may have taken the phrase, but the implications of "stand like a giant" cautioned against its acceptance without further contextual support. Another question about the presentation of the material concerns the question of redundancy. Unfortunately, two key aspects of the study require repetition of statements and protests, dreary as this can be at times. First, in trying to delineate Chinese images of Japan and to forecast future Chinese perceptions of Japanese behavior, it is necessary to demonstrate the frequency and intensity of the inputs derived from public statements. Their impact cannot be tested empirically by means of systematic polling in China, certainly not by a foreigner. The only recourse then is to repeat the statements as they occurred and demonstrate how they support the analysis. Second, to assess the impact of Chinese statements as they are reported in Japan, reiteration is necessary if the full frictional weight of these statements is to be felt, at least empathetically.

The decision to present a detailed description of events prior to their analysis is derived from the fact that most of the events covered in the following pages were only briefly summarized abroad, if reported at all. Therefore, a fairly full account of the actions and reactions in both countries is necessary before assessing their implications and striking a final balance. Chapter 9 provides a refreshing respite from details in this regard.

A final point is the imbalance between the treatment of China and Japan. Lacking knowledge of the Japanese language, I could not duplicate the research undertaken on Chinese materials, although my interviews in Japan, together with translated sources, are drawn on extensively. At the risk of being termed Sinocentric, the book concludes that the fundamental threat to the relationship comes from the Chinese side reacting to its perceptions of what is said and done in Japan. Therefore, the imbalance limits, but does not invalidate, the study.

I have deliberately tried to avoid judgmental observations on the respective merits of each side's position in controversial issues for two reasons. First, such observations lie beyond my competence in some instances, such as the disposition of the student dormitory in Kyoto, the ownership of which has been disputed by Taipei and Beijing in the Japanese courts for more than twenty years. In the case of the Nanjing Massacre, I have not attempted to validate the number of dead as calculated by different sources. Japanese newspaper correspondents put the figure at 20,000; Chinese Nationalist accounts claim 100,000; the official PRC history records 300,000, the number dominating the museum entrance in Nanjing. An atrocity did occur, but the actual death toll remains a provocative point of dispute between Chinese and Japanese writers.

But beyond my inability to determine the merits of the competing claims, a second and more important reason for avoiding this task is its irrelevance to demonstrating how the issues impact on the dynamics of Sino-Japanese relations. International relations are seldom determined by an objective assessment of right and wrong. Rather they are managed within a framework of mutual confrontation, competition, or cooperation, depending on the fundamental interests of each side as seen by its leadership. I have, however, attempted to show how misperception and deliberate distortion enter into official statements and mass media. This addresses a persistent problem in international relations and one that has plagued the Sino-Japanese interaction for more than a century. At the same time, I draw attention to the actual experiences, both past and present, that give life to the stereotypes held on the Chinese side.

An excellent example of the interaction between distortion and experience is the so-called Tanaka Memorial, which, according to many Chinese writers, spelled out in 1927 the Japanese plan for the conquest of China and Asia, a plan purportedly pursued with single-minded determination thereafter. There is a strong correlation between the strategy proposed by Prime Minister Tanaka Giichi at a cabinet meeting in July 1927 and actions taken in the following decade by different sectors of the Japanese military and civilian establishment. However, aside from the record of debate, conflict, and subversion of authority that attended the expansion into Manchuria, North China, and ultimately East Asia, the memorial was a post hoc fabrication, a fact that has been attested to by scrupulous scholars on both sides. Thus Lin Han-sheng writes, "This conference provided Chinese propagandists an opportunity to coin the famous 'Tanaka Memorial' to discredit the Japanese government."[4] Marius B. Jansen asserts, "There is not a scrap of evidence to authenticate the so-called 'Memorial' which became a convenient item of anti-Japanese propaganda before and during World War II."[5] Finally, Bunzo Hashikawa states, "In my opinion, the document is a forgery, not actually written by Tanaka at all."[6] Yet, as we shall see, it is still advanced in China as purported proof of a basic Japanese policy that may return in the future.

No foreigner can hope to plumb the depth and breadth of interaction and impression between any two peoples, especially, as in China and Japan, where language and culture screen so much from the foreigner's view. I have no illusion on this score. But it is sometimes possible for the foreigner to place interactions and impressions in a perspective that reveals what is unavoidable as compared with what might be better handled by one side or the other, or both. It is with this modest wish that I and those who assisted me offer this study for reflection and criticism.

2

From Past to Present

Her [Japan's] power is daily expanding, and her ambition is not small. . . . Although the various European powers are strong, they are still 70,000 li away from us, whereas Japan is as near as in the courtyard, or on the threshold, and is prying into our emptiness or solitude [i.e., the weakness of our defense measures]. Undoubtedly she will become China's permanent and great anxiety.

Li Hongzhang to
the emperor, 1874

In Asia, our two countries, China and Japan, are the closest neighbors, and moreover have the same language. How could we be enemies? Now for the time being we are fighting each other, but eventually we should work for permanent friendship. . . . If the diplomatic ministers of our two countries mutually and deeply understand this idea, we ought vigorously to maintain the general stability of Asia, and establish permanent peace and harmony between ourselves so that our Asiatic yellow race will not be encroached upon by the white race of Europe.

Li Hongzhang to
Itō Hirobumi, 1895

Li Hongzhang, managing foreign affairs for China's last imperial dynasty, correctly forecast fifty years of recurring confrontation and conflict with Japan in his pessimistic prognosis to the emperor.[1] From 1895 to 1945, Tokyo's military forces, through intermittent attacks, eventually overran China's main industrial areas, killing millions of Chinese and rendering many times that homeless. Despite this negative record, Li's optimistic admonition to Itō Hirobumi, his Japanese counterpart in negotiating an end to the Sino-Japanese War, also anticipated the positive emphasis of official Chinese and Japanese policies nearly a century later, albeit without Li's racial references. Since signing the Treaty of Peace and Friendship in 1978, Beijing and Tokyo have officially endorsed economic cooperation and political understanding, jointly sponsoring the Commission for Sino-Japanese Friendship in the Twenty-first Century.

Li's two statements capture the duality that has plagued this relationship throughout the past century and that continues to trouble Chinese views of it today. Chinese memories of the past and their subjective perceptions of present-day Japanese provocations combine to arouse private opposition and, on occasion, public protest against too close a relationship with an unreliable, powerful neighbor. Yet economic complementarity makes the two countries practical partners in Chinese modernization and their common strategic interest in balancing Soviet with American power in East Asia presents the possibility of a tacit, if limited, alignment.

Thus, Sino-Japanese relations are characterized by positive and negative aspects. On the positive side, Japan ranks first in trade, aid, and loans to China and leads all other countries in interpersonal contact with China, from the highest levels of state through business and tourism. But on the negative side, the Japanese invasion of 1937–45, replete with atrocities, which included the brutal Nanjing Massacre, is recurringly recalled in China, but ignored or downplayed in Japan.

China's memories of the past have been stirred by events such as the 1982 controversy over an attempt to suppress the historical record in a Japanese textbook and the commemoration of the fortieth anniversary of Japan's surrender in 1985. The vividly communicated accounts of wartime suffering that these events brought forth had an unanticipated impact on the subjective perceptions and attitudes of the younger generation in China. Dramatic evidence of this impact came in September 1985 when thousands of university students in Beijing and elsewhere, provoked by Prime Minister Nakasone Yasuhiro's tribute to Japan's fallen soldiers, publicly demonstrated against Japan's present role in China's economic modernization.

A similar duality of attitude exists between China's acceptance of the Japanese-American Security Treaty, with its attendant military cooperation, and repeated Chinese warnings against the revival of Japanese militarism. In 1987 Beijing criticized Tokyo's lifting of the ceiling on defense expenditures, fixed at 1 percent of

GNP since 1976, and cautioned against a further strengthening of Japan's armed forces as advocated by Washington.

These contrasting attitudes toward Japan can be seen in Chinese domestic politics. The ideologically sensitive and politically volatile subject of dependence on foreign capitalism in general and Japan in particular invites attack by opponents of the current policy. Such opposition may be opportunistically motivated or it may be based on genuine concern; regardless of its inception, its impact on public posture and policy can further complicate Sino-Japanese relations.

Before examining these recent dualities in detail, we must place them in historical perspective, reviewing some of the principal points of conflict and cooperation as they emerged between China and Japan during the period 1894–1978. Without recounting the entire record of the relationship, I will highlight those aspects that provide a precedent for the present relationship as well as the ones that are salient in understanding the recent Chinese treatment of this period, a period in which Japan appeared alternately as a military threat to be feared and a modernization model to be studied.

FROM THE ASHES OF DEFEAT

The Sino-Japanese War of 1894–95 remains a historic benchmark in Chinese perceptions of Japan. As one recent survey remarked, "From the launching of the Sino-Japanese War in 1894, Japanese imperialism recurrently invaded China throughout the subsequent half century."[2] Previous unequal treaties imposed by the Western powers had forcibly opened up China's ports to foreign commerce and extracted extraterritorial rights for foreign citizens. But now Japan seized Chinese territory outright. Although the war began over which of Korea's two Asian neighbors would exercise hegemony in the peninsula, Tokyo exploited its victory by annexing Taiwan and the adjacent Pescadore Islands. Thus in addition to giving up Korea as a tributary nation, China suffered its first loss of territory in modern times as a result of military defeat. Adding insult to injury, defeat came at the hands of a small country that had itself been forced by the Western powers to open its doors only four decades before. This challenged the Chinese in their assumptions of inherent superiority within the Confucian realm of East

Asia. Japan's rapid destruction of China's minimally Westernized forces shocked those who had believed "self-strengthening" was sufficient.

Yet from the ashes of defeat emerged a major effort by Chinese statesmen to emulate Japan's political and economic modernization. The paradox whereby some among the vanquished admired the victor as a potential teacher was matched by the victor's willingness to support Chinese reformers and revolutionaries in their search for a new course. Advocates of reform urged the Qing rulers to study the Meiji Restoration as a model of rapid modernization. Kang Youwei, a leader of this group, wrote many memoranda to the emperor to this effect, initially with some success. Thus during the Hundred Days of Reform in 1898, the emperor received Itō Hirobumi with these words:

> The government of your honorable country after its reforms has been praised by all nations. . . . The two countries, yours and ours, are geographically situated on the same continent [Asia] and are nearest to each other. At the present time reform is pressed upon our country by necessity. We are willing to hear an opinion expressed by your Excellency, and we request your Excellency to tell our princes and great ministers . . . in great detail the process and methods of reform, and give them advice.[3]

Soon, however, determined conservatives snuffed out the reform movement and its advocates were forced to flee for their lives. Japan offered both a sanctuary and a model. Liang Qichao, a leading reformer, evoked images of the Japanese as teachers and brothers as he approached the country on a Japanese ship: "Here is a land of superior men . . . its culture and people identical with ours."[4] Liang's colleague, Zhang Zhidong, argued forcefully that "it is better to study in the west for one year than to read western books for five years; better to study in a western school for one year than to study in Chinese schools for three years" and concluded:

> Japan is nearby and inexpensive for travel, so that many can go; it is close to China, and students will not forget their country. Japanese writing is similar to Chinese, and it can be translated easily. And western learning is extremely varied, and the Japanese have already selected its essentials.[5]

Lest the point still be missed, Zhang asked, "How did Japan rise, although it is only a small country? Itō, Yamagata, Enomoto, and

Mutsu were students in the west twenty years ago." In short, Japan was to be China's modernizing "West."

Zhang's advice proved well-taken. By 1900 more than a hundred Chinese students had entered a special school in Japan.[6] Within four years their number had grown to an estimated eight thousand. Not all graduated; some experienced discrimination and nationalism as manifested in anti-Chinese attitudes and behavior. But on balance the sense of Japan as a model for Chinese youth, even including its nationalistic aspects, sowed seeds of revolution that were to sprout in subsequent decades.

The seeming anomaly of Japan's victory prompting Chinese advocacy of Japan as a benign source of modernization is explained by more than Tokyo's stunning success. It also stemmed from the fact that the Qing dynasty was Manchu, not Chinese, and Japan's victory symbolized Qing, not Chinese, inadequacy. Chinese nationalists could relate positively to the modernized Japanese, who had already transcended the common cultural heritage of writing, architecture, and Confucian intellectual ethos. As one of the most prominent writers of the People's Republic subsequently remarked, "We studied Western culture through Japan. . . . At the same time that the study of Japan broke the feudalistic conventions of the past, it served to further China's progress toward modernity."[7]

One measure of the degree to which Japan transmitted Western concepts to China is the surge in the number of translations from Japanese into Chinese. Numbering more than three hundred by 1905, these translations constituted nearly two-thirds of all translated works in China in the first years of this century as against only 15 percent of those produced from 1850 to 1889.[8] Almost three dozen works focused on law and politics. These included both Japanese originals and works that had first been translated from Western sources. This further underscored Japan's image as a modernizing state.

Even Qing officials looked to Japan as teacher, although for reasons quite different from those of the reformers. In 1907 the court's representative in Tokyo endorsed Chinese enrollment in Japanese military academies, claiming "Japanese military education stresses loyalty and patriotism and subordination to superiors . . . and contains no dangers of unbridled indiscipline or opposition to government."[9] At the time he wrote these words, more than five hundred

Chinese had graduated from Japanese military academies and another three hundred and fifty were enrolled in military courses. Over the next two decades the majority of China's military leaders were to come from this group.

Japan nourished revolutionaries as well as reformers, although it did so with the thought of enhancing its future influence in China. No less a figure than Sun Yat-sen received emotional, political, and financial support from Japan at a critical time in his own fortunes. He repeatedly sojourned there between 1895 and 1907, often while being banned from China and Hong Kong. This prompted Sun to include "cooperation with Japan" in the six-point program of his Tongmenghui, or Revolutionary Alliance, formed in Tokyo in 1905. Although the government forced Sun to leave two years later as increased student activity aroused concern over all revolutionary groups, he received monetary compensation for the inconvenience.

In 1911 the Qing dynasty collapsed and was replaced by the Republic of China. Although the newly formed government failed to unite and govern the entire country, it won international recognition as the formal authority through which foreign powers could continue to extract concessions and enjoy privileges. The pretense of authority was enhanced by China's joining the Allies in World War I, hoping thereby to reacquire lost rights and to win genuine equality in the family of nations.

But this hope proved short-lived. In 1915 Japan levied the notorious Twenty-one Demands on China, including the virtual takeover of all German concessions. Despite this evidence of persistent expansionism Sun continued in his dream of pan-Asian solidarity and tried to persuade Tokyo that it could deal better with him and his revolutionary alternative than it could with the regime in Beijing.[10] Sun's political naïveté was exceeded only by his political impotence at this point; nothing came of his efforts. His pro-Japanese orientation serves, however, as a reminder of how reformers and revolutionaries alike saw a role for Japan in their goal of modernizing China, an attitude that persists today.

JAPAN'S ADVANCE INTO CHINA

Kang, Zhang, Liang, and Sun held that the logic of cultural compatibility and geographical proximity would facilitate Japanese cooperation in advancing China's interests. Unfortunately the logic of imperialism and power politics prompted Japanese military and civilian leaders to a policy of expansionism at China's expense. This negative record of expansionism, rather than the positive experiences and aspirations summarized above, provides the core of Chinese resentment and suspicion whenever the fear of revived Japanese militarism is expressed in the People's Republic.

Two years after Japan defeated Russia in the war of 1904–5, Tokyo and Saint Petersburg concluded a secret agreement dividing nearby Chinese territory into exclusive spheres of influence. Russia would have hegemony in Outer Mongolia and northern Manchuria while Japan could enjoy comparable privileges in Inner Mongolia and southern Manchuria.

With the outbreak of World War I, Japan moved to seize Germany's holdings in Shandong province. On November 7, 1914, Japanese gunboats bombarded and occupied the port of Qingdao. Beijing countered by asking that the special transit and military rights that Germany had held be returned to China. But Tokyo responded with the Twenty-one Demands, insisting that all German rights in Shandong become Japanese and that Japan enjoy special, and at times exclusive, privileges elsewhere.

Such demands from a presumed ally triggered student demonstrations, a boycott of Japanese goods, and the departure of the remaining revolutionaries from Japan back to China. More important, the day on which Tokyo's final ultimatum to sign the demands was delivered, May 7, 1915, subsequently became celebrated as National Humiliation Day. This designation explicitly linked Japanese expansionism in China with the rising tide of modern Chinese nationalism, foreshadowing developments that would poison relations between the two neighboring countries for the next thirty years.

The Shandong story did not end there. The 1919 Paris peace conference revealed that secret negotiations among Great Britain, France, and Italy two years before had approved Japan's retention of the German holdings. Worse still was the complicity of the Beijing regime, officially China's national government, but actually only a regional warlord enterprise. In September 1918 the Chinese minister to Tokyo had "gladly accepted" Japan's control of the Shandong railroad in return for large loans to the militarist clique in Beijing. Thus despite having sent 200,000 men to the Western front to dig trenches and despite the idealistic rhetoric of Woodrow Wilson, China was to remain exploited by its allies and its own nominal leaders for the benefit of Japan. The Paris peace conference, which formally ended World War I, far from satisfying Chinese nationalistic aspirations only intensified Chinese anger.

Ironically, it was the ally, Japan, rather than the enemy, Germany, which provoked the greatest antiforeign outburst of Chinese nationalism to that time. The May Fourth movement, as it became known, targeted the Paris accords in general and Japan along with its Beijing accomplices in particular. Initiated by Beijing University students on May 4, 1919, the protests swept through urban centers, uniting wide sectors of society in demonstrations, boycotts, and demands for the return of the Shandong concessions. Some compromises were finally reached at the 1920 Washington conference whereby China regained the main German holdings and Japan expressed a willingness to modify some of the Twenty-one Demands. But the damage was already done to the image of Japan as a potential friend of modern China.

In 1927 Shandong again became the scene of controversy when Japanese troops entered briefly to protect their interests and citizens, who were threatened by fighting between local Chinese forces. Although the Japanese withdrew shortly, a more serious intervention occurred in 1928 as successful Guomindang forces under the command of Chiang Kai-shek swept northward against the militarist regime in Beijing under the control of Zhang Zuolin. The Japanese commander forced a fight at Jinan, seized the city from Guomindang troops, and held it under martial law until a final settlement in 1929.

But Shandong soon paled into insignificance when compared with events in Manchuria, the southern half of which had remained a Japanese sphere of influence since the secret agreement with Russia in 1907. This sphere of influence included the key naval base at Port Arthur and Dalian, a port on the Liaodong Peninsula. The South Manchurian Railway zone joined this region with central Manchuria and ultimately the Chinese Eastern Railway. The zone included mines and ancillary facilities as well as portions of Mukden and Changchun. All areas were guarded by the Japanese Kwantung Army, which was directly responsible to the general staff in Tokyo.

In 1928, as Guomindang troops moved on Beijing in their successful drive to unite the country under Chiang Kai-shek, Zhang Zuolin retreated to make Manchuria his final redoubt. This threatened not only Japanese interests in Manchuria but also their larger goal of hegemony in Northeast Asia. In addition to direct involvement in the Chinese civil war, Tokyo faced the prospect of a unified and nationalistic China under a forceful Guomindang leader.

Leaders in Tokyo debated various responses but were preempted by a young Japanese Kwantung Army officer who took matters into his own hands. In June 1928 he blew up the retreating Zhang's train near Mukden, thereby hoping to provoke a Guomindang response that would justify a Kwantung Army occupation of Manchuria. His plot failed because of inadequate support among his own colleagues. The incident, however, further exacerbated Sino-Japanese relations, caused a cabinet crisis in Tokyo, which led to the collapse of the government, and established a precedent for unilateral military action in Manchuria, which proved successful three years later.

On September 18, 1931, the date commemorated by anti-Japanese student demonstrations in 1985, Japanese troops surreptitiously blew up a short section of the South Manchurian Railway north of Mukden. The commanding officer then seized the entire city. The Kwantung Army's ambitious plan to occupy all of Manchuria and Inner Mongolia encountered military and civilian opposition in Tokyo. But this fait accompli had passed the point of no return and the Japanese government accepted the Manchurian situation rather than admit its inability to control its own military. In March 1932 the Japanese created the independent state of Manchukuo and the last male descendant of the Manchu Qing dynasty was installed as its puppet ruler and regent.

The extent to which the various Japanese actions resulted from decisions by local officers, regional headquarters, the general staff, or high level consensus in Tokyo is irrelevant for our purposes. Regardless of the facts, many of which were obscure at the time, Chinese perceptions properly placed responsibility on the central regime ostensibly in power. Then and now, Chinese writings attribute these developments to a "militaristic, imperialistic, expansionist" government determined to achieve hegemony not only over China, but also over all of Asia. This line of analysis contributes to the contemporary Chinese sensitivity to Japanese militarism, whether it is perceived in the revision of Japanese textbooks concerning the past or in the present words and actions of Japanese leaders.

The Manchurian debacle triggered anti-Japanese boycotts and demonstrations. These in turn provoked the "Shanghai Incident," in which the local Japanese naval commander sent marines in to enforce order. Fierce resistance by the Chinese ultimately forced the Japanese to dispatch three divisions. Fighting continued for several months until an armistice was concluded in May 1932. Whereas Manchuria was remote from central China and activity there had been somewhat obscure, Shanghai was covered in word and picture on a daily basis for both a domestic and an international audience, which read about and watched the heroic Chinese stand against a superior enemy.

The loss of Manchuria transcended all the previous Japanese acts of expansion and intervention because it denied China its most valuable economic area. It was underpopulated relative to central China and enjoyed a food surplus. Its industry was more advanced and growing because of the infusion of Japanese capital, an excellent transportation infrastructure, and an abundance of local resources such as coal and iron ore. Its customs revenues constituted 15 percent of China's total. Thus the Chinese were justified in seeing Manchuria's role in China's economic modernization as crucial.

Equally important for the new Republic in Nanjing, established by Chiang Kai-shek in 1927–28, was the symbolic need to unify the country and resist foreign invasion. Tradition held that the Mandate of Heaven vested legitimacy in the ruler who could provide internal peace and external security. Cast in modern terms, the growing sense of Chinese nationalism should have prompted Chiang to respond aggressively to Japanese expansionism. He decided, however, to exterminate the Chinese communists before facing the Japanese. This prompted the Manchurian troops who had fled the Japanese to support Zhang's son, popularly known as "the Young Marshal," in forcing Chiang to reconsider his priorities. Thus in December 1936 the Young Marshal, in collusion with the top leadership of the Chinese Communist party, kidnapped Chiang and compelled him to agree on unity with all Chinese, including the communists, in resistance to further Japanese encroachments.

The year 1937 proved to the Chinese that their worst images of Japan were justified as Japan moved to invade and occupy the country's most populous and developed regions. As in Manchuria, a minor clash, this time at the Marco Polo bridge west of Beijing on the night of July 7, 1937, was exploited by local Japanese forces to enlarge the action. This quickly escalated to a full-scale war that ultimately killed or wounded twenty-two million Chinese according to official figures. Its impact on subsequent images of Japan is readily evident in the allegation that "the best historical records show that some 340,000 people died in Nanjing, 190,000 in group massacres and 150,000 in individual murders . . . [which] surpasses even the combined figure for Hiroshima and Nagasaki."[11]

It is impossible to recapitulate the full depth and breadth of Chinese suffering occasioned by the Japanese invasion. The bitterness remaining in the older generation with first-hand experience of this tragedy was recalled by one of my students who told of her mother spitting on the Japanese flag when it reappeared after the restoration of diplomatic relations in 1972. To the degree that this bitterness is transmitted to younger generations, either by personal accounts or by media images, the negative heritage from the past challenges exhortations for friendship in the present.

POSTWAR DEVELOPMENTS

When Japan broadcast its surrender on August 15, 1945, it did so to the allied powers, which included the Republic of China. But the American occupation of Japan delayed the formal ending by treaty of Japan's enemy status with China. Meanwhile the Republic of China was driven to refuge on the island of Taiwan as Mao Zedong's armies won the civil war and captured the entire mainland by 1949, the year in which the People's Republic of China was formally inaugurated.

On June 25, 1950, North Korea attacked South Korea. Washington responded with an American counterattack under United Nations auspices that ultimately drove the North Korean forces back across the thirty-eighth parallel, which had separated the two Korean regimes. Beijing warned that it would not stand by if American forces crossed the parallel, but Washington nonetheless authorized General Douglas MacArthur's march northward. In late November

1950 Chinese and American armies collided in combat that was not to end until July 1953 with the virtual restoration of the status quo ante and the two Koreas still divided.

At this time a series of American decisions impacted unfavorably on Sino-Japanese relations. First came the move to restore Japanese defensive military capabilities, reversing the immediate postwar demilitarization of the country. Despite a constitution, drafted by Americans, that prohibited any military establishment, Tokyo's police units became the first Japanese Self-Defense Forces. Next came Washington's willingness to end the occupation with a peace treaty provided that Tokyo would grant the United States the right to maintain bases and conclude a security treaty with the United States. In addition Japan had to forgo recognition of the People's Republic of China and conclude a peace treaty with the regime on Taiwan. Thus by the end of 1952 Japan was tied into the American military and political strategy that posited the containment of communism as the basic goal of foreign policy.

For its part, the People's Republic had concluded a military alliance with the Soviet Union on February 14, 1950, that pledged the two parties to mutual support in the event of an attack on either by Japan or any power allied therewith. The Sino-Soviet alliance served China well at the outset, providing it with access to loans, technical assistance, machinery, and military assistance sufficient to lay the foundation of economic and military modernization. It also deterred the United Nations forces in Korea from attacking China during more than two years of bloody stalemate. But the alliance also locked China into a posture of confrontation with the Japanese-American alliance.

As a further complication, on June 27, 1950, President Harry S. Truman interposed the U.S. Seventh Fleet in the Taiwan Strait, thereby forestalling Beijing's invasion of the Guomindang's last refuge. This intervention in the Chinese civil war was initially undertaken as a temporary presidential order in the context of the Korean war. In December 1954, however, it evolved into a formal treaty committing the United States to the defense of Taiwan, thereby adding another obstacle to relations between the People's Republic and the Japanese-American alliance.

Economic embargoes, imposed by Washington during the Korean war, further obstructed intercourse between the mainland and

Japan. These embargoes not only banned trade in the strategic commodities that were already proscribed for all communist countries and that had already been agreed to by members of the North Atlantic Treaty Organization. They also forbade the sale to the People's Republic of any item containing American-licensed material, whether the material was from the United States or any other country.

Despite these limitations private Japanese groups concluded an unofficial trade pact with mainland authorities in 1953. By 1956 the People's Republic constituted Japan's number one trade partner in East Asia with nearly 30 percent of its exchange in that region.[12] In the 1960s this "friendship trade" was joined by "memorandum trade" at a semiofficial level, moving Japan into first place as China's trading partner after the Sino-Soviet split brought ties with the socialist bloc to a near-total break. Chinese-Japanese political relations, however, remained frozen by American design.

President Richard Nixon's surprise dispatch of National Security Adviser Henry Kissinger to Beijing in July 1971 foreshadowed Nixon's own trip the following February. Although the resultant Shanghai Communiqué did not establish full diplomatic relations, it signaled an end to Sino-American confrontation. This freed Tokyo to pursue its own interests. In September 1972 Prime Minister Tanaka Kakuei transferred diplomatic recognition from Taiwan to the People's Republic, restoring normal relations between the two major East Asian countries. In August 1978 Prime Minister Fukuda Takeo took the final step by concluding a Treaty of Peace and Friendship with China. Thus for the first time in more than forty years Japan and China were able to interact without major obstacles, internal or external.

IN RETROSPECT

Li Hongzhang's privately voiced fears proved to be justified by Japan's subsequent aggression against China. But his diplomatically worded proposal for joint Sino-Japanese "friendship . . . to maintain the general stability of Asia" was echoed by various groups on both sides before and after the 1931–45 conflict. In short, his dual perceptions of the relationship's potential for conflict and cooperation proved genuinely prescient of what was to be seen and felt by different Chinese at different times in the subsequent hundred years.

The full record from 1894 to 1978 would provide a multitude of shadings, bright and dark, of this theme. The details, however, have been omitted in our attempt to capture only the most relevant highlights of this relationship. In particular a complete account of the policies advocated, and in some instances adopted, by different Japanese individuals and groups would shatter the image of unity implied by the convenient, but simplistic, term "Japan." But more than convenience justifies this shorthand reference to the complex system of politics after the Meiji Restoration. It is, in fact, the term that most commonly characterizes Chinese perceptions during the period under review. It is also the image most widely depicted by contemporary Chinese writers, with the notable exception of a few scholars and historians. Therefore, for the purposes of our inquiry, the term "Japan" is politically relevant, if historically simplistic. Likewise, the historical record that I have summarized shows the intermittent nature of Japanese expansionism. Many Chinese commentators, however, characterize this expansionism as being constant throughout the period. Similarly, the positive hopes for and experience of Japanese cooperation expressed by reformers and revolutionaries at the turn of the century go largely unmentioned in recent accounts, with one notable exception: regime responses to the student anti-Japanese demonstrations of 1985. These early hopes provide an important precedent to the efforts of Deng Xiaoping and his associates to make Japan a major participant in economic modernization.

To be sure, the dominant developments from the 1894–95 Sino-Japanese War to the 1972 reestablishment of normal diplomatic relations involved confrontation and conflict, not cooperation. Given this record with its extremely painful aspects, both material and psychological, it is no wonder that the historical heritage remains at or near the surface of Chinese consciousness more than forty years later. Seen from this perspective, the book clearly has not been closed on the past, as we will see in the next chapter.

3

The War as Historical Heritage

The Japanese invasion of 1937–45 surpassed any foreign aggression in modern Chinese history. The full cost can never be accurately computed. Chinese estimates suffice, however, to explain present-day perceptions of the pain inflicted by Japanese militarism: 21.8 million civilian and military dead and wounded and much of the country's industry destroyed or damaged.[1]

Needless to say, this history is viewed quite differently in the two countries. As a senior Japanese official frankly acknowledged, "We want to forget; they want to remember. Unfortunately we must say that Japan is a country with a long history and a short memory."[2] A retired diplomat recalled how a Chinese once challenged a Japanese aphorism to the effect that "water can wash away the past" by declaring, "We don't have that much water in China."[3] Underscoring his observation, an old Chinese proverb provides an omnipresent leitmotif for books, articles, and speeches addressing Sino-Japanese relations, "Past experience, if not forgotten, is a guide for the future" (*Qianshi buwang, houshi zhishi*).

The conflict between these two attitudes poses the single greatest obstacle to the stable, close, and enduring relationship based on trust and friendship that is officially advocated by Beijing. Provocative events in Japan associated with the war trigger an automatic response in China that combines anger over the past with apprehension about the future. When right-wing nationalists in Tokyo revise the sections on Japanese aggression in textbooks and challenge the validity of war crimes trials, the Chinese react bitterly and accuse the former enemy of nurturing the seeds of renewed militarism. These reactions are not confined to those who experienced wartime suffering first-hand. Their descendants articulate equally strong emotions when discussing Japan's responsibility for the war and its reliability as a partner, whether political or economic. A brief release of these feelings occurred in September 1985 when anti-Japanese student demonstrations occurred on at least half a dozen campuses, events that will be treated in the next chapter. The students, although relatively few in number, spoke for a wide sector of the urban populace in attacking Japanese attitudes toward the war and Japan's present "economic invasion."

Much of this sentiment stems from how the war is portrayed by scholars and publicists, particularly in the mass media aimed at youth. Images derived from these sources can affect the attitudes and expectations that the younger generation brings to present and future Sino-Japanese relations. A survey of academic and popular writings reveals the degree to which the historical heritage obstructs the officially espoused goal of Sino-Japanese friendship.

Before examining this evidence, however, several caveats deserve attention. We have little systematic information concerning Chinese responsiveness to the mass media and none on the topic at hand. Whether the images transmitted by word and picture impact on and are retained by the audience's memory can only be inferred or speculated on; no public opinion polls test this hypothesis. To the degree that observable behavior correlates with media messages, as when university students demonstrate against the danger of Japanese militarism, some conclusions may be logically warranted. They cannot, however, be empirically proven.

In addition, the assumption that there is a monolithic management of the media in a society as large as China belies reality. The editors of particular journals, such as *Renmin Ribao* (People's Daily) and *Zhongguo Qingnian Bao* (China Youth Daily) are well-informed on and sensitive to high-level policy on important domestic and foreign issues.[4] But it is wrong to assume that every article and photograph is controlled from a central point in Beijing. Single items should be examined with care. Analysis requires casting a wide net that captures a sufficient quantity of material to permit generalization, to establish trends and thematic emphasis, and to validate the significance attributed to idiosyncratic or deviant material.

Finally, of course, the media have no monopoly on attitude formation. Parental and family influences, peer pressures, and personal experience all contribute to individual and group perceptions and reactions. How these weigh in the net result depends on context, credibility, and consistency, both within and among the various inputs.

Having acknowledged these problems, however, the fact remains that media images, particularly of phenomena that are remote in time or space, can become stereotypes with a strong subliminal effect, positive or negative. The choice of words and pictures can increase or decrease emotional feelings. The past may be presented as pure history or as carrying a message for the present and the future. War offers fertile grounds for nourishing nostalgia for heroism and national unity and for mobilizing vigilance against a general or a specific threat. Any or all of these aspects may appear in combination, which then requires an evaluation as to what is the primary, as opposed to the secondary or minor, intent.

These guidelines will inform the following survey of general references to the 1937–45 war and, more particularly, two instances in which the war became the focus of special attention. The first instance concerns the 1982 controversy over the treatment of the war in Japanese textbooks. The second instance involves the fortieth anniversary of the war's end, Prime Minister Nakasone's visit to a military shrine on this occasion, and the 1985 anti-Japanese student demonstrations that occurred as a result.

SCHOLARLY HISTORICAL STUDIES

Two approaches differentiate Chinese scholarly works dealing with past Sino-Japanese relations. One approach necessarily includes reference to conflict, but concentrates instead on the positive aspects of mutual benefit. The other approach emphasizes the negative side while adding rhetorical reassurances on postwar interaction. Both approaches, however, tend to warn against the possible return of Japanese militarism.

Three major volumes exemplify these approaches. The most scholarly study is a collection of conference papers on the history of Sino-Japanese relations.[5] Held in Heilongjiang province on August 8–13, 1982, the meeting celebrated the tenth anniversary of the restoration of full diplomatic relations and as such prompted the twenty-three authors to emphasize positive themes. The occasion probably also prompted them to omit reference to another commemorative date, namely the fiftieth anniversary of the establishment of Manchukuo as a Japanese puppet state that included

Heilongjiang. Instead they ritualistically acknowledged "the historic friendship of two good neighbors separated by a narrow strip of water."

None of the authors focuses on the 1937 conflict, although one reviews "Three Wars of Ancient Time" and two deal with the non-military aspects of the 1894–95 war. A curious contrast, however, confronts the reader between the opening and closing pages of the symposium. The first chapter reviews the three early conflicts over Korea (663, 1274–81, and 1592–97). The authors conclude:

> The profound lesson of the three wars is that the two countries, China and Japan, should "make peace a priority, strengthen the stopping of war." . . . The three wars of ancient time were a brief interlude in the long enduring history of Sino-Japanese friendship and a record of defeat for the aggressors. . . . *Good neighborly friendship is the mainstream; mutual hostility is a minor tributary. History proves that Sino-Japanese friendship cannot be blocked.* History develops the trend; there is no reverse road, there is no prospect of turning back. "Changing arrows into jade," being good neighbors in peace, and having equality in friendship are the demands of the time and are in accord with the basic interests of both the Chinese and the Japanese nations and peoples [italics added].[6]

This unqualified statement of confidence in the basic relationship and its future evolution is not echoed in the final chapter, which reviews thirty years of post-World War II trade between the two countries. Although the central focus is economics, not politics, the author cautions his audience, "In Japan there are some forces that always cause trouble, that use every pretext to spoil Sino-Japanese relations, that strive to beautify past aggression against China and other Asian countries, and moreover carry out all kinds of activity in vain attempts to revive Japanese militarism."[7] The article concludes on a confident note, claiming that "these various threatening situations have already aroused the close attention and strict vigilance of the Chinese and Japanese peoples." Yet the final page also raises the specter of possible "trouble" and the revival of "Japanese militarism." The warning almost certainly resulted from the textbook controversy that erupted just prior to the conference.

A contrast to this predominantly positive volume is the thoroughly negative textbook appropriately titled *A Brief History of Japanese Imperialist Aggression Against China.*[8] More than two hundred pages of text and a detailed chronology covering the period 1870–1945 graphically recount the grim record. Published in 1984 with an initial run of 15,000 copies (the scholarly symposium had only 4,800 copies run), the book focuses on "fifty years of Japanese imperialism's insatiably greedy aggression against China . . . [which] caused the Chinese people to suffer endless hardships and vast casualties and seriously threatened the existence of the Chinese nation." These opening remarks reinforce the powerful image on the cover that depicts a crying baby in a bombed railway yard, probably the most widely distributed photograph from China in World War II.

The introduction notes that although the study recounts events it also analyzes the social basis and explosive character of Japan's aggression because "this can help the vast readership, *especially young readers*, to understand the ferocious features of the Japanese militarist ruling group and the resulting disaster, and moreover help us to cherish the present independence of our country and greatly stimulate our deep devotion to our socialist motherland" [italics added].[9] Frequent references to patriotism (*aiguo zhuyi*) follow. In this way, the recapitulation of historical suffering is justified as a means of enhancing national pride in the younger generation.

Consistent with the official emphasis on good contemporary relations, the reader is reassured that the past is truly past because "brotherhood remains after suffering a wave of catastrophes," which is exemplified by the long tradition of friendship and the demands of the two peoples. But the negative tone quickly returns:

> Of course, we must also see that in Japan there are still a small number of people who cling madly to the "Great Japanese Empire" of the past, frequently using any means and words to argue in defense of and to exonerate the past criminal aggression of the Japanese militarists. This goes against the will of the people. It not only encounters the natural denunciation of the Chinese people, but it also arouses the revulsion and condemnation of the Japanese people. Past experience, if not forgotten, is a guide for the future. We bring to light the true history of the Japanese militarists' aggression against China and this allows the two peoples of China and Japan and their descendants in later times to gain a lesson from history so as to consolidate and develop friendly relations between China and Japan.[10]

Thus in addition to arousing patriotic pride through an awareness of recent history, the book is designed to alert people to the possibility of the past returning in the future, a possibility allegedly made more likely by developments in Japan.

On the positive side the study closes with this reference to the half century under review:

> In the long flow of historical friendship between China and Japan, this was a single unfortunate moment. The Chinese people are consistently reasonable and sensible, differentiating good from evil from past to present. They draw a definite line between the small number of militarist elements and the broad Japanese people.

Nevertheless, the negative warning is reiterated: "The Chinese and Japanese people must firmly remember the cruel and bitter lesson given the two peoples by the extreme disasters brought on by the invasion of China by the Japanese militarists."[11]

This recurring theme of vigilance against a repetition of the past is succinctly stated in numerous scholarly works. Although usually balanced with assertions of overall friendship, the warning is of interest for two reasons. First, it signals a line of attack that is expressed more fully in popularly written material designed for wider audiences. This suggests the official approval of this theme. Second, the presence of this theme in works designed for college students makes it likely that this concern will become part of their perspective in adult life. One such book is a 552-page anthology of articles, chapters, and documents titled *The Foreign Strategy of Japanese Imperialism, 1931–1945.*[12] First published in 1975, a second edition was issued in 1983 in 11,000 copies. The wide selection of articles and topics and annotation make this comprehensive collection ideal for advanced courses and seminars. Unlike our other two examples, the anthology lacks any introduction or conclusion of a substantive or political nature. But the materials speak for themselves as a detailed chronicle of the expansionistic aggression by China's neighbor.

THE 1982 TEXTBOOK CAMPAIGN

A 1982 press campaign illustrates how the mass media, by giving attention to historical conflicts, can arouse contemporary Chinese youth over possible Japanese behavior in the future. On June 26, 1982, Tokyo newspapers charged the Ministry of Education with softening the language used in textbooks concerning Japan's aggression in Asia and particularly in China.[13] The subsequent domestic furor triggered angry reactions, both official and unofficial, throughout the region, from Korea to Singapore. Tokyo's belated pledge to amend the textbooks finally calmed the situation and smoothed relations with the offended regimes.

Nearly a month passed between the initial press reports and Beijing's public response. Not until July 20 did official protests and media accounts focus attention on the issue. Once these began, however, a full-scale campaign ensued, recapitulating the story of Japanese aggression and atrocities in vivid detail. Photographs, films, reminiscences, and political cartoons accompanied dramatically worded captions, headlines, and commentaries that specifically warned against the danger of renewed Japanese militarism. The simultaneous treatment in all media indicates direction from above despite the assertion of one official that "this was wholly spontaneous; we couldn't control the anger of the people."[14] Both the extent and the content of the campaign aimed at having domestic as well as international impact.

Zhongguo Qingnian Bao, the official youth newspaper with a circulation of three million, followed other national media on the textbook issue. Its initial news stories and the commentary of July 24 repeated Japanese press accounts with attribution and echoed official protests, adding the reported anger and the hurt feelings of Chinese and Japanese youth, who were united in friendship. A more volatile and concentrated reaction appeared one week later, after which clusters of articles and photographs intermittently filled the pages. These culminated in a strong attack by the paper's commentator on August 14.[15]

On July 31 the newspaper had intensified its coverage with two grim photographs, one of a young Chinese male about to be decapitated and the second showing a mutilated corpse. The accompanying caption claimed that the Nanjing Massacre of December 1937 had caused 340,000 deaths and it protested the suppression of this atrocity in Japanese textbooks. An adjacent article summarized a Japanese book that had revealed experiments in germ warfare that had been carried out on Chinese in Manchuria. It quoted the author's condemnation of this as inhuman, shameful, and the work of Satan's disciples. The book reportedly shocked all of Japan. A lengthy news roundup covered the initial Beijing-Tokyo exchanges over the textbooks, citing Japanese domestic protests against the Ministry of Education's insistence that this was a purely internal matter. It also reported editorial attacks in North Korea, Thailand, and Hong Kong.

Four days later a signed article ridiculed Japan's rejection of foreign protests as interference in its internal affairs. It also claimed that China's national integrity and sovereignty had been insulted by the textbook's use of the term "forward advance" instead of "invasion" and its refusal to describe the Nanjing Massacre as such, explaining instead that the "killing of many" was the result of "fierce resistance by Chinese troops." Seen in this perspective, the matter was clearly an international one that required an appropriate response from Tokyo.

A few positive notes emerged in this chorus of criticism. Japanese opposition to the revised textbooks won repeated reference, showing that a basic "unity and friendship" existed between the two countries despite "certain circles" in the Japanese government and the Liberal Democratic party (LDP) that sought to injure the relationship. For example, a Sino-Japanese children's choral group was featured in picture and story. The article noted that the children were jointly opposed to the return of Japanese militarism and the spiritual closeness of the children was compared with colors in a rainbow. Also, a letter from a Japanese professor, addressed to Chinese youth, protesting the textbooks was given a prominent place.

But the same issue of the newspaper also photoreproduced a Japanese army order establishing a "no-man's-land" and an adjacent article attacked the Japanese three-all policy—burn all, kill all, loot all—as extremely cruel, inhuman, and vicious. This scorched earth policy and its implementation in areas of Chinese resistance won repeated attention in this and other articles as vivid proof of the total barbarity of Japanese military behavior.

August 15, the anniversary of Tokyo's surrender broadcast, had been anticipated on the previous day: virtually the entire paper was devoted to this event and the textbook controversy. Under the headline "The Bloody History Must Not Be Written Off," a half-page recapitulation graphically summarized the events following the initial takeover of Manchuria in 1931. A map depicting "the invasion of Japanese militarism" identified the main points of advance, beginning with the loss of Taiwan after the 1894–95 war. Textual captions spelled out the details, accompanied by depictions of sword-bearing soldiers beheading people and burning buildings. Articles and photographs covered various aspects of the war with special emphasis on atrocities as revealed in the Tokyo war crimes trials and memoirs of Japanese soldiers.

The strongest statement came in an authoritatively signed "commentator" article entitled "Beware of the Revival of Militarism." Although it combined the themes of patriotic education, Sino-Japanese friendship, and vigilance against a repetition of history, the last point dominated the essay. After warning that "the ghost of Japanese militarism has come into sight and is giving us a lesson," the article continued:

> Are the officials of the Ministry of Education mentally unbalanced? Or do they misread the almanac? No! Of course not, they consider themselves smart. A few Japanese constantly bear in mind the profit they gained from the invasion of China and the war in Southeast Asia. Their hope of realizing their dream of reviving militarism is indefatigable. Their attempt to deceive the younger generation through education is deliberate. Their intention to revise history and to beautify militarism under the cover of ancestor worship is carefully thought out. Nevertheless how could historical facts written in blood be concealed by lies written in ink? Your "samurai" forebears used innocent Chinese to test bacteriological warfare and used them as living targets. They dismembered and chopped up Chinese captives who were tied to trees. You forced Chinese to dig holes and bury themselves alive. You adopted such savage means as the "iron maiden," pulling out fingernails, branding, belly cutting, electric grinding, and flesh eating to persecute Chinese compatriots. Thus even the German fascists labeled Japanese soldiers as a "group of beasts."

Rhetorically challenging Tokyo "Do you dare willfully to whitewash history and try to carry on the cover-up policy?" the writer paid ironic praise to Japanese militarism as a "teacher of negative lessons." He pointed to the tempering of the national will and the creation of numerous heroes that resulted, concluding that "those Chinese working in the area of the education of youth might well say 'thanks' to the officials of the Japanese Ministry of Education and 'appreciate' the way in which these officials are giving us a lesson that helps us to be even more alert and sober thirty-seven years after the war." This bitter sarcasm coupled with the admonition to "be even more alert and sober" contrasted with assertions earlier in the article that "unity and friendship" characterize Sino-Japanese relations, present and prospective.

The harsh verbal imagery of this commentary was visually paralleled a few days later in an article that reproduced paintings of wartime atrocities. Stacks of naked bodies, decapitated heads, and dismembered women communicated the savagery of Japanese troops in gruesome detail. The depiction of "Chinese traitors" working with Japanese soldiers and the identification of the painters as being from both countries countered the more nationalistic and xenophobic aspects. Amid this controversy, however, these were minor notes, barely audible compared to the major motif of Japanese militarism as a past and future threat. The text accompanying the pictures appropriately characterized the events portrayed therein as "stunning . . . unbearable . . . terrifying . . . unforgettable." The attendant call for Sino-Japanese solidarity against the general menace of war struck a somewhat hollow tone by comparison.

The campaign promptly ended at this point when Tokyo promised to review the disputed terminology. With Prime Minister Suzuki Zenkō scheduled to visit Beijing from September 26 to October 2, marking the tenth anniversary of normalized relations, both sides moved to defuse the heated subject. This, however, did not prevent Chinese Communist Party (CCP) General Secretary Hu Yaobang from publicly warning against the possible revival of Japanese militarism when he addressed the Twelfth Party Congress in mid-September. In addition Suzuki reportedly spent a considerable part of his visit reassuring the Chinese leadership on the matter.

The textbook issue did not disappear. In 1985 Beijing reacted quickly to a July 1 memorandum from Tokyo's Ministry of Education concerning primary school texts in history and social affairs. On the positive side, Xinhua, the Chinese news agency, noted that seven publishers now termed the invasion of China as "aggression" compared with only two in the past. And the number of textbooks that referred to the Nanjing Massacre increased from two to six. But on the negative side, Xinhua noted the failure to spell out the facts of the massacre, especially the omission of casualty estimates. It also criticized the failure to mention certain other atrocities, such as the germ warfare experiments in Manchuria.[16] More generalized references elsewhere to attempts at "beautifying aggression" kept the controversy alive for Chinese audiences. Then in 1986 the controversy erupted anew with another round of text-book review in Tokyo. This will be addressed below.

It is impossible to determine the full motivation behind *Zhong-guo Qingnian Bao*'s lengthy and bitter coverage of the war in 1982. Had it been contrary to official policy some shortening of duration or tempering of content would seem to have been in order. Hu Yaobang's past position as head of the youth league presumably equipped him to influence the journal's presentation of the issue. Yet Hu soon became Beijing's main promoter of Sino-Japanese relations. This raises the issue of a possible divergence of views within the leadership concerning the domestic treatment of the textbook issue and the more important matter of linking past conflict with the possibility of future Japanese militarism.

But whatever factors may have contributed to the campaign, its impact on the youthful readers of *Zhongguo Qingnian Bao* can be surmised. The journal's treatment of the war in general and the Nanjing Massacre in particular added a new dimension of "learning from the past" for a generation far removed from the events of 1937–45. In this regard, some of the seeds sown in 1982 bore fruit in the student demonstrations of 1985.

COMMEMORATING V-J DAY

August 15, 1985, marked the fortieth anniversary of Japan's defeat in World War II. The event occasioned a flood of articles, meetings, and special events in China, as it did elsewhere in the world. Museum exhibitions, plays, films, and television documentaries focused on the conflict. Personal reminiscences, heroic and grim, filled newspapers and magazines. A summer-long television series, "Four Generations Under One Roof," depicted the suffering of a typical Chinese family amid the horrors of the Japanese invasion and occupation. In Beijing ten thousand children gathered at the Monument to the People's Heroes for a mass ceremony. Plans were announced for a 20,000-square-meter memorial hall, to be completed in 1987 for the fiftieth anniversary of the beginning of the war. To be located at the Marco Polo bridge, the hall would include a model of a mass grave where several hundred Chinese soldiers and civilians were buried, forty rooms devoted to the war, and one room on postwar friendship between the two peoples.[17]

Another museum, this one devoted to the notorious Nanjing Massacre, won renewed attention at this time. Located on the outskirts of the former Nationalist capital, its starkly modern natural stone exterior bears the outsize numeral 300,000—the official total of civilian and military dead killed in six weeks of Japanese rapine, pillage, and slaughter. The museum's interior displays maps, photographs, newspaper reproductions, and documents, both contemporary and compiled after the war, testifying to the tragedy inflicted on this historic city after its surrender.[18]

Several new publications focused on the Nanjing Massacre in connection with the anniversary. A massive compilation titled *Source Materials Relating to the Horrible Massacre Committed by the Japanese Troops in Nanjing* had an initial printing of 10,300 copies.[19] A smaller booklet selected the most gruesome photographs from the museum collection to accompany a lengthy account issued in 34,000 copies.[20] The museum catalogue graphically reproduced the entire display of photos depicting piles of bodies found in the Yangtze River, rows of severed heads, the mutilated bodies of women and children, skeletal remains, and mass graves. Many came from snapshots taken by Japanese soldiers, others from postwar investigations.

The repeated references in the Chinese media to the Nanjing death toll as greater than the combined casualties from the atomic bombs dropped on Hiroshima and Nagasaki convey multiple messages. First, these references imply that there is a double standard at work: world attention focuses on the victims of the atomic bombs and ignores China's greater loss. Second, these references also seek to point out that Japan often wins sympathy as the victim and the United States is cast as the nuclear villain even though Japan started the war. This allows Japan to avoid any feelings of guilt for the invasion of China and the Nanjing atrocities. Third, these references make the point that the Nanjing Massacre was worse than Hiroshima and Nagasaki because it occurred piecemeal through the personal actions of individuals whereas the atomic holocausts occurred instantaneously from high-altitude bombing.

In my conversations in China in 1986, the first two points in particular emerged frequently as specific criticisms of the comparative attention given abroad to the two catastrophes. I found that the Nanjing Massacre repeatedly evoked genuine emotion, exemplifying for many the Japanese capacity for total brutality and inhumanity. For Chinese, young and old, the Nanjing Massacre epitomizes Japanese aggression.

The 1985 commemorative speeches did not treat Japanese militarism solely in historical terms. The principal speaker at Beijing's main assemblage specifically warned:

> Today a handful of people in Japan are again indulging in pipe dreams of a "Greater East Asia Co-Prosperity Sphere" and are even engaged in attempts to revive militarism, in complete violation of the will of both the Chinese and Japanese people and the trend of history. Homage paid by Japanese government officials at the Yasukuni Shrine, where, among others, the chief Japanese war criminals were venerated, hurt the feelings of the Chinese people.[21]

The implied linkage between "a handful of people" who "are even engaged in attempts to revive militarism" and Prime Minister Nakasone, one of the "Japanese government officials" who had paid "homage" at the shrine on August 15, gave this issue special significance. This linkage contributed to the student anger that erupted in demonstrations and that would return to plague the relationship in subsequent years.

The Yasukuni Shrine in Tokyo is dedicated to 2.4 million Japanese soldiers who died in various wars. Although it lacks any obvious military symbols, its Shinto ownership made the shrine a target of postwar reforms aimed at eliminating government sponsorship of religion. Nevertheless from 1956 to 1971 the Ministry of Health and Welfare was involved in enshrining war dead there.[22] In 1959 it decided to send the name cards of all class–B and class–C war criminals to the shrine. The ministry delayed until 1966, however, before sending the cards for fourteen class–A war criminals, including that of former Prime Minister Tōjō Hideki. The shrine in turn waited until 1978 on the latter group, reportedly to test public opinion. Meanwhile, by 1972 the ministry had decided to cease its involvement because of controversy over a state patronage bill for the shrine.

Prior to 1985 prime ministers had attended the shrine ceremony on a personal basis. These unofficial appearances prompted Chinese media comment, as in 1982 when Suzuki's visit provoked a *Zhongguo Qingnian Bao* article entitled "Whom Do They Mourn For?" But Nakasone broke precedent by attending the August 15 ceremony in his official capacity. Following the student demonstrations, the Chinese foreign ministry revealed that it had expressed concern in advance, asking Tokyo to "handle the matter with prudence. Regrettably, however, the Japanese side, ignoring our friendly exhortations, went ahead with the official visit to the shrine, thus hurting seriously the feelings of the Chinese people."[23] Apparently, concern over possible public reaction constrained the foreign ministry's immediate response to Nakasone's move because no formal protest was issued. In response to the question of whether China's commemorative activities might not arouse anti-Japanese feelings, Li Chuanhua, deputy director of the Propaganda Bureau of the CCP Central Propaganda Department, combined positive and cautionary themes:

> The Chinese people feel no hatred toward Japan now. Our purpose of solemnly commemorating the 40th anniversary of victory in the anti-Japanese war and reviewing the deep suffering of the Chinese people brought by foreign aggression is precisely to ensure that the two peoples of China and Japan will never again be involved in a war against each other and will live on good terms from generation to generation.[24]

Li then repeated an earlier statement by Minister of National Defense Zhang Aiping that opposition was directed against the Japanese fascists who committed the aggression, not the Japanese people or their present government.

But Zhang had justified the commemorative activities in more narrow and positive terms than Li. By "reviewing and exposing the aggressive crimes of the fascists, and of the Japanese fascists in particular . . . our purpose is to promote the friendly cooperation between the Chinese and Japanese people." Zhang had failed to specify Japan in warning that "if any country or government pursues a hegemonist, aggressive, and expansionist policy . . . we will resolutely oppose it together with all peace-loving people in the world." In addition, Zhang offered patriotic indoctrination as a second goal of the commemorative activities. By recalling wartime experiences, Zhang noted that "we can carry out various forms of education in patriotism and revolutionary traditions so as to invigorate the nation, and to realize the great targets set forth by the 12th CCP Congress." This was necessary because "the better the economic situation and our life are, the more constantly we should bear in mind how we have fought for the happy life we are living today. We should not forget that once we were faced with national extinction." Thus, Zhang's remarks struck a less cautionary tone than did those of Li and other speakers on the occasion.[25]

It is impossible to recapitulate the entire media output associated with the anniversary celebrations, particularly the tremendous coverage it received on radio and television, much less determine its actual impact on various audiences. In retrospect, numerous Chinese acknowledged that the twenty-eight chapter television series "Four Generations Under One Roof" especially affected younger viewers who lacked first-hand knowledge of the war. More generally there seems little doubt that the August events contributed to the anti-Japanese sentiments voiced by university students later that fall.[26]

1986: TEXTBOOK TROUBLES RETURN

Despite the furor aroused in both Japan and China by the issues of textbook revision and Yasukuni Shrine visits, these two issues subsequently returned as points of friction. Although both governments endeavored to dampen domestic reactions for the sake of better relations, the ensuing complications foreshadowed future problems as these and other incidents continued to enflame the war's historical heritage in China.

In August 1982, Chief Cabinet Secretary Miyazawa Kiichi pledged that "Japan will pay full heed to this [Chinese and South Korean] criticism . . . and the government will undertake on its own responsibility to make the necessary amendments."[27] The mechanism for implementing this pledge had been created under the American occupation in order to safeguard against the promotion of leftist views, which at that time were dominant among textbook writers and teachers.[28] A nongovernmental consultative group reviews initial drafts for the Ministry of Education, which then points out "errors" for the publisher's consideration. The revised draft then goes back to the consultative group for final approval or rejection, its recommendation presumably being accepted by the ministry. Although technically the ministry was free to differ with the findings of the consultative group, it could not dictate content to the publisher but only reject errors of fact.

Miyazawa's pledge failed to be realized. In November 1983 the education minister announced that the objectionable textbooks would be corrected the following spring. In January 1984, however, a junior high school text approved by the ministry appeared with some of the controversial wording unchanged. In particular, a foot-noted reference blamed the Nanjing Massacre on "shooting by some civilians in the confusion of the occupation" after which "Japanese soldiers killed numerous civilians, including women and children." [29] No total casualty figure was given.

The 1982 controversy prompted a right-wing group, the National Conference to Defend Japan, to produce a textbook that would make "young people love their country's history." [30] The submission of this textbook for review coincided with the August 1985 commemoration. The consultative group identified more than eight hundred points for reconsideration by the publisher, who was so notified in November.[31] In February 1986 a revised draft came back for a second review, which culminated in the consultative group's approval on May 27 after what was reported to be an unprecedented three-hour heated debate.

At this point leaks to the press triggered strong protests in Japan and abroad. On June 4, Beijing's initial reaction came in response to a question at the foreign ministry's weekly news briefing. Noting Japanese press reports, the spokesman recalled past Chinese statements and Japanese promises "to see to it that the errors in the textbooks [are] corrected. [But] regrettably the Ministry of Education of Japan has once again done something that hurts the feelings of the Chinese people. . . . How to look upon the facts about the war of aggression launched by the Japanese militarists in the past should be treated in a serious and cautious manner." [32] The spokesman warned that "we have always been and will continue to be in the future opposed to any statements and actions that distort historical fact and prettify the war of aggression."

Three days later the foreign ministry delivered a "stern note" to the acting Japanese chargé d'affaires, claiming that the textbook "grossly distorts" history and declaring, "To safeguard Sino-Japanese friendship and [to] guarantee a healthy development of relations between the two countries, the Chinese Government strongly demands that the Japanese Government implement its 1982 commitment . . . and eliminate the negative effects caused by the issue."[33] Tokyo's spokesman immediately announced that the book was still under examination. Accompanying Chinese press stories identified the "distortions" as including the justification of Japan's aggression as "necessary" and the "glossing over [of] the holocaust perpetrated by Japanese troops in Nanjing."

In contrast with 1982, no mass media campaign addressed the issue. In private, editors indicated that directives against such publicity had been issued.[34] A single lengthy comment appeared in *Renmin Ribao,* explaining that the controversial textbook was "only one of the approved versions" of which there were "quite a lot."[35] In spelling out its errors, the writer noted, "As for the brutal Nanjing Massacre that shocked people all over the world, the book deliberately refrains from mentioning the fact of the butchering of ordinary civilians by the Japanese troops, but on the contrary says that Japanese people did not know of this incident until after the war and that it is necessary to carry out a clear investigation regarding the 'truth' of the incident." The article recounted how "the book was first generally denounced in Japan by Japanese people of insight" and quoted *Asahi Shimbun* at length to this effect. Thus, "amid loud condemnation at home and abroad, the relevant departments in Japan could not help but" claim that no final approval had been given.

Meanwhile Prime Minister Nakasone, in the midst of campaigning for reelection, declared, "After studying the problems pointed out by China and other nations, I have reached the conclusion that certain portions of the textbook should be re-examined."[36] His remarks alarmed supporters of the Ministry of Education, who saw this as a precedent for the political control of education, but pleased those in the Ministry of Foreign Affairs who were anxious over Japan's relations with its neighbors. Nakasone's choice of words and timing made explicit the linkage between domestic politics and foreign policy. Nakasone, moderate nationalists, and right-wingers all agreed that the issue was an internal affair in which foreign interference had no place. A parallel linkage of Chinese domestic politics with foreign policy was hinted at by top Beijing officials who, according to their Japanese counterparts, asked them for "help" in dealing with internal divisions rather than "making demands."[37]

Finally, Tokyo moved to resolve the matter, alerting Beijing privately that the acceptance of a revised text would be announced on July 10. This prompted an authoritative "commentator" article in *Renmin Ribao* on July 7, the anniversary of the commencement of Sino-Japanese hostilities at the Marco Polo Bridge in 1937.[38] A major statement issued on an important national day, it was widely reprinted, thereby establishing a basic line of interpretation on Japan and Sino-Japanese relations.

The article declared: "Like the 'textbook incident' in 1982, this has evoked strong reactions among the Chinese people, other Asian peoples, and the Japanese public . . . because it is related to a basic question, that is, whether Japan admits or does not admit that the war which was launched by the Japanese militarists and which brought disaster to China and other Asian countries was a war of aggression." As proof it quoted the spurious Tanaka Memorial of 1927: "In order to conquer China, we must first conquer Manchuria and Mongolia; in order to conquer the world, we must first conquer China." After summarizing the events of 1931 and 1937 and contrasting them with the textbook's version, the writer concluded, "Historical facts have fully proved that the launching of the war of aggression against China by the Japanese militarists was a long etablished national policy of the Japanese ruling class, and this cannot be denied by any excuses and lies."

An ominous warning followed: "Although only a small number of people advocate and engineer a war at the beginning, if these people's activities are neglected or tolerated, the war will still become a horrible disaster that causes great suffering and misfortune to hundreds of millions of people." Since the author had paralleled other writers in repeatedly claiming that "only a small number" of Japanese want to revive militarism and "prettify aggression," whatever reassurance was implied was offset by these words.

The writer rejected two Japanese accusations concerning Beijing's public protest. First, denying that this was "attempting to settle old accounts," he insisted that China "has always distinguished the handful of Japanese militarists from the Japanese people as a whole." He also reiterated the standard line positing "more than 2,000 years of friendly exchange" against "a short and temporary adverse current." Second, rejecting Japanese charges of "interference in internal affairs," he acknowledged that this principle applied to the choice of textbooks except when they "wrongly described Japan's relations . . . distort the historic facts of Japanese aggression and expansion." In fact, "the 'textbook problem' . . . has not only despised the criteria of the international community and law, but also negated the solemn commitment of the Japanese Government to its international obligation."

The textbook's final version evoked qualified praise and criticism in China. On the positive side, Xinhua reported that the Tokyo government four times "instructed and urged" the Ministry of Education to make revisions, and that Nakasone himself "repeatedly stressed" this point.[39] Consequently the "revision of the textbook was completed basically at the prompting of the Japanese Government" to which "appreciation should be given." The revised language described the puppet state of Manchukuo, the Marco Polo Bridge Incident, the Shanghai Incident, and the Nanjing Massacre.

However, the Xinhua headline, "Distorted Facts Remain in Approved Japanese Textbook Observers Say," established the lead sentences, including the assertion that "not a word was mentioned about the aggressive policies of the Japanese militarists." This line was amplified by a foreign ministry spokesman who called the book "hardly satisfactory" and said that it "deliberately covers up the basic fact that the Japanese militarists launched the war of aggression against neighboring countries."[40] Beijing's ambivalent attitude was summed up in his comment, "We have taken note of the efforts made by the Japanese Government and the removal or revision of a number of obviously erroneous narrations in the textbook. However the textbook does not have a sound keynote."

Regardless of the dual tone sounded in official statements, I found a singular and strong negative attitude with respect to this issue in my private interviews throughout China in the summer of 1986. The Chinese I spoke with about the textbook issue charged the Japanese with the perfidious betrayal of past pledges and a pernicious tendency toward future militarism. A government analyst called it "a vital issue" and a specialist on Japan warned, "This case won't end the matter." A young historian agreed: "The issue is likely to arise every year that textbooks come up for approval," although he added that it might eventually fade in importance as a younger generation replaces those who had fought the Japanese.

Despite little media attention, many individuals showed a keen knowledge of the details and expressed considerable emotion in criticizing the Japanese handling of the matter. They rarely acknowledged Tokyo's improvement of the original language and never credited Nakasone personally for any of the changes. Blame invariably fell on a "small number of people," but this did not allow the issue to be trivialized. For most, the fact that this repeated the 1982 experience underscored the depth of the problem.

Compared with 1982, the 1986 controversy resulted in a relatively balanced compromise for both sides. Tokyo amended the textbook in part but stood by the final version without apology. Beijing protested the initial draft and approved the major revisions, but claimed more needed to have been done. Each muted the potential polemic and, to some extent, succeeded in accepting the other's position without surrendering its own. The two foreign ministries in particular worked diligently on behalf of the highest officials in both governments to save the relationship from further embarrassment.[41] Yet as an authoritative Chinese specialist on Japan remarked, "From the diplomatic point of view it is relatively easy to solve the textbook problem. But domestic politics want to educate the young people on the logic of aggression toward other nations. And this differs from diplomacy."

Domestic politics in Japan revived the textbook issue almost as soon as it had been settled. Reelected with one of the biggest LDP victories in years, Nakasone appointed a new cabinet with a staunch nationalist, Fujio Masayuki, as minister of education. In one of his first press appearances Fujio was quoted as suggesting that the same "guys" who had been complaining about the textbook were also guilty of aggression.[42] Beijing struck back briefly through a foreign ministry spokesman: "The statement was regrettable. We resent the statement. We are not going to make further comment on the issue considering the fact that the Japanese Government has been paying attention to the subsequent situation."[43] Fujio did not stop there, but before addressing "the subsequent situation," the Yasukuni Shrine deserves prior attention in order to reflect the proper sequence of events in 1986.

YASUKUNI SHRINE (NOT) REVISITED

As the textbook issue faded, the Yasukuni Shrine question flared briefly, only to end peacefully. But the very fact that it occurred at all, after the 1985 student demonstrations, showed the persistence of another irritant in the relationship. In the immediate aftermath of the demonstrations, Nakasone avoided the annual fall shrine ceremony. He did the same the following spring amid conflicting pressures at home and abroad.

Foreign Minister Wu Xueqian raised the matter in early April during a Tokyo visit, reportedly warning Foreign Minister Abe Shintarō that "unless this is settled smoothly it will hurt the Chinese people's feelings. It is important how correctly we will cope with past history." [44] Abe allegedly took issue with this, reminding Wu that Japan had already expressed "self-reflection on its past war record in the Sino-Japanese Joint Communique (1972) but as a problem on a different plane, the Japanese people have a feeling of mourning for the victims of war. . . . [It is] not that both Government and people are glorifying war criminals."

Wu discussed the issue with Abe, Nakasone, and LDP Secretary General Kanemaru Shin, and at the Foreign Press Club, prompting the conservative newspaper *Sankei Shimbun* to object that, because shrine visits are a domestic problem, his statements were "regrettable." [45] Taking a page from Beijing's book, the editorial claimed that persistent Chinese protests on this matter hurt the Japanese people's feelings.

Kanemaru was quoted as telling Wu that Nakasone "is also concerned and thinking of something new [to take the place of the Yasukuni Shrine], removing the color of religion, where the people will equally be able to pay homage . . . something like Arlington National Cemetery in the United States where . . . foreign leaders also can offer flowers, regardless of their religion." [46] He acknowledged that "there will be strong repulsion within the Party but I want to make efforts to materialize it while Secretary General."

When the shrine's spring festival arrived, Nakasone claimed that a heavy schedule prevented his attendance. But 148 Diet members or their proxies went (147 LDP, 1 New Liberal Club), led by a former minister of justice, who said Nakasone was "probably holding back because he doesn't want to offend the Chinese but it is necessary to take a resolute stance as Japanese." [47]

The next question concerned the August 1986 ceremonies. A resolution adopted by 300 LDP Diet members warned that "if Nakasone does not go to the shrine, Japan will forfeit its right as a sovereign state." The prime minister responded on the campaign trail that such visits were not "institutionalized."[48] My private conversations revealed equally heated views on both sides. An informed China expert in a major trading company said Nakasone would be "crazy" to visit the shrine again simply because of "domestic pressure." But a former diplomat called the Chinese "arrogant" for pressing the issue, declaring, "All of my generation, including Nakasone, share responsibility for the past and we should honor those who were hanged as taking the responsibility for all of us."[49]

On August 14, Chief Cabinet Secretary Gotoda Masaharu announced that "after careful and independent consideration" Nakasone had made a "prudent and independent" decision not to visit the shrine.[50] Referring to the "criticisms of neighboring countries," he added, "We must stress international ties and give appropriate consideration to the national sentiments of neighboring countries." On August 15, seven cabinet ministers attended the shrine ceremonies, including Education Minister Fujio, but not Foreign Minister Kuranari Sosuke.[51] Fujio took the occasion to claim that at least one of those enshrined, the wartime prime minister, Tōjō Hideki, was no war criminal because the Tokyo International Military Tribunal's verdict "cannot be considered as correct."[52]

In Beijing the day was marked by Japan's representative on the Commission for Friendship in the Twenty-first Century presenting Hu Yaobang with a bouquet of Japanese flowers after laying a similar bouquet at the monument in Tiananmen Square.[53] Hu acknowledged the flowers as "a symbol of peace as well as friendship" and said it was "wise" for Nakasone not to have gone to the shrine. Hu then softened the standard Chinese position by adding, "We always held that the Japanese people are also the victims of Japanese militarism. It is understandable for Japanese people to cherish the memory of their relatives who died in the war and pray for peace in various forms. They have our deep sympathy."

This exchange closed the question for the time being, at least between the two governments. It did not, however, close the question in Japan. A new group of eighteen young LDP Diet members, formed on July 31, attacked the "grovelling diplomacy" that was alleged to be manifest in textbook revision and Nakasone's absence at the shrine ceremony.[54] Its secretary general obliquely attacked Beijing by asking, "Can a country which rejects religion tell us not to follow our tradition?" He added his belief that the Tokyo War Crimes Trial had been illegal.

Nakasone felt compelled by domestic criticism to spell out his views at a press conference in late August. Asked why he had gone in 1985 but not in 1986, he answered at length with remarks of interest for both their international and their domestic implications. Nakasone began by admitting that "personally" he was "the one who wishes to visit the Yasukuni Shrine most" because his younger brother and "quite a few comrades" died in the war.[55] In addition he "wanted to establish the fact [that] that sort of procedure conforms to the Constitution." He claimed, however, that he "was not aware that permanent war criminals are enshrined there" but "it is natural for other countries to think that" a prime minister's visit "amounts to singing the praise of those leaders." He noted that, because "in China and in other countries opposition parties exist, that gives the opposition good material to attack the government. . . . Governments friendly with Japan will be driven into a corner and Japan's relations with them will deteriorate again—South Korea, China, and ASEAN, for instance." This will please "those farther north," meaning the Soviet Union.

Nakasone's reference to "opposition parties" in China reflected the previously mentioned intimations of disagreement on the Japanese relationship that had been communicated in Beijing to Tokyo's diplomats. His reference also sidestepped the Chinese claim of injured feelings among the people and thereby put the question in practical political terms, something, he declared, that "the spirits of the war dead would understand. I believed that they too would grieve if the country were driven into a predicament and isolated from Asia."

If the dead understood, the Minister of Education did not. In a somewhat rambling magazine interview, Fujio said that visiting the shrine to "express sympathy and solicitude for those who had laid down their lives for the country" was the "same as Chinese paying homage to the Confucius Temple and the Zhongshan [Sun Yat-sen] Mausoleum."[56] This gratuitously insulting comparison accompanied an equally provocative description of the Nanjing Massacre as an "unredressed incident" intended to "break down enemy resistance." Furthermore, he added that "war means killing people. It is not slaughtering as far as international law is concerned."

This time Seoul, not Beijing, took the stronger position sooner. Angered by Fujio's assertion that the 1910 annexation had been agreed to in advance by the Korean court, the foreign minister of the Republic of Korea canceled his imminent visit for the first Korean-Japanese foreign ministers meeting.[57] Nakasone thereupon fired Fujio, the first such cabinet dismissal in thirty-three years and only the third in postwar history. The chief cabinet secretary immediately declared, "Fujio's statements are strongly regrettable because they have caused useless doubts not only about Japan's reflections on the past war and determination for peace which our country has repeatedly expressed, but also about Japan's fundamental diplomatic policy which calls for maintaining and strengthening friendly and good relations with neighboring countries. . . . [The government] expresses deep regret to South Korea and China for having created such a situation."[58]

This effort at damage limitation met diplomatic needs, but probably failed to persuade doubters and cynics in China, given the deep distrust of Nakasone that had been expressed in my interviews that summer.[59] Few Chinese seemed aware of the peculiarities of Japanese politics in which factional opponents win appointments from victorious prime ministers in order to preserve party unity and maintain consensus. Such had been the case with Fujio, who was with Abe's faction, a rival to Nakasone. Instead, the appointment was more generally seen as reflecting Nakasone's true views with the dismissal resulting from their inadvertent revelation.[60]

THE TOKYO TRIAL: WHOSE VERDICT?

Among the various Japanese statements that provoke angry Chinese reactions, those alluding to the Tokyo War Crimes Trial are least frequent, but nonetheless produce a strong response. Typical is the review of a Japanese film "Tokyo Trial," which won lengthy publication in China's most prestigious journal devoted to Japan.[61] The writer linked the film with the shrine controversy, noting, "At first glance, this film looks as if the Tokyo trial was an unjust trial by the victor countries over a defeated nation and as if the chief war criminal was a martyr. No wonder the Japanese premier attended the shrine where major criminals were honored." Another standard comment followed: "In this film the destruction caused by the atomic bomb is more frequently presented than that of the Nanjing Massacre. In fact the number killed in Nanjing was far larger than those killed by the two atomic bombs."

In my private interviews, Chinese held that any Japanese questioning of the trial's legal basis showed both a refusal to admit guilt and a potential for repeating the aggression. When I countered that the American debate over the postwar trials' legitimacy is not centered on excusing Germany and Japan but, rather, revolves around other issues, the Chinese respondents invariably held their ground.

Along with the Nanjing Massacre museum, a Japanese experimental germ warfare laboratory outside of Harbin, which was cited in the Tokyo trial, is frequently mentioned in articles and books as further proof of war crimes. Officially opened on the fortieth anniversary of the war's end in August 1985, this modest exhibition recalls the grim record of 3,000 victims, almost all Chinese, who succumbed to the various diseases induced by injection and other means.[62]

In this context, Fujio's remarks and those of like-minded Japanese challenging the Tokyo trial's legitimacy and the execution of class-A war criminals understandably aroused Chinese anger over past aggression and suspicion about the future course of Japanese militarism. Together with the textbook controversy and the shrine visits, there is ample fuel to ignite popular sentiment against Japan, such as erupted in the student demonstrations of September 1985. At a later point, I shall examine the societal impulses in Japan that generate these provocative nationalistic outbursts. It suffices at this point to note the syndrome of stimulus and response that generates a loop of political interaction beyond the control of top policymakers in both countries.

4

The Anti-Japanese Student
Demonstrations

Student demonstrations are important political phenomena in many countries, but they carry special import in China because of their historical role in challenging authority. Articulate advocates of nationalism, students sparked widespread dissent after the wars of 1894–95 and 1914–18. As we noted earlier, the celebrated May Fourth movement began at Beijing University when news of China's "sell-out" by the Allies at the 1919 Paris peace conference became known. The student protest triggered a wave of urban demonstrations embracing various socio-economic sectors in the country's first manifestation of modern nationalism.

As willing martyrs for reform and revolution, students proved to be politically powerful in opposing the Nationalist regime in 1946–47. In 1966–68, rioting Red Guards followed Mao's dictum to "bombard the headquarters of capitalist roaders." Conversely, student moderates, ostensibly honoring the late Zhou Enlai, mobilized against the radicals in a massive demonstration in Tiananmen Square on April 5, 1976. This prompted the Gang of Four to attack the participants as counterrevolutionary and to oust Deng Xiaoping from all his positions for allegedly having instigated the students.

After the nationwide turmoil unleashed by the rampaging Red Guards, Mao's successors moved to control student dissidence. Although the 1978 constitution guaranteed the freedoms of association and debate and the freedom to put up wall posters, these guarantees proved worthless in 1979–80 with the suppression of the short-lived democracy movement.[1] The 1980 constitution pointedly removed permission to put up wall posters, a major means of student communication in the absence of campus newspapers. Meanwhile the regime's reopening of the universities, its emphasis on technological training for career advancement, and its modernization program were assumed to assure compliant student behavior.

Against this background, the anti-Japanese demonstrations that began in Beijing on September 18, 1985, and subsequently spread to other cities, deserve special attention. This date marked the 1931 Mukden Incident in which a bomb explosion on a Japanese railroad was used by the Japanese to justify the seizure of Manchuria. This historical event fixed the particular date of the demonstrations. But the larger context within which the Chinese reaction to Nakasone's Yasukuni Shrine visit occurred was the fortieth anniversary of the war's end. This anniversary furnished the nationalistic referent that allowed the demonstrators to attack Japan's role in China's economic modernization as "a second invasion." Finally, it also offered a protective nationalistic shield for opposing the regime. Because the regime was politically vulnerable on this point of foreign policy, a wide range of domestic practices could also be criticized at the same time that the students criticized Japan.

The regime's responses also deserve study. This was the first time since Mao's death that widespread public demonstrations had challenged authority. Mindful of the students' potential power and anxious to avoid violence, much less create martyrs, the leadership reacted ambivalently but prudently, mixing minimum force with maximum persuasion. As such, the confrontation provided a precedent for the much larger and more critical challenge posed by student demonstrations in December 1986.

ACTIONS AND REACTIONS

Ostensibly commemorating the 1931 Mukden Incident, thousands of students gathered on the campuses of Beijing, Qinghua, and People's Universities early on September 18, 1985. Behind locked gates at the latter two schools, mass meetings applauded anti-Japanese speeches and chanted slogans. At Beijing University, however, the gates remained open and several hundred students marched several miles to Tiananmen Square where they were joined by those from the other campuses who had climbed over the walls.[2]

Xinhua reported that the Beijing University assemblage was solely concerned with the historical past and quoted expressions of Sino-Japanese friendship.[3] Foreign press accounts, however, presented the demonstrations as wholly contemporary in focus. Slogans on wall posters and those shouted by the marchers included: "Down with Japanese militarism!" "Down with Nakasone!" and "Down with the second occupation!" the last referring to Japan's prominence in China's economic modernization.

Anti-Japanese sentiment exploded at other widely separated points, but this was only partially reported abroad. Two weeks after the Beijing occurrences, some one thousand university students staged similar demonstrations over a three-day period in Xian. Parading to the provincial offices, they shouted "Boycott Japanese goods!" and "Oppose the resurgence of Japanese militarism!"[4] In mid-October similar student gatherings in Chengdu led to the stoning of Japanese cars and the manhandling of pedestrians. Faced with the imminent visit of Vice President George Bush, the authorities locked the campus gates and substituted Chinese cars for Japanese ones in the motorcade.[5] As elsewhere, the Chengdu demonstrators shouted slogans against the Japanese role in China's economy. In Harbin the university authorities preempted student organizers by showing Western movies in the auditorium.[6] In Wuhan, students of the normal school were permitted to meet in the cafeteria, which they plastered with anti-Nakasone posters. Kunming also reported demonstrations and others were rumored elsewhere, albeit without confirmation.

The Beijing demonstrations coincided with the CCP Conference of Party Delegates and plenary sessions of the CCP Central Committee. In addition to the potential embarrassment of this timing, the students' linkage of historical and economic issues challenged the policy of reliance on Japan for economic modernization. An additional way that this policy was vulnerable to political controversy was suggested by a slogan reported from Xian, "Return the Diaoyu Islands to China!"[7] These unpopulated rocky outcroppings located between Taiwan and the Ryukyu Islands had long been a point of dispute between Beijing and Tokyo, especially after the early 1970s when experts estimated that large oil deposits might be located on the continental shelf. Returned to Japanese control by the United States after the Okinawa reversion, the Senkakus, as they are called in Japan, rarely occasioned open controversy. But in May 1978 more than one hundred Chinese fishing boats, equipped with electronic gear, sailed around the islands with signs claiming them for

China. That fall Deng Xiaoping turned away queries at a Tokyo press conference by suggesting the issue could "be handled better by the next generation."[8] Since then both sides had avoided public reference to the dispute.

Under these circumstances the timing and content of the demonstrations posed both domestic and foreign problems for the Chinese leadership. Yet no preventive measures were taken in advance and regime responses were inconsistent, suggesting uncertainty and division at various levels. A well-informed foreign correspondent later claimed that the demonstrations were organized using the telephone and mail networks among campuses, beginning with the return to classes in late August, and that they had official approval at this time.[9] The initial student poster, which openly called for demonstrations on September 18 against Japanese militarism and economic domination, appeared six days before the scheduled event.[10] Three days later the authorities rescinded permission. Party and Youth League officials tried to persuade the students to cancel their plans but to no avail; a vice mayor of Beijing appealed personally to the students, but was shouted down.

On September 17 a large number of police blocked off access to Beijing University and authorities announced that a "September 18" meeting would be held to commemorate the Mukden Incident. Meanwhile students who had eluded control ordered floral wreaths to place at the Tiananmen monument. As quickly as anti-Japanese posters were removed new ones appeared, accompanied by enlarged photos of wartime atrocities and suffering.[11] The Beijing University president was later quoted as saying that he sat up the entire night, worried over the prospect of escalating violence should police enter the campus. But in the end nothing happened.[12]

On September 28, Hu Qili and Li Peng, two rising luminaries, met with students of various persuasions in the central offices of Zhongnanhai, the locus of top party and governmental power. Subsequent reports claim that the meeting addressed the main student complaints and praised the basic motivation behind the demonstration as patriotic and consistent with university tradition. To the student accusation of official tolerance toward the offensive Japanese textbook terminology and Nakasone's Yasukuni Shrine visit, Li Peng justified a soft approach as diplomatically necessary. Against the allegation that the open door policy resulted in China being servile to Japan, he conceded that "some cadres" had misapplied the policy, but asserted that basically it preserved independence and initiative for China. To balance these "soft" responses, Li countered the student calls for democracy and freedom by referring to the constitution's specific limits and the need for protecting social stability and unity.

Despite these initial leadership efforts, demonstrations occurred the next month in Xian, Chengdu, and Wuhan. In addition to distributing circulars, Beijing students visited other cities to encourage further activity. This had the effect of nationalizing the protests. At the same time, foreign news reports emphasized the anti-Japanese slogans and behavior of the protesters and made the demonstrations an international issue. A major response was required on both accounts. The regime reacted with lengthy articles, meetings with students, and high-level diplomacy. In general, a soft approach prevailed, only occasionally tinged with a hard line. On the one hand, the students required careful handling lest they be further provoked and require more forceful suppression. On the other hand, the current policy had to be defended, especially if Japanese sensitivities were to be soothed so as to assure increased investment and technology transfer.

Zhongguo Qingnian Bao addressed the students under the heading "Patriotism and Opening up to the World." [13] It argued that "the Chinese people have totally washed away that national shame in history that caused us so much grief and have completely buried that old era in which the Chinese people suffered insults and bullying." It went on to claim that "mutual respect and equality and mutual benefit have become the foundation of the relationship between China and the nations of the world, including those that formerly committed aggression against us." The article urged that "when recalling history we should not ignore the change of era" and concluded that, although "after opening the door it is impossible not to allow a single fly or mosquito to come in," shutting the door "would be called giving up eating for fear of choking. We must establish national self-confidence." In short, student nationalism was well-meant but misguided in its attack on Japan's economic role in China.

Renmin Ribao devoted two pages to an article with the hortatory heading, "Cherish Sino-Japanese Friendly Relations Forged with

Such Arduous Effort." [14] Both the length and the content were unusual for this newspaper, signaling the seriousness with which the subject was viewed. A positive tone emerged at the outset in recounting how, "even during the period [when] the Japanese imperialists invaded China," Sun Yat-sen and other revolutionaries won support from sympathetic Japanese. After citing renowned Chinese intellectuals who had studied in Japan and then become revolutionaries, the authors stated that they would focus on post–World War II relations, thus avoiding the most painful period.

The article asserted that normal relations had resulted from "the strenuous, tortuous, unremitting, and tremendous efforts of various quarters and strata and of the farsighted politicians of the two countries for more than two decades after the founding of the PRC." In this regard, the article singled out numerous Japanese personages in a virtual panegyric. Former Japanese officers and organizations of enlisted men won pointed praise for promoting the restoration of diplomatic ties. Statements by Zhou Enlai underscored the tribute paid to those who had worked to bring the two countries closer together. This section served audiences in Japan as well as in China. Only one negative reference broke the otherwise positive tone of the presentation, the so-called Nagasaki flag controversy of 1958, and this was covered in a single paragraph.

However, the need to work continuously for improved relations was argued in terms of "forces in Japan which are opposed to Sino-Japanese friendship and are trying to beautify the aggressive war and restore militarism." To illustrate this point, the article noted that "the textbook incident in 1982 and the Yasukuni Shrine visit, which took place earlier this year, are examples known to all." Because "various problems are to be expected . . . it is necessary for the people of the two countries to make further efforts to safeguard Sino-Japanese friendship. Otherwise a small number of Japanese militarists will succeed in realizing their desire and this will be detrimental to the fundamental interests of the people of the two countries." With this token acknowledgment that there was some justification for the student demonstrations, the article ended.

Meanwhile Nakasone, responding to the student protests, had already canceled a scheduled appearance at the fall Yasukuni Shrine festival, explaining his earlier visit as "only natural to pay homage to those who fought for their country and fell in the war." [15] At the same time, Foreign Minister Abe was reportedly asked by his Chinese counterpart to understand the sentiment behind the student demonstrations and Li Peng reassured him of China's "understanding" of Japanese feelings in the controversy.[16]

Yet the issue continued to fester in both countries. Nikaidō Susumu, number two in the LDP, told the Chinese ambassador that he had not known that Tōjō and other war criminals had been enshrined and under the circumstances Nikaidō "had second thoughts" about the visit. But simultaneously a senior Japanese foreign ministry official denied that there were any plans to end the prime minister's official visits to the shrine.[17] The same week two Japanese rightists in Fukuoka were arrested for using a car to block a bus with Chinese visitors on a "friendship voyage" and shouting insults at them.[18] Diet questioning prompted an official cabinet reply that Nakasone's visit had not aimed at rehabilitating war criminals, whose sentences were accepted as just, nor did the visit establish any precedent for future prime ministers, who would decide what to do on their own.[19]

In Beijing Hu Yaobang told a meeting of the Commission for Sino-Japanese Friendship in the Twenty-first Century that those responsible for the war should not receive sympathetic treatment and no revival of militarism should be allowed. He added, however, that the Chinese people should distinguish between war criminals and the Japanese people.[20] This two-sided approach, aimed at placating the students and the Japanese alike, was expanded on by State Councillor Gu Mu when he was interviewed by the managing editor of Kyodo news service. Gu declared that his government opposed student attacks on Japanese economic activity as "aggression." But he explained that such attacks were the result of injured feelings after the shrine visit and that this sentiment was fully shared by the Chinese government. Although Gu gave a positive evaluation of Sino-Japanese economic cooperation, he added that it was important for both countries to avoid hurting each other's feelings.[21] Chinese officials meanwhile fanned out to various campuses for informal exchanges of view with student groups. The former ambassador to Japan, for instance, reportedly told Xian students that while he understood their feelings, their perception of Japan as economically aggressive was wrong.[22]

Despite these major media messages and official statements,

anti-Japanese student agitation continued. An inflammatory circular pushed under doorways at Beijing University called for a demonstration on November 20. This would celebrate anticipated victories in a Sino-Japanese women's volleyball game and a Sino-Japanese chess tournament.[23] The circular merits attention, not because of its impact, which proved to be slight, but because it demonstrates how the student protesters joined the Japanese issue with a broader challenge to authority.

After recalling how "the events of September 18 [1931] degraded the Chinese nation into a race that was being invaded and suppressed," the message asserted that "at present, in an era of openness and reform, confronting a critical moment of Japanese economic aggression, we need to awaken people into making efforts to catch up with Japan economically and to save the Chinese nation from its decay." This theme, however, was not developed any further. Instead the circular shifted to a domestic attack on "those in power [who] take advantage of reform, plotting for their private interests." These "bloodsucker princes" are "undermining the image of the party so much that the party has thus far not restored its prestigious position in the minds of the people."

The remedy for the situation, according to the circular, is "for you Beida [Beijing University] students to stand up bravely and demonstrate a strong sense of responsibility and fearless mettle, which is exactly the great significance of the September 18 assembly." While supporting the principle of democratic centralism, the circular noted that "it is not centralism but democracy that is the 'principal aspect and guiding function'" of political behavior. Alluding to the celebrated twin symbols of the May Fourth movement, the circular asserted that "'Mr. Science' has not awakened the people. It is inconceivable to stand up in the world without democracy. . . . Democracy is the liberalization of thinking. It is the beginning of openness and the foundation of the larger-scale reform." Thus the message moves from an initial reference to "Japanese economic aggression" to an attack on the privileged positions of the leadership's offspring, the so-called bloodsucker princes, and culminates in a call for greater liberalization and democracy. This last theme was to become central in the massive student demonstrations a year later.

The circular targeted November 20 for a Tiananmen massing of students because victory in the scheduled volleyball and chess competitions would make that day the day "in contemporary Sino-Japanese history, when the Chinese will feel proudest and most elated and national patriotism will be at an unprecedented height." Actually, however, the assemblage was designed to "celebrate 'Democracy '85,' precede commemoration of 'December 9,' and accomplish the unfinished tasks of the 'September 18' gathering." The reference to December 9 called forth another nationalistic, anti-Japanese memory. On this date in 1935, university students in Beijing had tried to mobilize pressure on Chiang Kai-shek to abandon his anticommunist campaign and form a united front against Japanese aggression. The circular ended with detailed instructions on maintaining absolute secrecy and using different routes to Tiananmen Square so as to elude the authorities.

Whether because the distribution of the circular alerted the regime to take preventive measures or because post-September 18 developments dampened student activism, the November 20 demonstration was sparsely attended compared with the earlier event. As the new minister of public security told *Beijing Review* later, "On November 20 some persons disrupted public order at Tiananmen Square. They were reprimanded by the police and were afterwards taken back by their units." [24]

But December 9 still posed a problem for the authorities. According to an informed Hong Kong report, a "national command headquarters" issued an "appeal" at the end of October for a nationwide demonstration on December 9, alleging that Sino-Japanese trade was resulting in losses for China and accusing Tokyo of an "economic invasion." [25] Delivered at campuses in eight major cities, the appeal broadened its attack to include other student grievances, citing the bureaucratic system, unhealthy social trends, and the suppression of democratic rights. Although the appeal paralleled the clandestine circular in this sense, it went further in identifying additional complaints.

The official response was immediate. Eschewing forceful suppression, the regime preempted and coopted the December 9 activities with a week of campus seminars, highly publicized reminiscences by surviving participants of the 1935 demonstrations, speeches by major figures, and authoritative media articles. In the only event open to foreign observation, four thousand high school students braved zero-degree weather in a government-organized rally at the monument to the People's Heroes in Tiananmen Square. There they swore loyalty to the regime and to the Communist Youth League.[26]

Li Peng's address to six thousand youths assembled at the Great Hall of the People on December 8 summarized the main themes that were to guide student behavior. He noted that the "December 9th movement" showed "that a youth movement can contribute to the development of history only when it conforms with the trend of times . . . and, under the leadership of the Communist Party, becomes an organized and disciplined force and maintains unity with the masses."[27] In 1935 "the central task was to resist Japan and save the country. . . . Now the central task is to build our motherland into a strong and prosperous socialist power." Chinese youth help by "studying diligently now and working hard in the future." Li continued, "They are also welcome to offer opinions, criticism, and suggestions," but he warned, "The youth today . . . have unavoidable weaknesses, which are manifested mainly in a separation from realities and a lack of practical experience. It is impossible for one to correctly understand and solve any practical problems by acquiring knowledge from books but scoffing at putting theory into practice."

Renmin Ribao's editorial carried Li's words one step further, remarking, "One cannot deny that young people, with passionate enthusiasm but little experience, are sometimes dominated by radical feelings and show one weakness or another. We who have had experience in this respect should show understanding and make allowances for them, actively guide and teach them, thus helping them to mature earlier."[28] The editorial also developed another of Li's themes more bluntly:

> History indicates that the development of Chinese youth movements is closely bound up with the future and fate of our nation and state and with the direction and process of social progress and historical developments. . . . When the direction of the student movement or youth movement is in line with the development of history, it will forcefully propel history forward. . . . *However if the student movement or youth movement runs counter to the demands of the times,* not only will there be twists and turns, but *the movement itself will suffer*

serious setbacks and the youth of a generation, or even several generations
will be held back or wasted. The Red Guard movement during the
"Great Cultural Revolution" was such a negative case in point [ital-
ics added].

These warnings and allusions sounded an ominous note for both
officials and students, underscoring the seriousness with which
the situation was viewed by the authorities.

ANTI-JAPANESE PROTESTS
IN PERSPECTIVE

Observations at the time and interviews later both agree that more
than anti-Japanese sentiment motivated the student demonstrators. Although official explanations along this line aimed at reassuring audiences in Japan, especially businessmen, independent
evidence testifies to a coalition of critics that capitalized on extant
anti-Japanese feelings in order to advance a broader attack against
current policy.

Thus a senior Shanghai official explained the absence of demonstrations in his city by acknowledging "other grievances that we
acted on."[29] Inflation was one such grievance, for which student
allowances were raised 50 percent, from forty to sixty yuan. Also,
the cafeteria menu was improved, as was bus transportation into
the city. Other informants admitted that corruption, official privileges, and the bureaucratic blockage of reforms caused complaint
during the demonstrations and the discussions that followed. Some
of the older students had been Red Guards or had absorbed the
Cultural Revolution values of austerity and sacrifice. Some had seen
relatives advance during the Cultural Revolution only to suffer subsequently in power and privilege. These groups resented Deng's virtual dumping of Mao's vaunted stress on self-reliance, equality, and
political as against material motivation. Others who cherished a
sense of Chinese identity based on more traditional values feared
the vulgarization of society through the foreign content of modernization and the official approval of personal enrichment. All
could unite against the so-called princes, whose parental influence
advanced them ahead of others in competition for study abroad
and high-ranking jobs at home. Finally, various personal drives,

whether idealistic, egotistic, or opportunistic, also prompted some individual participation aside from these general issues.

By attacking inequality, bureaucracy, corruption, pornography, and other social practices in the name of nationalism, the critics hoped to avoid punishment. Students in the social sciences, who generally avoided participation because their postgraduate assignments depended on political acceptability, tended to be cautious in their criticisms. By comparison many more students from the natural sciences took part, knowing that laboratory jobs would probably be available regardless of their political record.[30]

But the existence of these multiple motivations did not exclude genuine anti-Japanese sentiment. This was testified to later by many, especially in the younger age brackets. The stimulus for this sentiment undoubtedly had come, in many cases, from family and relatives who had suffered personal loss as the result of Japanese aggression. It also came from various media messages that dramatically portrayed the agony of 1937–45 (some of which were examined in the previous chapter). The 1982 campaign against Tokyo's textbooks and the fortieth anniversary of the war's end unleashed a surge of historical reminiscences that aroused nationalistic passions.[31] These passions were readily aroused by the Nakasone shrine visit, which quite literally added insult to injury in Chinese eyes, much as President Ronald Reagan's 1985 visit to a German cemetery containing the graves of Hitler's infamous SS troops enflamed the feelings of Jews in the United States and elsewhere.

The degree of anti-Japanese feeling associated with the war emerged in my interviews that focused on the student demonstrations. A research institute director in northeast China repeated the standard criticism that Nakasone's shrine visit "hurt the feelings of the Chinese people," but then said, "The student demonstrations were also wrong because they hurt the feelings of the Japanese people."[32] This provoked a woman in her early twenties immediately on leaving the discussion to protest vehemently, "The students were right! How would anybody feel who had lost a father or an uncle in the war?" She went on to categorize Japanese behavior as "bestial," citing the Nanjing Massacre.[33]

In Beijing a man in his mid-thirties spoke bluntly, "Young people hate the Japanese. They cannot forget the war and the brutal behavior to so many for so long." A research specialist echoed his sentiments, "We all feel bitterness from our families, without any propaganda. Our father, our mother, our grandfather—they all suffered so much for so long. We cannot forget that." A young scholar in Nanjing declared forcefully, "What Japan has done in the past will be remembered *forever!* If the Japanese government won't admit it, Chinese feelings will be greatly harmed."

These powerful feelings condition Chinese views of their economic relationship with Japan. We will examine this relationship in a subsequent chapter. It is worth noting at this point, however, that charges of shoddy goods, cheating on contracts, and the holding back of technology were leveled against the Japanese. Paradoxically, none of these accusations deters the Chinese from purchasing Japanese products and few, if any, are echoed by Chinese economists or specialists in foreign trade. Nonetheless they constitute an important component of student sentiment.

Another factor contributing to the 1985 demonstrations was the resentment aroused by the highly touted visit of three thousand Japanese "youths" in October 1984. Invited by Hu Yaobang on his trip to Japan in 1983, the group, not all of whom were young, received special treatment as guests of the government, including banquets and parties.[34] The Japanese had anticipated a simple sight-seeing tour without any political overtones. Moreover, their previsit stereotype of China included the standard romanticized views of the Great Wall, the Forbidden City, the Temple of Heaven, and the Grand Canal. They expected China to be beautiful and culturally sophisticated. Coming from some of the most modern cities in the world, however, the visitors were shocked at conditions in China and did not hide their reaction. At the end, many left behind the souvenirs and mementos given to them by their Chinese hosts.[35]

The amount of money that the Chinese government spent on the tour was not only far above what was necessary for simple hospitality, but it contrasted sharply with what Chinese students had for living and entertainment. As a young man commented concerning the dance he attended in Tianjin, "I wouldn't have gone because of the Japanese, but we don't get to go to parties like that very often!" Critics also attacked the relative lack of reciprocity despite the gross disparity in wealth between the two countries.

Tokyo only reciprocated after "repeated demands of the Chinese side" and then "only 300 people were invited."[36]

In sum, 1985 proved to be an important year in Sino-Japanese relations on three negative counts. First, the student demonstrations challenged the policy of reliance on Japan as a partner in economic modernization. The summary label, "pro-Japanese faction," reportedly circulated during the demonstrations with obvious reference to Hu Yaobang, among others.[37] This term of opprobrium captured the fundamental feeling at the time. Second, the publicity given these demonstrations in Japan weakened business confidence in accepting the role of partner, especially where that role involved capital investment over a long period of time. And third, both governments were embarrassed politically in their efforts to cope with domestic opposition while maintaining and strengthening their mutual relationship. In the short run, at least, the prospects of Sino-Japanese friendship in the twenty-first century had paled significantly.

5

Japan as Role Model

It would be wrong to assume that Chinese audiences are fed an exclusive diet of anti-Japanese propaganda or that all media messages portray Japanese society unfavorably. Although these assumptions could be applied to the years before 1972, the situation changed fundamentally following the establishment of diplomatic relations between China and Japan.

The negative media treatment of past Sino-Japanese conflict coexists with positive images of contemporary Japan that portray the country as a role model that should be emulated in selective ways. Embodied in descriptions of Japanese society and its postwar evolution, these images counter war memories and facilitate the leadership's efforts to promote good relations. But negative descriptions of Japanese life do exist in the Chinese media and, although they are far less numerous than favorable descriptions, this suggests a partial rejection of the Japanese model.

The People's Republic has experienced one intensive effort at promoting a foreign role model. In the 1950s, "Learn from the Soviet Union" was an omnipresent injunction in education, economics, and politics. In the 1960s and 1970s, however, Soviet revisionism was anathematized as a corrupt betrayal of Marxism-Leninism. Then, in the 1980s, as Beijing sought detente with Moscow, the domestic policies of the Soviet Union received more favorable treatment although its foreign policy was still condemned.

This contradictory precedent cautions against any simplistic projection from recent images to future images, much less to future policies toward Japan. The Chinese leadership will shape the mass media to fit its foreign policy, changing messages as it sees fit regardless of objective reality or subjective attitudes. This does not, however, vitiate the utility of examining public images in a particular period. Such images constitute one element of influence on perceptions, expectations, and attitudes. They may not determine private opinion, especially if they are contradicted by personal experience or inconsistent among themselves. Contradiction can reduce credibility and inconsistency can lead to the promulgation of divergent views. Nevertheless, while indeterminate in impact, media images warrant attention both as reflections of authorized opinion in communist systems and as inputs to public consciousness. Whether different images reflect different policy positions at higher levels depends on the issue, the sources, and the larger political context. At a minimum, however, conflicting images can contribute to a debate, especially at lower levels. This is particularly relevant to the issue of Japan and its perceived utility as a partner in China's modernization.

Materials published from 1984 through 1986, following the establishment of the Commission for Sino-Japanese Friendship in the Twenty-first Century, reveal wide variation in the way that Japan is depicted, running the gamut from unstinting praise to harsh criticism. The apparent failure of the leadership to force the commission's declared goals on all authors and publishers stands in marked contrast to the ubiquitous panegyrics that supported Sino-Soviet friendship in the 1950s. As might be expected, those items directly associated with the commission's activities and people-to-people diplomacy, such as the exchange of visits by delegations and individuals, are purely positive. We therefore omit these from our survey in order to strike as accurate a balance as possible on the basis of the less obviously propagandistic publications.

YOUTH AND EDUCATION

Zhongguo Qingnian's treatment of a managers' training center exemplifies the cautious yet positive emphasis given to Japanese practices that are thought to be instructive for Chinese behavior. Bankrupt Japanese businessmen who have become discouraged reportedly rebuild their confidence at this center.[1] A rigorous hardship regimen replaces traditional teaching and textbooks so that in the end the participants can finally shout "I'm the best!" and "I can win!" The author's conclusion is expressly hortatory:

> We are not here talking about setting up a similar school in China, but what we should consider is the objective of the school. Our traditional teaching encourages students to be the opposite. Whoever has a little bit of individualism will be accused of arrogance and ambition. A man without self-confidence will be without any drive.

A nation without self-confidence will not be vigorous. As young
people we should break through the traditional image of "a modest
gentleman" to encourage ourselves, develop ourselves, and do more
for our country.

The next issue of this magazine discusses the sensitive subject of
social contacts among youth. It frankly praises Japanese practice as
offering more opportunities in which active initiative is encouraged.[2] The article notes that Japanese college freshmen and sopho-
mores not only mix with juniors and seniors of the same department, but also mix with students from other departments, a sharp
contrast to the highly compartmentalized campus in China. Most
Japanese students belong to clubs that enhance their nonacademic
life. Business firms also organize gatherings for people to get ac-
quainted and socialize. The article pointedly concludes that in
Japan feudal morals "are not popular" and that society has no ob-
jection to normal contact among young people.

One Chinese writer notes that Japanese inventiveness goes well
beyond these modest arrangements with nearly five thousand
"love connection" centers that match up singles for possible marriage.[3] Many of these centers are computer-based, including one
that reportedly has 27,000 registrants who are analyzed on 755 aspects. Because marriage may be "very expensive," some of the
larger corporations not only offer marriage introduction services,
but also offer to provide the ceremony itself.

Japanese education receives high praise from another writer
who cites both explicit and implicit models for Chinese emulation.
Shijie Zhishi rated Japan as second to the United States with 50.5
percent of its youth entering high school.[4] (The actual figure is over
95%.) A *Renmin Ribao* writer found several aspects of an inves-
tigatory visit relevant to reforms in the organization of Chinese
education.[5] In particular he cited the "roster" system whereby primary, middle, and high school teachers are reassigned every three
to five years, beginning further from home and moving progres-
sively closer. He also admired the grouping of primary students
after the third grade according to performance "in order to offer a
better environment for learning." Another *Renmin Ribao* article
notes that investment in education, long regarded as part of the
overall investment in Japan's economy, has paid off handsomely,
especially in science and technology.[6] In addition, higher education is described as being geared toward the fostering of "creative,

diligent persons armed with an international outlook," a tacit criticism of the Chinese stress on rote learning and unquestioned acceptance of professors' lectures. Support for these points emerged in a separate story on a forty-one-member computer development research center where, except for the director, the average age of the research staff is under thirty-two.[7] This contrasts with Chinese research centers, which are burdened with older personnel who lack the knowledge and drive to innovate and compete abroad.

Negative reports are much less frequent, but they do occur. Chinese students in Japan express surprise at the number of unemployed youths and the association of youth with suicide.[8] *Shijie Zhishi* went further when it harshly indicted Japan's younger generation for having lost the "Japanese spirit of hard work and enthusiasm."[9] It noted that many are bored and depressed by modern life as shown by a 25 percent increase in suicide over the past ten years with the highest rate for youth anywhere in the world. Violence at school and crime are also on the increase and the traditional respect for the old and the protection of the young are disappearing. The writer blamed these social ills on material modernization, urbanization, women working, and the rigid educational system. In another issue this journal carried first-hand impressions of life on a Japanese campus, echoing these negative observations. Getting to bed late, coming late to class, and growing long hair seemed to typify male student behavior.[10]

But whether measured quantitatively or qualitatively, favorable descriptions of Japanese youth and education clearly outweighed the unfavorable descriptions during these years. We cannot assess the impact of either emphasis. The most disturbing reports probably concerned rising suicide rates. These may have reminded older readers of a similar phenomenon during the Cultural Revolution and thereby reduced respect for Japanese modernization as a model for China. In this regard it is worth noting that similar critical views that focused on suicide among Japanese adults also emerged at this time.

IMAGES OF JAPANESE SOCIETY

Although in general articles on Japanese society lack the emulative thrust found in analyses on education and economics, their tone is distinctly favorable and at times admiring. For example, one item recalls how before the war Chinese often referred to the "small

Japanese," but that now newer generations were growing taller because of dietary changes, especially in the use of dairy products.[11] Given the importance of the quantity, quality, and variety of food in China, this analysis touched on a sensitive nerve in view of Beijing's failure to improve the daily diet for most of the population between 1958 and 1978.

The favorable depiction of the quality of life in Japan extends beyond food. For instance, one article describes how sixteen regions have been designated for the development of cities that specialize in high technology. Planning not only focuses on industry and science, but also stresses the construction of beautiful modern residential areas with all the facilities necessary for good living.[12] Tokyo wins praise for the more than one hundred libraries, large and small, scattered throughout the capital, most of which have good reading and study conditions, excellent service, and all books open to the public.[13] These conditions, especially the last, stand in marked contrast to Chinese libraries.

The more personal side of life provides additional items for possible emulation. According to *Renmin Ribao*, a survey of sixteen thousand Japanese reported a decline in smoking, with smokers constituting less than 39 percent of the population, a figure that must have seemed incredible to Chinese readers.[14] Even family behavior wins positive attention. One article entitled "Seven Japanese Ways to Accomplish Marital Harmony" summarizes a survey by Japanese psychologists and family specialists who emphasize mutual trust, tolerance, self-restraint, and positive thinking or faith as desirable behavior.[15] Undesirable behavior includes arguing in front of the children or forcing them to take sides and telling outsiders about family problems.

Even accounts of unfavorable events often end with the author giving credit to Japanese society. Thus, when a nitrogen fertilizer factory at Minamata poisoned fish and, through the fish, the local population, the factory officials were eventually convicted. This led a Chinese reporter to conclude that "justice prevailed."[16]

A more balanced study was made by a young Chinese trade commissioner who not only visited Japan many times but lived there for up to three years at a stretch.[17] On the positive side, he claims that unlike China where a personal connection, or "going through the back door," is helpful if not essential, in Japan "there is no back door. . . . People are judged by their ability; personal relationships do not help." On the negative side, however, he describes growing youth problems, an aging society, and a proclivity to ignore politics and hard work in favor of entertainment.

These latter themes were spelled out more fully in a long *Renmin Ribao* analysis commemorating the one hundredth anniversary of Japanese cabinet government and the fortieth anniversary of the Japanese surrender in World War II. The writer declares that "hard work" and "efficiency" hold less attraction for the Japanese of today and notes that some are actually concerned that being first in the world economy may result in chauvinism.[18] The article raised questions such as, "Will Japanese forget about the war? Will the tendency of young people to have no interest in politics give way to fascism?" Although no answers were given, by implication they were unfavorable.

Another critical analysis uses economic dislocations resulting from the rise in the value of the yen in 1986 for a much broader indictment of the psychological stress that allegedly racks the country.[19] Reaching back several years, the writer cites the 1982 Japan Air Lines crash in Tokyo Bay that was caused by a mentally disturbed pilot as proof "that the whole of Japanese society is under pressure." The negative implications of the Japanese model are identified as "coming not only from economic competition, but also from rapid technological developments . . . and the changing values concerning the family system." Without explicit reference to Beijing's goal of economic modernization, the reader nevertheless can probably discern the lesson to be learned. Job-related absences in Japan nearly doubled between 1975 and 1984 and increased alcoholism and suicide are symptomatic of the long-term mental stress that results from pressures to conceal true emotions and feelings.

As with the topics of youth and education, however, such critical articles are relatively few and moderate in tone. Despite the political concern, expressed elsewhere in the Chinese media, over the danger of revived militarism, analyses of Japanese society offer no supporting evidence. Even when the topic of fascism is raised, as in the question about Japanese youth cited above, there is no express linkage with militarism. Prostitution, corruption, and crime receive little attention. Overall, the image of contemporary Japanese society presented to the Chinese reader is quite favorable.

JAPAN AS AN ECONOMIC MODEL

In addition to articles on subjects of general interest aimed at a wide audience, Japan's value as a model for economic development concerns a narrower public, but one with actual or potential influence on public policy. Articles in specialized journals and professional monographs supplement the mass media in that they provide images of contemporary Japan that conflict with the images derived from its prewar evolution.

An analysis of Japan's postwar economic strategy by a respected scholar, Kong Fanjing, explicitly addresses the utility of the Japanese experience for China.[20] The author states three key questions at the outset:

> How did postwar Japan achieve such a fast rate of development on a foundation of "total ruin?" How did it achieve the modernization of its national economy and realize the long-held desire of eliminating the disparity with Europe and America 100 years after the Meiji Restoration? Are there some basic experiences on which we can draw?

Although acknowledging that some aspects of Japan's development are unique, other aspects "definitely include experiences of general significance that can be drawn upon on the basis of each country's concrete conditions." Kong then expresses the modest hope that his work will "make some slight contribution to Chinese socialist economic modernization." The author first summarizes the main factors behind Japanese economic development. He then examines them in detail through a relatively objective, nonideological, data-based analysis. Finally, he enumerates them again in a concluding chapter as italicized points of emphasis. Although he eschews direct admonition of what China should and should not emulate, the threefold reiteration of these factors conveys his message clearly. These factors deserve brief recapitulation as a professional portrayal of the potential of Japan as a model.

First and foremost, Kong claims that economic development prevailed over domestic and foreign policy in general and military and educational matters in particular. Tacitly refuting the intermittent alarm sounded in the mass media concerning the possible return of Japanese militarism, he notes that all postwar prime ministers curtailed military spending in favor of economic development.

This admittedly required subordination to the United States, but in return Japan enjoyed the benefit of American military protection. Indeed, whenever Washington pressed Tokyo to increase military spending, Tokyo responded by citing the "peace constitution," which had been drafted by the American occupation authorities. He observes that this tactic has also been used in response to more recent American pressure in the early 1980s.

Kong implies admiration for Tokyo's tactics in "using U.S.-Soviet-Chinese contradictions, [and] especially U.S.-Soviet hegemonic contradictions," to win Washington's support in military affairs, foreign policy, and economics. Thus, by adopting "a posture of depending on the U.S. . . . Japan thereby developed its own economy and realized its goal of genuine independence." The parallel possibility of China's exploiting Soviet-American tension did not need elaboration for his reader to get the point. The author hastens to add that "this of course is not to say that the Japanese ruling groups have no thought of expanding their military strength, but rather that the heart of their economic strategy makes the development of the economy more important." Nowhere does he suggest that this policy might be changed in the near future, despite the obstacles to continued economic growth that are identified at the end of his analysis. Instead he argues that Japan has "made foreign policy subordinate to domestic policy and domestic policy subordinate to economics."

Second, Japan chose the proper course at each stage of development, moving step by step toward the main goal. The successive shifts of emphasis in the 1950s, 1960s, and 1970s are evidence of flexibility amid stability.

Third, the government kept consumption increasing, but at a level that would make possible the capital accumulation necessary to develop heavy and chemical industries.

Fourth, Japan concentrated on the importation, copying, and improvement of technology in order to catch up with the level of the advanced world. This proved to be a more advantageous approach than one emphasizing wholly independent research and development because it provided a training ground for Japanese technology experts and eventually Japan was able to produce better technology than other countries.

Fifth, Japanese management gave priority to quality and labor productivity was raised by studying American methods and adapting them to local conditions. As a result, Japan became "number one," its annual production increases from 1960–73 averaging 10.7 percent against only 3.6 percent for the United States and 5.9 percent for West Germany. Kong explicitly credits cooperation between labor and capital for this record, omitting any reference to the evils of monopoly capitalism or the benefits of class struggle.

Sixth and last, Kong praises the Japanese educational system because it is designed to develop human resources and liberate intelligence. After describing the present and prospective problems confronting the economy, his emphasis on the human factor leads to the following panegyric: "The Japanese people's ability to adapt to circumstances is head and shoulders above all others. This point has been made manifest by the course of Japanese history since the Meiji Restoration, by the pace and attainments of postwar economic recovery, and by events since the oil shock." Moreover, Kong concludes that Japan will always adapt to new problems and that China should study this closely.

This final note contrasts with the warnings in the historical works that call for watchfulness against the threat of renewed militarism and expansionism. Kong's only negative note comes when he depicts the objective constraints on Japan's ability to guarantee sustained growth without causing diffticulties with its trading partners, particularly the United States.

Kong is not alone in praising qualities allegedly inherent in the Japanese people. A professional journal devoted to modernization reviewed how resource scarcity stimulated the development of energy-saving technology in Japan noting, "Japan has a much shorter history of civilization than China, but it has never stopped learning from other cultures about that which it lacks. The Japanese do not feel inferior for the fact that they are always borrowing things from others. They are never frightened by anything foreign."[21] This obvious thrust at conservative opposition to the open door policy cut particularly deep by being couched in an implied comparison with Japan.

The role of government is central in Chinese writings on Japan's economic success; private enterprise receives only secondary attention. In contrast to the American style of enterprise independence and competition, the Ministry of International Trade and Industry (MITI) is credited with coordinating private enterprise.[22] This coordination is reported to facilitate superiority in high technology. The government provides several important services including commercial intelligence, annual economic forecasts, statistical surveys, and plans, both mid-range and long-range.[23] The official promotion of high technology has also resulted in increased grants for research and a new information center.[24] Also of potential relevance to China is Tokyo's approach to provincial economic development in which specialization is stressed, but within an overall plan.[25] Some provinces will specialize in electronics, others in agriculture. The report claims that this approach aimed at a change "from urbanization to localization," an effort Beijing is also struggling to implement.

Japanese policies toward the consumer have also been examined. A survey of postwar policies recalls that the initial step was to raise the price of agricultural products, which had the effect of increasing the farmer's purchasing power for personal needs as well as for goods involved in agricultural production.[26] Later, the annual income of workers was raised so that it grew by 1.7 times from 1961–70, the highest rate of any capitalist country during this period. The government also adopted a flexible loan policy. Although these steps did not completely solve the problem of production versus consumption, they reduced it over time.

Turning to the private sector, Japanese career training is held to be the best in the world thanks to the public schools and employee programs.[27] Three aspects win attention: upgrading skills, adapting to the requirements of internationalization, and retraining older employees. The need for both upgrading and retraining is illustrated by an account of office automation in which the reader learns that computers and other equipment have virtually replaced the use of pen and paper.[28]

One article focuses on an "innovative reform by the Japanese retailing industry," namely mail-order sales through television and catalogues.[29] Apparently ignorant of much earlier American practice, the writer considers this the first "major innovation [in retailing] since the introduction of the supermarket." Chinese shoppers, facing the daily crush in the stores, would envy this alternative.

A more balanced presentation appeared in an unusual three-part series carried by *Renmin Ribao* in 1985 that recounted an extensive tour of Japan.[30] The reporter praises computer training centers that make room for preschool children learning to count. He describes a city where more than 1,400 traditional textile workshops succeeded in converting to Western styles through technological reforms, market surveys, and a flexible system of management. Similarly, a small town that encountered severe unemployment when modern agricultural machinery became available had managed to set up twenty-five factories between 1975 and 1983, attracting investment by offering tax-free incentives and other inducements.

The writer warns, however, that new problems emerge with developments such as high technology. When the most efficient work is done by machines, not only will people feel helpless but "large-scale unemployment will certainly result." This ominous forecast carried special significance for the newspaper's readers, who are well aware that there have been problems in coping with China's burgeoning population even before high technology systems enter daily life.

Robotization, the ultimate threat to workers, is a field in which Japan is preeminent worldwide according to *Shijie Zhishi*.[31] With production increasing fivefold from 1982 to 1985, and already accounting for 56 percent of the total world output, Japan's dominant position derives from a favorable market environment, breakthroughs in microelectronic technologies, and governmental support that promotes this industry. Robots were first used in the manufacture of automobiles, moved on to big and then to small industries, and now characterize "tripartite enterprise" in which two persons work with a robot. Although the writer did not make the point, it seems fair to assert that this aspect of Japanese development may merit admiration but certainly not emulation as far as China is concerned.

These last few negative notes notwithstanding, the image of Japan pointing the way to China's economic future is dominant, whether expressed or implied, in the majority of writings on economics. Reflecting this professional perspective in popular terms, a report on Japan's 1985 Exhibition of International Science and Technology was headed "Walking into the Twenty-first Century" and ran in a journal appropriately titled *Knowledge Is Strength*.[32] "Imaginative" and "a wonderland" characterize the reporter's awe in describing the exhibition halls and displays.

THE MODEL: PARTS OF A WHOLE

The obvious differences between the two countries in terms of population, territory, and levels of human as well as material development defy any simplistic application of Japanese practices to Chinese modernization. As Kong Fanjing concedes in his introduction, Japan's specific historical conditions have given its development many unique objective and subjective aspects.[33] He nevertheless justifies his proposal for selective study by citing Mao Zedong's claim that the close coexistence of both unique and general contradictions is universal. This allows Kong to examine Japan's postwar economic strategy with the express hope that it could help guide China's future course.

These admittedly brief glimpses of Japanese youth, education, society, and economy, seldom accord fully with reality, much less address the problem of adapting Japanese practices in China. They also do not stand alone in shaping perceptions of Japan and the Japanese because they coexist with the revived images of historical enmity. Finally, they do not necessarily agree with or outweigh the impressions the Chinese derive from daily contact with Japanese businessmen and tourists in China.

No writer presents Japan as a complete model, political as well as economic, for the Chinese to study, evaluate, and possibly emulate. One survey of the political system and its postwar development presents an impressive and comprehensive description complete with numerous tables and figures covering the domestic and foreign record up to 1982.[34] Its thirty-page chronology and its non-ideological, nonpolemical tone make this a useful handbook of information on most aspects of the country. But it differs from our selected articles in its straightforward treatment; it offers no evaluation, express or implied.

These limitations notwithstanding, the fact remains that Japan's image in Chinese nonfiction publications, except those in the historical genre, was distinctly favorable during 1984–86. In many respects it was offered as a positive model for selective emulation in the Chinese effort to modernize society and catch up with the advanced economies of the Western world. The contrast between this recent image and the way in which Japan and the Japanese were depicted to Chinese readers during the decades prior to 1972 cannot be overstated.

Because our concern is with Sino-Japanese relations, we are not surveying the Chinese image of other countries such as the United States.[35] Varying views exist on the utility of borrowing exclusively from a single role model as opposed to forming a synthesis that borrows from several, including the Soviet Union. But as an antidote to the historical heritage of brutal Japanese military aggression, the positive attention given to that country in recent years may have a salutary effect, especially should the Japanese avoid provocations that trigger hostile Chinese reactions that reinforce negative stereotypes.

6

Sino-Japanese Economic Relations

Amid various political controversies between Beijing and Tokyo, the *Far Eastern Economic Review* dubbed Sino-Japanese economic relations "the ties that bind."[1] The facts would seem to justify this imagery. For more than a decade Japan has consistently held first place in China's foreign trade, averaging roughly one-fourth of the total. Japan has also offered more loans, both governmental and private, than any other country, totaling more than $7 billion for the seventh five-year plan. Also, Japan's aid program to China, although not large, outranks that of all the other countries. Japanese economic representatives stationed in China, whether in banking or trading, likewise outnumber those from any other country.

Yet the same duality of positive and negative aspects that beclouds the relationship in other areas affects Chinese attitudes and expectations here as well, albeit to a far lesser degree. A recurring bilateral trade deficit, which exceeded $5 billion in 1986, raises continuous demands for opening Japanese markets to improve the balance, demands that have won little response in previous years. Japanese investments in China, smaller than American and at times West German investments, are attacked as grossly incommensurate with the size of Sino-Japanese trade and the Japanese surplus. Japanese technology transfer is criticized as both slow and low, the implication being that Japan is keeping China backward and dependent on its more advanced neighbor.

Writing in 1983, the leading American analyst of this relationship, Chae-jin Lee, concluded, "There is no doubt that the intelligent and resourceful people of China and Japan can find a way to sustain their peaceful and friendly relations if they so wish and that they can obtain substantial economic benefits from each other in the future."[2] Lee, however, tempers his forecast by making it conditional on several factors in China:

> Yet the exact course of their economic relationship is more likely to depend on China than on Japan. . . . As long as the Chinese can

sustain a stable domestic political basis for their four modernizations policy and can improve their bureaucratic and managerial performance, the normalization of economic and diplomatic relations between China and Japan suggests that both will be able to learn from their past achievements and mistakes and to work out a mature and viable system of mutually beneficial economic cooperation in the years to come.

Another analysis two years later echoed Lee's optimism, but added two more factors: "So long as the congruence of economic interests exists between Japan and China, and so long as they share common concern over the Soviet military buildup in Asia, it is reasonable to expect the continuation of Sino-Japanese economic cooperation in the future."[3]

The variables cited in the preceding paragraph, whether domestic and political or foreign and strategic, complicate long-range forecasting. It is easy to posit the favorable factors that make for complementarity between the two economies. China's resources serve Japan; Japan's markets serve China. Proximity facilitates trade. Cultural commonalities, particularly linguistic, ease technology transfer. But it is very difficult to weigh the importance of these factors against the political, strategic, and economic variables, much less develop a wholly integrated model that can project alternative futures.

Forecasting is further impeded by special developments that make the mid-1980s an invalid point of departure for trend analysis. Sino-Japanese trade fluctuated wildly between 1983 and 1986, both in amount and composition. In 1984, Beijing's experiment with decentralized foreign exchange controls coincided with increased demand for consumer goods. This caused foreign exchange reserves to plummet in 1984–85. As a result, consumer imports were drastically cut and foreign exchange access sharply curtailed in 1986. Conversely, the persistently low level of foreign investment in China prompted Beijing to legislate major changes in late 1986 that, if properly implemented, could raise this level significantly in coming years. Despite these transient events, it is still possible to highlight the positive prospects and negative problems that confront the Sino-Japanese economic relationship and how they might affect its stability or growth.

Equally important, however, is the political relevance of economics in the overall relationship. As we have seen, student demonstrations in the fall of 1985 attacked Japan's "economic invasion," forcing the leadership to explain why the relationship was both necessary and beneficial to China. Japanese business practices are widely criticized among those who are not professional economists. Project failures or shortcomings are readily blamed on the foreigner, rightly or wrongly, especially if the foreigner is Japanese. The cumulative effect of these perceptions is such that it can erode Chinese confidence in Japanese cooperation and the Japanese willingness to risk capital in Chinese modernization efforts.

To place these alternative emphases in perspective, we need first to sketch the background against which recent developments have taken place. We will then examine the specific aspects of trade, foreign investment, technology transfer, loans, grants, and other forms of interaction. This will provide an objective framework within which we can examine the subjective perceptions at different levels in the two countries. Again, I will give special emphasis to Chinese assessments and expectations.

DEVELOPING THE RELATIONSHIP: 1972–86

Sino-Japanese trade overcame serious political obstacles prior to the establishment of diplomatic relations in 1972.[4] Despite the absence of such relations and Washington's embargo against all PRC trade involving American-licensed materials, Mainland China was Japan's leading trade partner in Northeast Asia in 1956. In 1967 even after the Cultural Revolution erupted, Japan's mainland trade still exceeded its trade with Taiwan and South Korea.

During the prerecognition period, Japanese nongovernmental organizations played a key role in facilitating trade. Given the fact that by 1975 the mainland's share of total Japanese foreign trade was only 3.34 percent, their importance was more symbolic than substantive. The symbolism, however, helped to maintain commercial contact despite political separation. It also established personal relationships that were to serve the subsequent expansion of trade.

Diplomatic ties permitted governmental involvement on the part of Japan. The timing was welcome in China where economic development had stagnated since the withdrawal of Soviet advisers and assistance in 1960 and the self-imposed isolation of the Cultural Revolution. Bilateral trade grew from $1.1 billion in 1972 to nearly

$3.8 billion in 1975. Beijing particularly valued the importation of whole plants for synthetic fiber, ethylene, ammonia, urea, and rolled steel.

But this period proved short-lived, partly because of China's reluctance to import more than could be paid for by exports in the present or the near future. In addition, Zhou Enlai's death in January 1976 opened the way for the so-called Gang of Four, who demanded self-reliance, which eventually led to the virtual exclusion of foreign technology imports.

Mao's death in September 1976 and the fall of the gang soon thereafter allowed his immediate successor, Hua Guofeng, together with the rehabilitated Deng Xiaoping, to resume Zhou's policy with full, indeed excessive, force. A flood of contract commitments emerged from the newly liberated Chinese bureaucracy. In the case of Japan, the value of trade soared from $3 billion in 1976 to more than $10 billion only five years later. The Long-Term Trade Agreement, based on the principle of balanced exchange, was signed on February 16, 1978. It targeted a total trade of $20 billion over five years. Chinese exports of crude oil were to grow from 7,000 to 15,000 tons per year by 1982, coking coal exports were to go up from 300 to 2,000 tons each year, and steam coal from 200 to 1,700 tons annually. In return, Japan was to sell $7–8 billion in plants and industrial technology plus $2–3 billion in construction machinery and materials on the basis of low-interest, deferred payment.

Nearly four dozen contracts were concluded in this bullish atmosphere by 1979. They added up to more than $3.8 billion in plant equipment.[5] The most spectacular agreement concerned a gigantic steel plant to be built at Baoshan, near Shanghai, with an annual capacity of six million tons. Several billion dollars more of ongoing contract negotiations whetted the appetite of Japanese entrepreneurs, who were described at the time as succumbing to "China fever."

Chinese assumptions, however, proved wholly unjustified. Oil output did not increase, but domestic demand did. Foreign exchange earnings fell far short of expectations. Moreover, Chen Yun, China's top planning official, who had only recently been restored to power, severely criticized the overall design. On February 26, 1979, Beijing suspended nearly thirty contracts with Japanese manufacturers of plant equipment, worth $2.5 billion. Then in 1980–81, Beijing hit the Japanese with another $1.64 billion in suspensions.[6] The 1979 and 1980–81 cancellations together constituted 59.1 percent of all foreign plant contracts concluded at the time. By comparison, West German suspensions totaled only $783 million and both American and British totals were well under $100 million each.

The Baoshan steel mill lost an estimated $1.3 billion in Japanese orders as a result of the cancellations. In addition, Beijing announced that the second phase would not begin until well after the first phase was in full operation, thereby cutting its original output target in half, from six to three million tons per year. The Japanese firms involved in the project protested and demanded compensation for the costs already undergone in plant preparation. After prolonged negotiations, Tokyo provided $1.33 billion in development loans at 3 percent for thirty years with a ten-year grace period. The loan would fund six major construction projects, including Baoshan. Meanwhile, Sino-Japanese trade fell from $10.38 billion in 1981 to $8.86 billion in 1982.

This seesaw pattern of trade and contracts between 1978 and 1982 occasioned wild swings of euphoria and resentment in Japan. The perceived vast potential of the China market contrasted with the seemingly unpredictable nature of Chinese economic policy. The Japanese vividly remember this period and their subsequent cautious approach to investment in China is readily understood, especially in the aftermath of anti-Japanese demonstrations.

Japanese gains during this period, however, should not be underestimated. The Japan-China Economic Association estimates that China concluded $11.7 billion in contracts for "whole plants and technology" from 1978 to 1984, of which Japan won 52.4 percent for more than $6 billion.[7] In contrast, West Europe's share was 38.2 percent and that of the United States only 7.1 percent. Of the ninety-seven contracts signed for whole plants, fifty-four had been completed or nearly so by 1983, with Japan taking a leading role among all foreign countries in steel, petrochemicals, chemical fertilizers, and synthetic textiles. Sino-Japanese trade meanwhile recovered most of its pre-1982 level, just exceeding the $10 billion total in 1983, and remained in rough balance. Both sides were reassured that there would continue to be growth in trade.

These statistics notwithstanding, the 1978 Long-Term Trade Agreement had clearly failed to foresee the problems, particularly on the Chinese side, that were impeding the realization of the agreement's goals. By the time the agreement expired, neither side was interested in negotiating a successor. Instead, there was general agreement that if a genuinely close and harmonious relationship were to be sustained, a serious and systematic mutual effort would be required to cope with both new and old problems.

One new problem was the sudden rise and fall in Chinese consumer orders during 1985–86. This problem warrants attention both for the way it reflects some recurring problems in Chinese economic planning and for the way it impacts on Japanese perceptions of the China market.

Japanese exports to China increased 73 percent in 1985 over 1984, but declined by 21 percent in 1986. Three factors accounted for the sudden increase in 1985. First, the overheated economy raised demand for producer goods as capital construction and private investment expanded in 1984–85.[8] As a result, Japanese shipments of steel products, constituting 25.6 percent of total exports to China, rose sixfold for pig iron and doubled for steel bars. Second, Chinese consumer orders skyrocketed as a result of increased purchasing power from rising incomes. This triggered inflation and prompted Beijing to approve massive imports of consumer durables. Japanese television orders rose fivefold in 1984 and tripled in 1985, with only somewhat lesser increases in orders for refrigerators, washing machines, and other electrical appliances. Electrical equipment (including consumer goods) and industrial machinery together accounted for 36.2 percent of Japanese exports to China in 1985. Third, two of Deng's major economic reforms included granting local enterprises and governments greater import authority and decentralized foreign exchange control. These two reforms led to widespread profiteering as scarce luxury goods were imported and resold. As a result, Japanese automobile shipments—mainly for officials and taxis—quadrupled in 1984 and trebled in 1985. In 1985, transportation equipment constituted 17.6 percent of overall Japanese exports to China.

In combination, these developments caused China's foreign exchange reserves to plummet from $17 billion in July 1984 to $10 billion in March 1986. The crisis worsened as oil, which constituted nearly 34 percent of China's 1985 exports to Japan, dropped sharply in price while the yen steadily rose in value. Beijing reacted by limiting import channels and foreign exchange access, banning the import of finished products in transportation and consumer goods, and promoting domestic production for import substitution.

The impact of these actions was immediate and, for some Japanese firms, drastic. The Japan International Trade Promotion Association polled its members in early 1986 and found nearly one hundred unimplemented contracts amounting to sixteen billion yen.[9] The estimates of threatened orders ranged from fifty to one hundred billion yen, with some small firms driven to bankruptcy in the absence of alternative markets for products designed to meet Chinese specifications. As a result, 1986 shipments to China of machinery and equipment fell 30.2 percent, electrical appliances dropped 39.7 percent, and transport equipment, including automobiles and ships, plunged 58 percent.[10] In short, Sino-Japanese trade once again experienced the seesaw phenomenon.

The problem of contract suspension or cancellation was made worse by the Japanese failure to insist on arbitration and compensation clauses. According to informed sources, however, even if the clauses had existed, the Japanese would not have pressed them because they believed that Beijing retaliated against Japanese compensation awards in the Baoshan case by favoring West German firms in the next round of contracts. One result is that the Chinese side may feel less compelled to observe contracts and the Japanese side less willing to enter into them.[11]

SINO-JAPANESE TRADE PROSPECTS

Sino-Japanese trade is of grossly disproportionate importance to the two economies. Despite all the disturbing developments, Japan was still China's most important trade partner in 1986, with more than one-fourth of the PRC's total foreign trade, while China ranked fourth for Japan with only 4.7 percent of its total trade.[12] Chinese sensitivity to this asymmetry prompted Deng Xiaoping's April 1985 remark to former British Prime Minister Edward Heath that Japan's share was too high and trade with Europe must be increased accordingly.[13]

In addition to the quantitative difference, qualitative factors also favor Japan over China. Although particular Japanese industries, such as electrical appliances and steel, rely on China as their main market, overall Japanese economic health depends far more on the United States and West Europe than it does on China. Conversely, Japanese purchases of Chinese oil and coal are essential to the PRC's foreign exchange earnings. Nearly half of China's crude oil goes to Japan, for whom the supply is only 6.5 percent of total oil imports.[14] Much of China's oil has a high paraffin content, which requires special refining processes. It is difficult to sell elsewhere because only Japanese companies, anticipating the large shipments scheduled under the 1978 Long-Term Trade Agreement have invested in the necessary facilities. Meanwhile, Chinese coal faces competition in price and reliability of delivery from Australia and Canada.

This asymmetry is in large part structural given the different stages of economic development in the two countries and the standard inequality of exchange between primary products and manufactured goods.[15] It is also in part geographically determined: Japan is much closer to China than the United States and West Europe. Proximity not only lowers transportation costs for bulk shipments, but also facilitates the exchange of information, especially in market development where knowing the territory is easier if headquarters and home are only a few hours away. Japanese field representatives can return for firm and family needs with less dislocation in time, cost, and jet lag than their American and West European competitors. These factors help explain the Japanese edge in market development in China. By 1987, more than 300 Japanese firms had offices in Beijing as compared to 170 American concerns. For example, Nissho Iwai Corporation had offices in Beijing, Guangzhou (Canton), Shanghai, Nanjing, Tianjin, Dalian, and Shenzhen, but International Business Machines Corporation had offices only in Beijing and Shanghai.

Japanese barriers to Chinese exports, however, add to the trade imbalance and are identified as doing such in public complaints, both official and academic. For example, in mid-1986 one specialist claimed that Japan was banning Chinese fruits and vegetables even though similar items were being imported from elsewhere.[16] Similarly, South Korean straw mats could be imported, but Chinese mats could not. Both categories were seen as potentially helpful in redressing the trade imbalance. A second complaint concerns Chinese raw silk and satins, traditional exports to Japan, which must endure declining quotas under annual governmental agreements that resulted from special restrictions imposed by Tokyo. Also, differential tariffs allegedly discriminate against China as compared with the United States, with rugs and tea representing specific cases. A responsible Chinese official privately substantiated these charges.[17] He identified sixteen products restricted by Japanese import controls, including straw mats, which are ubiquitous in Japanese homes, beef and pork, Chinese medicines, cigarettes, and famous fruits such as Hami melons and Tianjin pears. Silk and soybeans come under tight quotas and high tariffs limit the import of Chinese shoes and leather goods, workers' gloves, tin, canned goods, artificial carpets, tea, and seven other items. The official remonstrated against Japanese advice to "import less" as a remedy for the trade imbalance, noting that Chinese modernization requires machinery and consumer goods to increase productivity and raise living standards. Instead, he argued that it was up to Japan to "import more" by opening its markets, a demand voiced worldwide in the mid-1980s. The official noted, however, that Tokyo seemed more responsive to this demand when it came from Washington than when it came from Beijing.

This same foreign trade specialist conceded that Chinese producers needed to improve their quality control and their ability to meet delivery schedules. He also acknowledged that it would be several years before the trade imbalance could be eliminated. Even if the Japanese cooperated in the identified areas, only incremental improvements would result. But the specialist noted that in the meantime any evidence of genuine concessions by Japan would ease trade frictions, which had reached serious levels.[18]

The Japanese concurred in identifying the Chinese items with the potential for increased importation, but differed in certain cases in explaining the obstacles. For instance, the Japanese preferred the oil content of American soybeans, but were loathe to tell this to the Chinese. Instead, they complained about stones and dust in the shipments.[19] Trading specialists admitted the virtual exclusion of leather and bags, but claimed "impurities" and "inconsistencies" prompted the restrictions on straw mats.

These complaints were enlarged on in a survey of Japanese trading companies, department stores, and chain stores that documented the Chinese official's admission that quality control and delivery schedules needed improvement.[20] These criticisms were made credible by comparing China's share of consumer product markets with those of other countries, such as South Korea and Taiwan. In 1984 China ranked fifth in footwear, eighth in travel goods, ninth in toys, and eleventh in sporting goods. Only in apparel did it hold 19.2 percent of the market, second to South Korea.

Among the litany of complaints, quality control was first in frequency of reference. Chinese fabrics often arrived stained and dirty, either because they were improperly handled at the factory or because they were loaded on open trucks. Wearing apparel sometimes required repressing and repackaging in fresh polyethylene bags. Food occasionally spoiled in transportation. Delivery delays posed the greatest challenge for trading companies. Timing is critical with regard to primary products because of wide market fluctuations and manufactured goods because of seasonality. In the latter case, one department store reported that its imports of Chinese fall wear had not arrived by October. Taiwan and South Korea each account for 30 percent of Japan's imports of knitted wear. China's fourth place rank is blamed on "difficulty in meeting delivery deadlines."[21]

Another area of criticism concerns pricing, in which the Chinese are alleged to be unresponsive to international mechanisms, such as the Chicago grain market, the Dallas cotton market, and the London Metal Exchange. Department and chain stores also complain that the Chinese offer different prices to retail stores and trading companies and that they even offer different prices to American and European buyers as compared to Japanese.

More generally, mainland manufacturers lack initiative and the ability to respond quickly to the development of new products, whether to expand into existing markets or to meet competition. Up to a year can be consumed in getting approval for new designs. An experienced exporter in Wuhan confirmed this, claiming that bureaucratic delays invariably lose machinery export opportunities to Taiwanese competition whenever product redesign and development is required.[22]

Japanese specialists noted that the demand for rattan furniture and chairs has increased rapidly in recent years, with Taiwan winning 80–90 percent of the market whereas "China should be able to increase its exports if it puts sufficient effort into marketing."[23] Similarly, Taiwan held 60 percent of Japan's frozen vegetable purchases in 1986. China ranked fourth behind the United States and New Zealand: "The problem is guaranteeing the products' frozen state from the production site to Japan."

"Knowing the territory" sums up China's greatest need as far as Japanese traders and analysts are concerned.[24] Japanese tastes differ markedly from American, particularly in attention to detail, design, and quality. This dictates a far more informed approach to exports, at least as perceived from Tokyo. Japanese firms and trading companies have assisted in this process through joint production enterprises, which will be examined in the following section. But it is clear that much time and effort will be required if Chinese exports are to play an important role in redressing the trade imbalance between the two countries.

Returning to the import side, the Chinese frequently complain about shoddy goods, suggesting that the Japanese "send their best products to the United States and West Europe, while leaving their second best for China."[25] In mid-1985, the Chinese press reported that thousands of Mitsubishi trucks broke down. Privately other allegations arose, such as television sets being sold from Japanese subsidiaries in Taiwan and South Korea without proper identification. An informed Beijing official acknowledged this problem, but discounted its importance by saying "these incidents occur in all international trade; it is no worse with Japan than others."

Specialists in Japan frankly admitted that serious deficiencies had arisen in specific product lines shipped to China and offered varying explanations that attributed blame to both sides.[26] Apparently the Mitsubishi trucks that broke down included some new designs that had not been adequately tested, requiring parts to be replaced in some cases and the entire truck in others. Toyota encountered a different problem. Huge numbers of Toyotas were ordered from Hainan and then resold throughout China, including the northeast. Not knowing of their eventual destination, the Hainan shipments were prepared for a tropical climate, but the extreme winter conditions in the places that many of the vehicles ended up caused them to break down completely.[27]

In the rush to utilize local authority and foreign exchange before these powers were rescinded, many Japanese taxis were imported into China without provision for spare parts. As a result, taxis gradually became idle, causing the Chinese to complain about Japanese sales practices. This problem was further complicated by the rapidly rising yen, which affected parts prices.[28]

The previously mentioned flood of orders for Japanese television sets, refrigerators, washing machines, and tape recorders prompted Japanese manufacturers and traders to utilize all the resources in their offshore networks. In the rush to meet demand, however, they often overlooked standard quality control and frequently failed to identify the point of manufacture.

Aside from these specific cases, several Japanese traders called attention to the absence of adequate distribution and service systems in China. With orders placed at one point, sales occurring elsewhere, and no systematic communication from any point back to the manufacturer, consumer complaints do not reach the headquarters until problems have become widespread and long-standing. As one specialist explained, "No product is perfect; no company can control everything. But without timely information, nothing can be done before it reaches serious proportions."

Last and least significant in the Japanese view, but nonetheless troublesome, are the communication and behavior gaps between the two societies. Instructions for installation, proper use, and preventive maintenance are often misunderstood or ignored in China. The consequent product failure is then blamed on the manufacturer or trader. Identifying responsibility for a problem is sometimes perceived to be politically or socially sensitive, so the Japanese firm simply accepts the Chinese complaint in order to maintain the relationship for future sales. Meanwhile, the fundamental problem remains to threaten future interaction.

Despite their complaints the Chinese generally agree that, given a choice, consumers will buy a Japanese product instead of a local one even if it entails a higher cost. An occasional conversation reveals complete satisfaction with the Chinese counterpart but overwhelmingly it is compared unfavorably with its Japanese competitor.

Despite consumer preferences, Chinese officials repeatedly threaten to cut future imports if Tokyo does not lift its trade restrictions and open its market to Chinese goods. Addressing more than one hundred Japanese business leaders in February 1987, Zhu Rongji, vice minister of the State Economic Commission, warned that "economic relations between the two countries will not grow unless the Chinese trade deficit with Japan declines." Zhu further suggested the possibility that trade might actually decrease.[29] Beijing had already switched suppliers in some items, the United States replacing Japan in office equipment with 53 percent of Chinese imports in 1986 compared with 32 percent in 1985.[30] West Germany also improved sales of metalworking machinery and telecommunications equipment at the expense of Japan.

Chinese and Japanese analysts both agree that aside from the problems in marketing, quality control, and delivery reliability, modifying the Chinese export mix to meet changing Japanese demand is an even more fundamental challenge. As one Tokyo specialist remarked, "I am worried about our financial and technical assistance for developing Chinese coal production. What will they say when our imports fail to expand at the same rate? Where will they sell it?"[31]

Chinese experts call attention to structural changes in the Japanese economy toward less energy-intensive industries.[32] Thus, not only are low prices likely to prevail in raw materials and fuel resources, but their market share in Japan will also shrink. The magnitude of the problem is demonstrated by Japanese customs figures for 1985, which show that China's exports consisted of crude oil and other petroleum products (43.1 percent), foodstuffs (15.6 percent), and only 27 percent processed goods, mainly textiles.

On the positive side, Chinese analysts point to the abundance of "relatively untapped labor . . . [which] will give China considerable competitive edge in the field of processed and semiprocessed exports."[33] They note that the share of manufactures in Japanese imports rose from 22.8 percent in 1980 to 31 percent in 1985 according to Chinese calculations. In part this was because of market liberalization, but it also reflected the shift in Japan toward technology-intensive and knowledge-intensive industries and away from labor-intensive and capital-intensive industries.

The Japanese foresaw that the trade imbalance would lessen in the short run as the appreciation of the yen inhibited Chinese consumer imports and encouraged exports.[34] However, China's seventh five-year plan calls for economic growth of seven to eight percent. This will require imports of industrial machinery for use in large projects with fixed assets, such as power stations and harbors. Regardless of immediate developments, the longer-run view on each side cautions against expectations of balanced trade. At a major meeting of governmental and private specialists in Beijing in May 1986, the Japanese frankly warned that it could take up to twenty years for China to achieve this goal.[35] They pointed to their own record in trade with the United States between the 1950s and the 1970s as an example of how patience and persistence can pay off in the end.

Similarly, Chinese analysts focusing on the longer view emphasize the need to shift exports from primary products to processed goods and, within that sector, to concentrate on value-added exports rather than simple manufactures.[36] In short, the Chinese economy needs to restructure fundamentally its export capabilities. For this to succeed, however, Chinese analysts call on "the Japanese government to extend assistance in . . . expanding the size of Japanese investment and raising the level of technological transfer. To this end, it is also hoped that the Japanese government will help China overhaul its technologically backward enterprises."

This linkage between exports, on the one hand, and investment and technology transfer, on the other hand, adds another dimension of complexity to overall trade. Whereas it is possible for Tokyo to improve market conditions through governmental action, Japanese investment and technology transfer depend primarily on private enterprise. This in turn shifts the focus outside of trade per se to the far less quantifiable realm of joint ventures and other forms of foreign investment.

JAPANESE CAPITAL INVESTMENT

In addition to Japanese market restrictions, the Chinese also complain about the low level of Japanese investment in China, contrasting it with the large trade surplus, and the relatively small number of large production ventures. These themes dominated Sino-Japanese discourse through 1986, at which time Beijing finally acknowledged that some of the causes for Japanese and other foreign financial caution stemmed from the investment environment in China. That October the State Council enacted extensive legislation that

Table 1   Foreign Investment in China
(number of cases)

Form of Investment	1979–85	1985	1986
Joint ventures[a]	2,343	1,412	870
Cooperative ventures[b]	3,823	1,611	560
Wholly foreign-owned ventures[c]	120	46	18
Total	6,286	3,069	1,448

Sources: The 1979–85 data are compiled from Chinese sources by the Japan External Trade Organization (JETRO) and are cited in Takashi Uehara, "Changes in China's Policy Regarding the Introduction of Foreign Capital," *China Newsletter*, no. 66 (January–February 1987): 17. The 1986 data are compiled by the Chinese Ministry of Foreign Economic Relations and Trade (MOFERT) and are cited in *China Daily*, January 24, 1987, in FBIS, January 28, 1987, K15. In addition, six offshore oil contracts were listed separately.
[a] Projects in which the Chinese and the foreign investors share both the investment and the management. The Chinese side is usually the majority investor.
[b] Projects in which the Chinese pay royalties for production using foreign equipment and know-how. There is no foreign investment.
[c] Projects in which all investment is provided by foreign concerns.

was designed to remedy the situation. The inevitable delays in implementation and the uncertainty about local responsiveness, however, left the near-term future subject to the problems inherited from the recent past.

As with trade, the pace of foreign investment in China fluctuated widely up to 1987 as shown in Table 1. Three reservations attend these figures. First, they include contracts signed but not yet implemented. Thus, the Ministry of Foreign Economic Relations and Trade (MOFERT) acknowledged that more than half of the contracts concluded between 1979 and 1986 were not in operation by 1987. Similarly, during 1979–85, direct investment totaled $16.2 billion in contracts, but only $4.6 billion in actual terms.[37] Of the record $5.85 billion committed in 1985, only $1.57 billion arrived that year.[38] In 1986, contract commitments fell to $3.3 billion and although $2.1 billion was utilized, most of this was from previous commitments.[39]

Second, Beijing's definition of foreign investment includes Hong Kong and Macao, which during 1984 provided 86.3 percent of the companies involved and 75.6 percent of the total investment committed.[40] Although some genuine foreign investment passes through Hong Kong intermediaries, the overwhelming majority of such investment represents local Chinese activity. In addition to the standard profit motivation, Hong Kong investment in China is often facilitated by special mainland connections and encouraged by parochial interest in privileges for relatives, anticipated rewards after the Chinese takeover of Hong Kong in 1997, and simple patriotic identification with Chinese modernization.[41]

This in turn relates to the third and substantively most important reservation about the figures in Table 1: the figures do not reveal what proportion of the contracts are in productive enterprises as opposed to the so-called third industry or service sector, which includes hotels, restaurants, and office buildings. Although most foreign investment goes into this latter category, that from Hong Kong and Macao is especially concentrated in this sector because of local experience and anticipated quick returns.

As Table 1 shows, the number of contracts negotiated in 1985 surged to constitute nearly half of the total for 1979–85. But in 1986 the number of contracts signed fell by almost 50 percent, with roughly a two-thirds decline in the number of cooperative and wholly foreign-owned ventures. Japanese behavior paralleled this general pattern: only ten joint ventures in 1980–83, but forty-seven in 1984 and ninety-five in 1985.[42] Tokyo's Ministry of Finance reported that 78.6 percent of the funds went into the nonmanufacturing sector, although this sector won only 60 percent of total Japanese direct investment, both in Asia and in the world as a whole.[43] Moreover, most of the manufacturing projects were relatively small and did not involve large amounts of capital or technology. By the end of 1985 Japanese investment in China, at 355 million yen, ranked second (excluding Hong Kong) to American investment, which stood at 381 million yen.

Chinese officials emphasize that increased productivity, technology transfer, and export growth are the main objectives for seeking foreign investment. Viewed in these terms, the open door policy had fallen far short of these goals by 1986, whether examined with respect to all countries or by the level of Japanese investment in particular. At the most general level, the problem lay in the divergence between Chinese goals and those of foreign investors, who envisaged high returns from the large domestic market. This underlying conflict of interest only surfaced in 1985–86 when the fall in China's reserves prompted Beijing to restrict access to foreign exchange. These restrictions applied to foreign-owned enterprises as well as indigenous firms.

The impact of this development became dramatically evident in the Fujian-Hitachi television plant that had been widely touted in China and Japan as a model joint venture.[44] Formed in February 1981, the new management had turned a 1975–80 loss of 417,500 yuan into a 475,000 yuan profit for the period starting in June 1981 and ending in December 1982. By 1983 the company's annual output of 140,000 color television sets constituted 27 percent of total PRC production.[45] But in mid-1986 the factory shut down after operating at a loss.[46] Profits on the domestic market had been high despite a heavy import tax of 40–60 percent on parts constituting nearly 60 percent of the finished product. Because of the tax these parts had cost approximately $100 million over five years. Then in late 1985 the appreciation of the yen raised their cost further and in early 1986 access to foreign exchange was cut. Rather than rely on local parts of inferior quality, the management reduced output, but this slashed profits. Meanwhile costs continued to rise and there was no import tax relief to compensate for the higher yen. After weeks of intensive high-level discussions on both sides, new measures won agreement and operations resumed. Several dozen television kit-making factories in various provinces came under the control of a holding company, which was financed by China, but which received technical assistance from Hitachi. Local components in the Fujian-Hitachi sets would be increased from 40 percent to 85 percent by 1987. This would have the effect of cutting costs 20 to 30 percent and would enhance export competitiveness. Beijing's determination to preserve a favorable image for joint ventures prompted these extraordinary measures, but could not eliminate the negative impact of foreign reports, especially in Japan.[47]

More persistent, if less dramatic, problems explain why a late-1985 survey of 115 foreign firms in Beijing revealed widespread discontent, with the highest percentage of discontented firms being Japanese.[48] The intensity of their feelings showed as well. On a scale of 1 to 5 measuring satisfaction, with 1.0 representing strong dissatisfaction, the Japanese companies averaged 1.9 as against 2.9 for American firms. More than two-thirds of those unhappy with the projected financial return were Japanese; more than three-fourths of Japanese firms said China's legal framework provided inadequate safeguards for foreign investment.

The litany of private complaints from foreign businessmen became a chorus of public criticism in 1986. A sharp fall in the rate of investment (by June investment levels stood at only about half of the levels they reached in 1985 at the same point in the year) and widespread publicity in Japanese- and English-language journals finally moved Beijing to action. Speaking to Japanese businessmen in September, Deng Xiaoping frankly admitted, "We cannot ask foreign investors to come and then not let them make money. But high rent and other expenses are making profits difficult for them."[49] One of the most surprising of the "other expenses" Deng referred to was labor. The Foreign Enterprises Service Corporation (FESCO) monopolizes the supply of Chinese workers for foreign firms. Not only does this limit the employer's choice, but the mandatory wages are higher than elsewhere in Asia. According to reports, 85 percent of the wages is kicked back to FESCO, as are most incentive bonuses.[50] Office costs include greatly inflated charges for telephones, telex, materials, as well as secretaries, translators, and drivers.[51] Foreign banks operate at a loss in hopes of eventually making a profit. In the meantime, however, they are taxed locally on all income. Import tariffs average 40 percent and duties and adjustment taxes can double the cost on such items as personal computers. Unofficial charges include illicit commissions, gifts, and "inspection trips" to foreign firms abroad.[52] Some of these problems combined with the sudden drop in oil prices to create a crisis in the Sino-Japanese joint venture at Bohai Bay.[53] In 1980, a Japanese consortium began exploration and development at this site, which ultimately cost more than $600 million. The first offshore returns, however, only began in October 1985. In 1980, oil prices were moving upward, from $20 a barrel to a peak of $32 in 1981, with an average of $25 until the sudden 1985–86 plunge to $14. At that point profits became impossible, losses mounted, and both sides publicly aired their complaints, repeating many charges reported elsewhere and further inhibiting Japanese investment.

Chinese officials accused the Japanese side of favoring minority shareholders, which included trading companies more interested in selling equipment and services than producing oil. This allegedly excluded Western firms from submitting tenders. For their part, the Japanese claimed that Chinese servicing won priority over competing bids. These situations raised costs unnecessarily, but as a Japanese executive admitted, "People were expecting oil prices to climb further and there wasn't much control over costs." For example, even though Mitsubishi Heavy Industries won a contract for two oil production platforms, as was later acknowledged by both the Chinese and the Japanese, China Offshore Platform Engineering still received one of the two bids as a compromise. Similarly, China France Bohai Geoservices, a joint Sino-French venture, admitted charging 40 percent more for maintenance and other services than in the South China Sea, where keener competition exists. Office rent likewise exceeded the highest Hong Kong rates. Low productivity per worker resulted from doubling the number of persons necessary to work an offshore platform, with twenty-eight Japanese and more than fifty Chinese technicians on board. The Chinese claimed there were too many "expensive" foreign experts; the Japanese retorted that the excess personnel were Chinese whom they had agreed to train. In addition they explained that every one-person job required three people: a Japanese technician, a Chinese trainee, and a translator.

The cumulative effect of these uneconomic concessions and compromises proved fatal once oil prices plummeted. In June 1986 a top official in Tokyo explained, "We started with the expectation of 1985 output earning $30–35 a barrel. At present Indonesian oil is $10 a barrel and that is light, so Bohai should sell at $4 less, being heavy. But there is no profit at $6!"[54] However, as in the case of Fujian-Hitachi, when faced with a shutdown and the attendant publicity abroad, Beijing took drastic action. The Tokyo official characterized these actions as "unique to Sino-Japanese relations and not imaginable in other oil producing countries." First, Beijing paid $20 a barrel to keep production profitable. Second, it increased the Japanese share of production beyond the contract agreement that had made output sharing proportionate to investment. Third, all of the initial production went to the Japanese side, the Chinese delaying on their receipt. Fourth, the Chinese agreed to replace the Japanese with lower-salaried Chinese and to phase out the costly Chinese service companies.

Both economic and political considerations forced the Chinese concessions. A local official responsible for employing fifteen thousand workers, many of whom worked on this project, protested, "You can't ask us to lay off our people. Where shall they go? This is still a socialist country." In addition, a Japanese executive noted the political importance of this project. "This is the biggest and one of the first Sino-Japanese joint ventures, and China is eager to see that it will succeed. If this one fails, there is little hope for further Japanese investment." [55]

Emergency measures enabled the Fujian-Hitachi and Bohai Bay operations to survive. But much more would be required to realize the seventh five-year plan's goal of $80 billion in foreign capital, double that won in the sixth five-year plan, of which one-third was to come from direct investment. Thus in October 1986, the State Council announced twenty-two "Provisions Encouraging Foreign Investment" to supplement the various inducements adopted by many provinces and municipalities. [56]

In November State Councillor Gu Mu, amplifying on Deng's earlier remarks as he spoke before an audience of joint venture company representatives, admitted, "The first requirement . . . is to make real improvements in the investment environment and to introduce to China the latest in business management experience from abroad. The second requirement is to guarantee the legitimate earnings of foreign enterprises, to have them manage their business in China, and to allow them to reach a stage where they can make real money." [57]

Gu's emphasis on management touched on a critical point at issue throughout China as well as among joint ventures, namely the authority of local party secretaries versus the authority of factory managers. This posed one of the greatest obstacles to Deng's economic reforms in 1986–87 because the entrenched party officials resisted losing power to the more knowledgeable plant officials. It also confronted joint venture managers with such practical questions as authority over the appointment and dismissal of personnel. [58]

Seen in these terms, 1986 marked a watershed for foreign investment in China. On the one hand, long-standing grievances that had been allowed to fester burst into the open as crises threatened Sino-Japanese model projects. On the other hand, the Chinese leadership abandoned its unrealistic, one-sided demand that investment be commensurate with trade and acknowledged the need for a drastic improvement in the investment environment. These two developments cleared the air and opened the way for a gradual improvement in meeting mutual needs. But the actual course of foreign investment in China will ultimately depend on how the 1986–87 reforms are implemented throughout the country.

TECHNOLOGY TRANSFER

An integral part of Beijing's foreign investment strategy is the acquisition of technology that can enable the Chinese economy to overcome the quantitative and qualitative gaps that accumulated during the twenty-year period that saw the disaster of the Great Leap Forward, the withdrawal of Soviet assistance, and the nihilism of the Cultural Revolution.

Technology transfer in its fullest sense is defined by a British specialist as "the pool of knowledge concerning industrial, agricultural, and medical arts. This concerns both physical and social phenomena, the knowledge about the application of basic principles to practical work, as well as information and know-how derived from participation in the production process." The transfer of technology can take three forms: physical goods, information, and human.[59] An American analyst identifies the main channels for technology transfer as "training programs, joint technical services, joint management, and joint production."[60]

Until the post-Mao period, the Chinese adopted a much simpler approach, equating the import of equipment with the transfer of technology. Thus beginning with Soviet assistance programs in the 1950s, extending through the brief periods of foreign plant purchases in the mid-1960s and early 1970s, and including the extensive contracts in the late 1970s, the acquisition of physical goods took almost exclusive priority over the acquisition of information. Little genuine assimilation of foreign technology occurred, except in selected military-related areas under Soviet auspices.[61]

This approach was not wholly abandoned. The 1978 Long-Term Trade Agreement, for example, included seventy-four whole plant contracts and another twenty-three were signed through other arrangements.[62] In 1981, however, the State Economic Commission formulated a plan to upgrade the production capacity of small and medium enterprises through the importation of specific technology and key equipment. This plan was to serve the twofold purpose of conserving foreign exchange and maximizing the applicability of carefully selected technology. Some three thousand projects were identified as part of this plan, of which Chinese officials hoped that Japanese technology would assist with three hundred. Overall, Japan's share in the $11.7 billion of contracts concluded for whole plants and technology in 1978–84 exceeded $6 billion, or 52.4 percent, with 38.2 percent from West Europe, and only 7.1 percent from the United States.

The Japan-China Association on Economy and Trade (JCAET), in consultation with the PRC State Economic Commission (SEC), had extended cooperation in 106 cases by mid-1986.[63] Thirty-six factories underwent upgrading studies by the Japan International Cooperation Agency (JICA). Through mid-1986, 651 Japanese experts had diagnosed factories in China through official and private channels and four hundred Chinese technicians had visited hundreds of Japanese factories. In all, some sixty cases of technology and facility contracts totaling $111 million were concluded during 1981– 85. The principal industries studied or serviced by contracts included machinery (general, electrical, and precision), chemicals, and plastics.

The joint procedures for technological cooperation deserve attention in view of the political criticisms in China that popularly depict the Japanese as slow to help and reluctant to provide what China really needs.[64] Tokyo's two main agencies, JICA and JCAET, operate quite differently.[65] JICA, a wholly governmental technical assistance program, only surveys plants. The plants it surveys are those selected by the SEC as needing standardized or older technologies. Between 1978 and 1984, some 934 persons engaged in JICA developmental surveys.

JCAET, however, is jointly funded by the government and more than four hundred corporate members. It plays an extensive and primary role in Sino-Japanese trade as the only organization that systematically monitors technology transfer and factory renovation, serving its members' interests as well as China's. After the SEC selects projects that have been nominated by provincial and city governments and vetted by the relevant ministries, JCAET translates and distributes the list to its member firms. If they show interest, singly or jointly, interchange begins with the appropriate Chinese enterprises. If no firms are interested, JCAET discusses their reasons and, if nothing can be arranged, notifies the SEC accordingly.

The Chinese side submits factory profiles and reform plans, followed by survey teams to the interested Japanese firms. After exchanges of view, the Chinese determine the best matchup from among the candidates. The corporation selected then sends technicians, who make a free diagnosis of factory production technology, facilities, and management. The diagnosis goes to the SEC with suggestions for improved production, better quality, new product development, and energy conservation. It also indicates what technology and facilities should be acquired.

The Chinese enterprise then prepares a feasibility report for approval at appropriate levels, including the SEC, where the report is thoroughly reviewed and a careful market study is made. After these steps, the project then goes to three Japanese firms, including the one initially chosen for the diagnostic study, to assure competitive bidding. The initial firm has preference, provided that it can match other bids or make some concessions. In 1983, only five out of nineteen negotiations proved unsuccessful.

Despite these carefully developed procedures, problems that are viewed differently on each side inevitably arise.[66] Japanese firms complain that Chinese information is often inadequate for determining the sources of problems, yet the Chinese seek guarantees on the finished product that can be difficult or impossible to make given this lack of information. They also claim that the Chinese want the most sophisticated technology regardless of applicability and that they underestimate personnel needs. Reciprocally, the Chinese claim that the Japanese often do not want to supply technologies, sometimes withholding blueprints or certain data and sometimes keeping secret patented information. In addition the Chinese say that they have been compelled to purchase unnecessary machines and that some products have have serious quality problems. They also insist that they fully appreciate human support needs.

Tokyo addressed this last item in 1982 with the creation of the Japan-China Software Center. In the next three years Nippon Electric Corporation (NEC) trained more than one thousand Chinese technicians, many of them through the center, in software development and use. Both sides were served by this program: China through human-embodied technology transfer and NEC through the provision of needed software engineers in the form of Chinese trainees.[67]

One reason that the Japanese withhold technology and information from the Chinese touches on the politically sensitive subject, rarely alluded to publicly by either side, of export controls. The North Atlantic Alliance Coordinating Committee for Export to Communist Countries (COCOM) includes Japan in its joint efforts to prevent the spread of strategic technology. For example, it took one year for Japan to gain approval for VCR shipments to China and then certain components remained secret. Similarly, when the Chinese manager of a joint venture television factory asked his Japanese counterpart how a small part functioned he was told, "I'm sorry. I cannot discuss that."[68]

Some relief to this problem came in 1986 when COCOM restrictions were considerably loosened for China, following a major relaxation of American export licensing procedures. This allowed Canon to sell exposure systems for producing very large-scale integrated circuits (VLSI); previously only the sale of lower-integrated linear integrated circuits production facilities had been permitted.[69] Canon's mask-aligners furnished one of the most important front-end semiconductor production facilities, providing 64-kilobit dynamic random access memories and other highly sophisticated VLSIs. Fuji Electric Company began shipment of high-purity silicon wafers for semiconductors to serve a radio factory that had earlier contracted for a high-voltage silicon diode manufacturing facility and production technology from Fuji.[70] Sino-Japanese joint production of optical fibers and cable began in 1987, with the formerly prohibited technology, machinery, and testing instruments coming from Japan.[71]

These developments signaled a new era in possible technology transfer, yet many Chinese privately complained that Japan continued to obstruct COCOM approval. Informed American as well as Japanese sources flatly denied that this was true.[72] However, as we have noted, perception is often more important in politics than reality. Incidents on both sides in 1987 aggravated this problem. In March a Japanese trading company and four businessmen allegedly exported high technology equipment to China that was potentially utilizable for advanced weaponry according to information provided by the Ministry of International Trade and Industry.[73] The equipment, however, was purportedly for the manufacture of television sets and the affair soon dropped from sight. Far more serious was the aftermath in June of the Toshiba Machinery Company having subverted COCOM restrictions by the sale to the Soviet Union of machinery for the manufacture of quieter submarine propellers. With Washington already in a "Japan-bashing" mood because of trade imbalances, this incident touched off a political storm that caused Tokyo to react precipitously on exports to all communist countries. As a result, Toshiba was forced to cancel many of its contracts in China.[74] After several months of negotiations and reassurances from Nakasone, Beijing reacted publicly and sharply. An authoritative article claimed that "great losses" had been suffered, "strong resentment" had been expressed, and compensation had been demanded of Japanese firms failing to deliver on time.[75] The writer warned, "It should be pointed out that China insists on the principles of equality and mutual benefits in foreign economic transactions. China also insists that no dependent relationship exist." In December Kyodo reported that the Chinese canceled a number of import contracts in retaliation, including machinery, electrical goods, and measuring instruments, allegedly as a result of central directives to provincial and municipal trade offices.[76]

The practical problems encountered in using technology transfer to upgrade existing plants are well illustrated in the plastics industry.[77] For polyethylene, mainly used in plastic bags, the Chinese grading of raw materials is so variable that it is unacceptable in Japan. Also, molding conditions may vary with every batch. Polyvinyl chloride, which is used for construction in hotels and apartments, has poor heat resistance because of basic inferiorities. Engineering plastics suffer from inadequate grading, designed to meet different uses, so that molded components are often rejected as substandard.

The industry's inventory of molding equipment ranges from thirty-year-old hand-operated machines to the latest equipment from Europe and Japan. It also includes Chinese machines indigenized with parts and direction from Japan or other foreign countries, copies of imports that lack their capabilities, and wholly Chinese designed and manufactured equipment. A single plant may mix several of these types, operating them for a wide variety of product lines. This situation obstructs specialization in production and quality control therefore suffers.

As in most Chinese industries, overstaffing is common; five or more times the number of workers are employed at a Chinese plant compared with similar firms in Japan. With productivity per capita and per machine both low, costs are inordinately high. Without cost accounting, small lots often receive disproportionate care and effort, which is uneconomic. One Japanese specialist tactfully concluded, "It is necessary to remain somewhat humble when called upon for advice."[78]

Problems external to the factory further complicate the situation. Products are sometimes stacked in the open, uncovered; in dry areas, plastics become electrically charged, acquiring more dirt. Power may vary in voltage or suddenly stop, ruining whole batches and possibly damaging the equipment as well. Voltage fluctuations of 20 percent result in nonuniform products; thus, even the most advanced molding machines cannot meet the specifications of the Japanese market when operated in China.

These obstacles limit the expansion of compensatory trade, in which machinery imports are paid for by the export of that machinery's output. Despite the Chinese preference for compensatory trade as a solution to foreign exchange shortages and rising yen rates, the Japanese resist these arrangements. Because plastic items "presently manufactured under China's production system are all but unacceptable quality-wise in Japanese eyes," few such compensatory arrangements exist.[79] Meanwhile, the competition for Japanese subcontracting is increasing in Taiwan, Korea, and other newly industrializing Asian countries. They will eventually learn the manufacturing techniques for plastic parts, further limiting China's export position.

A leading Japanese specialist summarized the problems on both sides that will make technology transfer a slow, difficult, and sensitive issue for some time to come.[80] On the Chinese side, he stressed the need for greatly increased expenditure on information and servicing, noting that sometimes the Chinese require separate prices for the equipment and the software (the information necessary to run and maintain the equipment) and then drop the latter, pleading budgetary limitations. Another complication that stems from this practice is that the prices for training and service are negotiated on a case-by-case basis. Although there are world prices for equipment, there are no such prices for training and service. This raises Chinese objections and suspicions of unfair practices.

Given the low absorption capacity of their factories, the Chinese resistance to software acquisition becomes a more serious problem the higher the technology they demand. Furthermore, "in most cases the Chinese ask the Japanese corporations to guarantee the final product" even when they "must use existing equipment wherever possible and keep new equipment purchases to a minimum." The combination of inadequate software and unreliable equipment degrades technology performance, yet "it must be said that the Chinese tend to blame failure entirely on their foreign partner."

This Japanese analyst admitted that there are problems on his own side. He noted that "the undue wariness and even anti-Chinese feelings among some Japanese company people need to be overcome." Cultural similarities may not be meaningful in commercial transactions and "it may be advisable to think of China as completely different in terms of social system and culture so as to temper the expectations of success based on some inapplicable sense of affinity." Finally, "Japanese corporations often fail to put themselves in their Chinese counterparts' shoes. . . . They should be aware that Chinese history and the present social system are intimately wrapped up with wars, revolution, and cultural revolution."

This Japanese writer's attention to "the wide differences between the cultural and social systems of the two countries" echoed the observation made by a young Chinese professor whom I cited in an earlier chapter. It addresses a basic problem that has only recently begun to receive attention in business and academic circles on both sides. An annual seminar on the theme "Economic Affairs in Japan and China," held in Japan April 11–13, 1987, found the forty participants in a "frank exchange—and even heated discussion" which, to a Japanese analyst, "confirmed once more the immense gap between perceptions held in Japan and China."[81]

This analyst summarized the standard complaints on both sides, addressing subjective as well as objective aspects. The downturn in Japanese investment momentum during 1986–87 had multiple explanations: "subtle policy changes that tend to accompany changes of top leadership in China; lack of transparency regarding approval procedures; administrative red tape; inflexible Chinese demands for hard currency balance; lack of adequate infrastructural facilities, such as water and power supply, drainage, transportation, ports, and communications facilities; and uncertainty regarding raw materials supply and costs." Further obstacles include: "Chinese inexperience in established international trade practices; inability to secure capital and operating funds; difficulty in determining the amount of capitalization; and a tendency to go back on negotiated deals; also an inadequacy of information necessary for wise investment [and] difficulty in determining the proportion of finished products for domestic consumption and export."

The Chinese complained in particular that technology transfer was inadequate, evidenced by the fact that whereas 48 percent of hardware imports came from Japan as against 13 percent from the United States and 10 percent from Germany, only 13 percent of the production know-how came from Japan as against 26 percent from the United States. Again the Japanese explanation was multiple, illuminating not because it is necessarily correct, but rather because of the viewpoint expressed. The writer suggested that some of this difference stemmed from "accounting" in which European and American firms begin broadly on the basis of future potential while Japanese businessmen start each project on its own terms, starting small and developing gradually. He saw European and American investors as selling off unprofitable operations faster than their Japanese counterparts and therefore the "difference in strategy" could explain the initial gap in levels of investment and technology transfer. Stylistic differences also exist. European and American businessmen are "more accommodating to various demands" at the start, but express reservations later, while Japanese businessmen "prefer to convey their inability to accept certain conditions" at the outset. He suggested that the Chinese prefer the "yes, but . . ." approach of Europeans and Americans to the "no, but . . ." approach of the Japanese. Finally, he noted that "language itself sometimes becomes a major impediment." The use of Chinese characters by both sides did not lead to a common meaning and interpretation. Time was required to work out the legal implications.

More fundamentally, the writer called attention to the successive stages of economic development and the relationship of technology transfer to each stage, by implication suggesting that the Chinese would have to be patient and take a long view paralleling the Japanese experience. In his approach, the initial stage finds foreign technology costly and without immediate benefit. In the second stage it becomes "sufficiently established to compete with the indigenous modes of production, thus creating a dual economic structure." This leads to its eventual assimilation into the domestic economy "resulting in greater technological sophistication and economic efficiency." He then points out that the mode of technology transfer should fit the importer's level of development, with licensing arrangements suitable for more advanced stages. He denied that the degree of willingness to transfer technology could be inferred from the mode or the level of technology exports to China. His admonitions for "mutual cooperation and trust when problems arise" are dutifully echoed in Chinese writings, but the Chinese are likely to perceive that the implied burden of waiting for high technology imports is one-sided against them.

Alleviating misunderstandings can reduce the tensions associated with technology transfer. Many of the difficulties, however, are inherent in this relationship, which embodies both a historical role reversal of the teacher-student relationship and a contemporary economic conflict between Japanese profit maximization and Chinese developmental needs.

LOANS, GRANTS, AND OTHER COOPERATION

The strongest evidence of Japanese cooperation in China's economic modernization is the record of loans extended between 1979 and 1986. The seven-year total of $3.4 billion (at 1986 exchange rates) in long-term government credits, together with their relatively liberal terms of repayment, proved responsive to successive Chinese demands as fiscal crises repeatedly threatened key projects.[82] In addition, a succession of short-term Export-Import Bank and commercial credits pushed the total amount of credit available to China to nearly $20 billion. A brief recapitulation of this record reveals why, despite the gross trade imbalance and associated complaints, Chinese officials tenaciously defended Japanese economic relations when challenged by student demonstrations in 1985.[83]

The first loan agreement of May 15, 1979, for $2 billion came from the Export-Import Bank of Japan. Its purpose was to keep alive the contracts that were threatened with suspension because of the Chinese failure to earn foreign exchange through oil sales. Payable in fifteen years at 6.25 percent, it was followed three months later with two commercial loans for a total of $8 billion, $6 billion of which was lent for six months at 0.25 percent above the Eurodollar rate and $2 billion of which was lent for four and a half years at 0.5 percent over the Eurodollar rate.

I have already noted the December 1979 pledge by Prime Minister Ōhira to loan 300 billion yen, apportioned in annual installments, for six major construction projects, all of which were completed by 1987.[84] This loan saved the Baoshan steel complex and also provided for three major railroads, two ports, and one hydroelectric power plant. Repayable in thirty years at 3 percent with a ten-year grace period, the loan was not tied to Japanese purchases.

When the next contract crunch came in 1981, Tokyo provided a $1.3 billion package consisting of $560 million in government commodity loans, $430 million in Export-Import Bank supplier credit guarantees, and $300 million in syndicated commercial loans. Among other things, this enabled Baoshan to complete its first phase and enter production as scheduled in September 1985. It also facilitated Beijing's compensation for Japanese firms whose contracts had been canceled in 1979–80.

As the 1979 loan approached exhaustion in 1983, Beijing requested another $6 billion for projects over the next five years. After feasibility studies, Prime Minister Nakasone agreed in March 1984 to provide a second aid package of $2.1 billion for the next seven years, payable in thirty years, with a ten-year grace period, at 3.5 percent. This would cover seven key projects, including two railroads, three ports, one hydroelectric plant, and one telecommunications plant. In addition, Export-Import Bank funds were offered for developing coal and petroleum resources. The terms were agreed to in December 1984: the loan would be for $2.4 billion over five years, payable in fifteen years at 7.15 percent, and would cover two coal and four petroleum exploration projects.

The Export-Import Bank also provided small and medium loans

in cooperation with four Japanese commercial banks. Since 1982 these loans have made five billion yen available for small-scale plant and machinery imports from Japan. Repayable in two to five years at 7.5 percent, approximately one-third of these loans had been drawn on by 1985. Also in 1985, the Bank of Tokyo headed a consortium that concluded a $2 billion loan agreement with China for ten years, the interest rate of 8.5 percent being slightly above the prevailing interbank loan rate in London.

Last and least sizable in the Japanese record of lending to China is the Tokyo bond market, where Chinese institutions had raised 65 billion yen by mid-1985. The Chinese have floated bonds in increasing amounts: 5 billion in August 1983, 20 billion in November 1984, and 30 billion in January 1985. The rising yen threatened to eliminate this option, at least until rates stabilized.

Tokyo's financial behavior throughout these years has stemmed from mixed motives. At a minimum, the loans salvaged Japanese contracts that were threatened by suspension or cancellation and, failing that, funded compensatory payments. They also helped to preserve and expand economic relations that would benefit future Japanese trade and investment. Beyond this, however, a genuine desire to help China develop, regardless of risk, underlay the loans with generous terms in which the repayment will depend on unpredictable political conditions over several decades.

This latter consideration prompted one experienced foreign banker in Hong Kong to remark, "Financially these loans make no sense. Politically they are really disguised reparations."[85] In my interviews, Japanese officials asserted, "We owe it to China. We must help after all the damage we did to them." Yet in China, except among economists, Zhou Enlai is widely criticized for his failure to demand reparations in 1972. Many Chinese asserted that "this was his worst mistake!"[86] Not only did I find no knowledge in China that Chiang Kai-shek forswore reparations in 1951 and, in doing so, virtually excluded this option when Zhou sought Japan's transfer of recognition from Taiwan. There was also no awareness of the size, conditions, and timing of Japanese loans over the period 1979–86, much less a perception that these loans might be surrogate reparations.

To be sure, loans, unlike reparations, must be repaid at some point and repaid with interest. Unforeseen problems emerged in

1986–87 to cast a shadow over this situation. As of March 1986, China's yen-denominated debt constituted between 35 and 45 percent of its $5.87 billion total, with $1.5 billion in yen-denominated bond issues and $500 million in government-to-government soft loans.[87] With exports denominated mainly in dollars and the yen-dollar exchange rate plummeting from 220–250 per dollar in the early 1980s to 120–130 per dollar by late 1987, a serious repayment squeeze loomed ahead. Fortunately, most of this particular debt is not due until around 1990 by which time remedial measures or exchange reversals may occur.

The seventh five-year plan's goal of $80 billion in foreign funds anticipates one-third in public loans and another third in private financing. Given the sudden rise in the yen, the proportion that will come from Japan is impossible to forecast. Japanese banks, however, are in a leading position to extend loans to China: twenty-two of the seventy-five banks listed in Beijing are Japanese, compared with only seven each from France and the United States.[88] The Japanese banks' reputation for undercutting the London rate provides an additional advantage.

As one of Prime Minister Nakasone's final gestures, he celebrated the fifteenth anniversary of the Japan-China Friendship Association in September 1987 by announcing a 100 billion yen loan for the promotion of Chinese exports.[89] Tokyo officials explained that this loan would be part of the $20 billion Nakasone had said Japan would recycle to help developing countries. Precisely how the new loan would be implemented was to be worked out between the two sides at a future date.

Japan also occupies first place in grants to China, totaling $800 million between 1980–84 with a commitment to double overall foreign aid by 1992. Funds from the Office of Development Assistance flow through the Overseas Economic Cooperation Fund, some to the JICA for plant surveys and the rest to specific projects. For example, in 1986 Japan granted more than 2.0 billion yen to establish a rehabilitation center in Beijing for the physically handicapped and another 1.4 billion yen for water purification facilities in Changchun, both to be completed in 1988.[90] Presumably China will benefit proportionately should Japan's overall aid program expand as planned, although grants will always be small compared with loans.

Other forms of economic cooperation between China and Japan

illustrate the range of interactions. In most instances, these interactions benefit China more than Japan. For example, in 1986 40 percent of the more than ten thousand "foreign experts" in China were Japanese.[91] In late 1985 the two countries agreed on a program that would provide Japanese volunteers between twenty and thirty years of age for two years of service in China. Also, a "silver volunteers" association, with government support, provides retired engineers. This group, the Japan-China Personnel Exchange Association, comprises Japanese politicians, economists, and entrepreneurs, who meet regularly with their Chinese counterparts.[92] Retired specialists help Chinese managers to study Japanese entrepreneurial methods.

In April 1985, the third session of the Sino-Japanese Scientific and Technological Cooperation Joint Committee signed more agreements than had been made in all previous years.[93] Among the thirty projects under way were promising new antibiotics, some that might be used to make safer and less toxic insecticides and others that may be effective against leukemia and other cancers and tumors. Another joint effort succeeded in extracting niobium from molten iron. Although these developments occurred with Japanese cooperation, China is seeking patent rights in several countries for their future use. China's Biotechnology Development Center has signed a contract with Nippon Zeon Company, a leader in chemicals and natural materials development, that establishes a five-year research effort in biotechnological processes that will focus on tissue cultures for drugs, spices, and other animal products.[94]

An agreement between the Japan China Agricultural Farmer Exchange Association of Tokyo and the Sichuan Scientific and Technological Commission has resulted in a joint survey of underground resources in Sichuan, the first such survey in China since the 1950s.[95] Equally important for its possible long-run implications is an agreement signed at the Fourth Sino-Japanese Government Members Conference in Tokyo in July 1985 on the peaceful uses of nuclear energy.[96]

Japanese assistance in human development exists at various levels. A management training center in Tianjin, begun in March 1986 with China providing the land and the buildings, receives Japanese teaching materials, books, computers, and video equipment as well as assistance in training the Chinese faculty. Through 1987, some

1,500 Chinese graduate students had researched three hundred subjects in Japan with Japanese funding. Also, a private sector project has supported 750 workers in Japanese factories as of mid-1986. Beijing covers the workers' airfares and the Japanese firms pay their wages.[97] The program works as follows: Beijing lists the industries seeking better trained employees. The Japanese firms review the lists and agree selectively. After public competition in China for spots in the program, the qualifications of the best applicants are submitted to the firms. The final selection of Chinese participants is based on their knowledge of Japanese and their demonstrated hard work. Mostly between twenty-five and thirty-five years old, the workers reportedly interact well with their Japanese cohorts. Because of the language requirement, most Chinese participants initially came from the northeast, which Japan had occupied from 1931 to 1945. More recently, however, Shanghai workers have also participated.

MUTUAL PERCEPTIONS AND
EXPECTATIONS

This by no means exhausts the instances of economic interaction outside of trade, loans, and grants, but it suffices to demonstrate the wide variety of activities that fall under the heading of cooperation. In practical as well as in philosophical terms, "the ties that bind" seems an apt depiction of Sino-Japanese economic interactions, even if some of the time the ties that bind also seem to get tangled.

But perceptions and expectations do not always accord with actual circumstances, especially when they are embedded in a relationship plagued by historical and emotional tensions. I have alluded to this problem at various points, yet because its potential impact is so great, I reexamine it here. Stated subtly by a Japanese scholar, "It is very difficult when the Chinese have always been the teacher and we have always been the student. They cannot change to being the student very easily; they don't like it. We have not had much experience at being the teacher and we don't do it very well."[98] I found in my extended informal conversations that each side bluntly accuses the other of arrogance and displays reciprocal contempt that at times borders on hatred. Such attitudes are more common among younger Japanese. Their elders express genuine feelings of guilt and feel that they have an obligation to help China. But this hostility is more generally shared among all people in China. The only exception to this hostility is the most senior Chinese officials whose early years in Japan and intimate involvement in "friendship trade" nurtured a relationship through the years up to 1972.

No solid or conclusive evidence on personal attitudes can be derived from three months of selected interviews, but certain recurring references suggest core perceptions that may underlie differences articulated in purely economic or technical terms. Thus, one Chinese stereotype depicts the Japanese as "cunning." This term, *jiao hua*, may be used for sharp business practices, but it also connotes being tricky, crafty, or sly. It is the most commonly encountered adjective when the Chinese talk about the Japanese. Other expressions often heard include "thinking only of the wallet," "looking down on us," "determined to hold China back," and, at times, "cheating." By comparison, West Germans are frequently depicted as "really wanting to help China develop."

Reciprocally a Japanese stereotype depicts Chinese officials as "greedy" and "unappreciative" and Chinese workers as "lazy" and "ignorant." Japanese factory representatives resent being forced to fight the bureaucracy and live in poor conditions "when we can make more money faster elsewhere. But the boss says we owe it to them." Negotiations take too long and contracts are not reliable; factories are filthy and the workers undisciplined.

On a more positive note, a 1984 survey of Chinese factory cadres, mid-level managers, and persons associated with government organizations in seven major cities produced predominantly favorable views of both Japan and China's relationship with her.[99] Of the 675 responses to 1,500 mailed questionnaires, 90 percent said Japanese capital and financial cooperation were necessary for China's modernization. Forty-four percent thought Japan had done more in terms of economic cooperation than any other country, while only 19 percent denied this (the rest marked "don't know").

Both the Chinese and the Japanese agree that ten years of post-Mao interaction has provided valuable learning experiences for each side. This was particularly reflected at the Second Sino-Japanese Economic Seminar held in Tokyo in November 1986 and jointly sponsored by *Renmin Ribao* and *Nihon Keizai Shimbun*.[100] Nearly two hundred economists, academics, and journalists exchanged papers and views. As a Chinese report noted, "Compared with the last seminar [in November 1984], the two sides were really sincere and frank and they look forward to the future in a realistic manner, bringing great hope to the people concerning prospects of economic cooperation between the two countries." After reviewing most of the problems examined above, the allusion to "great hope" was argued in the standard cliché, "Japan has what China lacks, funds and technology, and China has what Japan lacks, resources and manpower. Close combination of these two aspects will produce wonderful economic results."

Foreign analysts generally hold similar views, if somewhat more modestly expressed. As one forecast put it, "In the long run, Japan can hardly fail to be by far the most important supplier of technology, capital goods, and management knowhow to China, while China seems bound to go on looking to Japan as the major market for its minerals and farm products—to say nothing of manufactured products."[101]

But two points of rancor, sounded privately in Japan, caution against too confident a forecast. First, although all foreign investors exhibit similar restraint in investment and express similar reservations concerning the Chinese investment environment, Japan is repeatedly singled out for special criticism by Chinese officials. This is resented. Second, and associated with this, whereas Japanese entrepreneurs tend to separate economics from politics, the Chinese tend to link the two, both at home and in representations to Japanese officials. Yet the Japanese government has proven cooperative in many areas other than trade and is limited in what it can do to affect decisions in private industry.

On balance, Sino-Japanese economic relations are fundamentally strong because of mutual interests, political as well as economic. However, as with Sino-Soviet relations in the 1950s, in China politics can take priority over economics. This tendency puts a premium on the mutual management of the overall relationship in both Tokyo and Beijing. If effective, such management will prevent short-run problems from determining long-run prospects.

7

Japan's Pacific Role

Chinese analysis and forecasting of Japan's Pacific role is a subject of major strategic as well as political sensitivity. Consequently, much of this analysis is confined to restricted publications that are circulated only within the government. The two most important centers for research and analysis are the Institute of International Studies (IIS), directly under the Ministry of Foreign Affairs, and the Institute for Contemporary International Relations (ICIR), which serves the State Council. The IIS journal carried ten articles on Japan between January 1981 and January 1986, seven of which dealt with foreign policy.[1] During this same period, the ICIR journal carried only one article on this subject. Yet discussions with strategic analysts and specialists on Japan in both institutes reveal that considerable interest and attention is given to Japan's prospective role in the Pacific basin. Although the bulk of their writing is used in inner policy circles, some analysts are permitted to place articles in noninstitute publications, either under their own name or under a pseudonym.[2]

In addition to the limited availability of these policy-oriented studies, our analysis is further complicated by the linkage between Japan and superpower competition in the Pacific. Chinese perspectives must view Japan in a larger strategic context, as an object of superpower interests as well as a regional actor in its own right. This larger context also conditions Chinese positions on Japan: as Chinese policies toward the superpowers change, Chinese policies toward Japan will also change.

An excellent example of how China's view of Japan can be subsumed within the larger superpower context emerged in 1979–80 when alignment with Washington and opposition to Moscow dictated policy toward Japan. In early 1979, Deng Xiaoping declared that China, Japan, and the United States "must further develop the relationship in a deepening way. If we really want to place curbs on the polar bear, the only realistic thing is for us to unite."[3] A year later Deputy Chief of Staff Wu Xiuquan went even further, "I am all for Japan's increasing its self-defense capabilities. . . . Generally speaking, Japan is one of the economic powers and it is entitled to become a big power militarily, too. . . . It would not seriously affect the Japanese economy even if defense spending were increased to 2 percent of the gross national product."[4]

As we will see, none of these sentiments were repeated during our period of focus, 1982–87. On the contrary, in 1987 Tokyo's lifting of the 1 percent of GNP ceiling on Japanese defense expenditures elicited critical comment in China. Also, by this time, Sino-Soviet detente precluded Chinese attempts to form an anti-Soviet united front, tacit or otherwise. This allowed the Chinese to publicly express their concern over Japan's future role in the Pacific.

Inferring Chinese views on Japan is somewhat constrained by limited information and the practical need to separate the Chinese treatment of Japan per se from the much larger body of writing that deals with global and superpower strategic matters. These constraints, however, do not preclude addressing the prospects for Sino-Japanese military cooperation, a subject that has aroused considerable concern or hope, depending on the particular vantage point, in Moscow and Washington.

In the 1970s, Soviet anxiety focused on the threat of China's massive population being strengthened militarily by Japan's technologically advanced economy as part of an American global strategy. The resulting "yellow peril" specter prompted a Soviet Sinologist in the Tokyo embassy to warn me, "Watch out! One day it will be 'them' against 'us'!"[5] Although this line of analysis disappeared from Soviet commentaries in the 1980s when Beijing began to reciprocate Moscow's detente probes, it doubtless remains a "worst-case" concern of Soviet military planners.

Conversely, a tacit anti-Soviet coalition linking China and Japan recurringly inspired hope in Washington, which was initially encouraged by Deng's call for a united front in 1979. Five years later, Hu Yaobang offered a less explicit variant of this proposal in comparing China and Japan to rival heroes in Chinese traditional tales: "When they fought, both sides were weakened. But when they were united, they were invincible."[6] Chinese allusions to Sino-Japanese friendship and cooperation as leaving "little prospect of war" in Asia or "contributing to the peace and security of Asia" hint at joint understanding, if not actual collaboration, in maintaining a favorable balance of power.[7]

On the surface, the slow but steady expansion of personal interaction between the military establishments of the two countries appears to foreshadow closer relations in this area. This interaction followed a dramatic change in Beijing's posture toward the Japanese-American security treaty, from vocal opposition to explicitly acknowledged approval. But these developments may be weighed against Chinese analyses of Japan's military potential and the persistent efforts of successive prime ministers to expand Tokyo's role in the Pacific basin. In particular, Nakasone's successful drive to abolish the limit on defense spending strengthened Chinese perceptions of a dangerous, growing nationalism in Japan. According to this analysis, growing Japanese nationalism presages the possible reemergence of a Japanese military threat to all Pacific countries, including the United States.

MILITARY CONTACTS

The following section, unless otherwise noted, is based on my interviews with military and civilian officials in the Japanese Self-Defense Agency, June 1986. None of the persons spoke in their official capacity and no attribution of information can be made.

Until the 1980s, military exchange visits between the two countries involved retired officers or those of low rank, who always acted as private individuals and had no official mission.[8] Little publicity and no protocol or ceremony attended these visits, but they inevitably drew attention abroad, especially in the Soviet press.

Gradually, however, an asymmetry developed in the level of military personnel coming from China to Japan as compared with those coming from Japan to China. By 1986, Beijing's representatives had included a national defense minister, his vice minister, and a deputy chief of staff, in addition to Deng Xiaoping himself, chairman of the Central Military Commission.[9] To be sure, Deng's public identification was not military and the other visitors had stopped in Japan "informally" en route to or from the United States. But even allowing for the differences in nomenclature between the People's Liberation Army (PLA) and the Japanese Defense Agency (JDA), no officials of comparable rank from Tokyo visited China in any capacity.

This asymmetry is particularly noticeable because more retired Japanese generals were invited to China than vice versa. One explanation offered in Tokyo was bureaucratic. It claimed that Beijing had a greater variety of agencies with more funds to host such visits and that, in addition, hospitality was much less expensive in China than it was in Japan. But a more plausible view emerged from other JDA officials, who claimed that the Chinese had a greater interest in developing the relationship because it could help in modernizing the PLA. In short, China had more to gain from military visits than Japan. Also, Tokyo was more averse to signaling any military relationship than was Beijing. Domestic opposition and Soviet sensitivity cautioned against any actions that might be misinterpreted.

Whatever the actual Chinese intent, a curious contradiction emerged in 1986. On the one hand, visiting PLA officials pressed for closer relations than Tokyo seemed willing to develop. On the other hand, concern in Beijing over incipient Japanese militarism prompted attacks on textbook revisionism and visits by the prime minister to the Yasukuni Shrine. Thus in May, PLA Chief of Staff Yang Dezhi reportedly told JDA Director General Kato, "Japan and China are big powers in the Asia-Pacific region and they are responsible for the maintenance of security and stability in this region." [10] Yang then saw the JDA joint staff chairman and allegedly proposed an "active exchange of personnel and views in the military field, not limiting such exchanges to political, economic, and cultural fields." Yang subsequently saw Nakasone, the highest level contact in Japan by a PLA figure to that time, despite the official claim that he was only "stopping by on the way back from the United States" for an "informal" visit. In their exchange of remarks, Yang declared, "Friendly relations between Japan and China will contribute to peace in the Asia-Pacific region." Nakasone, however, avoided a parallel response, suggesting, "Let's expand friendship to the remotest generations by abiding by the four principles, such as equality and reciprocity." [11]

The next month PLA Deputy Chief of Staff Xu Xin came to Japan on an official invitation in response to the JDA deputy director general's trip to China in May 1985. Xu's visit had been postponed twice, suggesting controversy in Beijing over its desirability after the anti-Japanese student demonstrations. Having finally arrived, Xu's exchanges with JDA officials went unreported in the Chinese press in contrast to Yang's earlier visit, perhaps in deference to sensitivities on both sides.

The contradiction between the PLA pushing military cooperation in Tokyo and commentaries in Beijing warning against a revival of Japanese militarism most likely stems from the coexistence of PLA tactics aimed at the acquisition of help in military modernization and strategic concerns over Japan's future military power. Japanese policy explicitly prohibits the transfer of military technology and weapons abroad, although an exception has been made for the United States. In addition Prime Minister Ōhira, in December 1979, declared that no military cooperation with China would be permitted; his successors accepted this restriction. Therefore, it is assumed in Tokyo that PLA interests center on studying Japanese methods of modernization and possibly sending PLA personnel to train at Japanese military academies.

JDA specialists expressed cautious estimates of what might lie ahead. A well-informed and experienced officer anticipated an eventual Chinese desire for exhanges involving logistics, air and naval technologies, and personnel management. But he believed that the PLA would require the rest of this century to modernize its own weaponry in terms of design, production, and operational capability. Therefore, he saw no urgency in the relationship.

As an additional impediment, this individual noted that few PLA officers could speak Japanese and those who did often had little background in military affairs. He concluded that the Chinese appeared to be exploring for the best in foreign models, whether Japanese, American, or other, and that they might ultimately develop their own synthesis. Another source remarked that it would be quite some time before any Chinese could attend military academies because it would have to be on a reciprocal basis and there was no political possibility or practical need for Japanese soldiers to attend Chinese academies.

In sum, the gradual growth of military contact between high-ranking individuals in the two countries symbolized little and substantively had accomplished nothing through 1987. Despite much speculation in the press in Japan and abroad concerning the significance of such visits, there is no evidence that they were prompted by Tokyo or that they served Beijing except perhaps in the sense that they sent a signal to Moscow. As a reminder of China's options in seeking support against worst-case Soviet threats, these visits may be of some value. But this tactic falls far short of the threatened alliance alleged by some Soviet commentaries or the strategic entente sought by some American planners.

JAPAN'S FUTURE ROLE:
THE PUBLIC COMMENTARY

Chinese public projections of Japan's future role in the Pacific basin have persistently expressed low-level concern, although Chinese concerns increased somewhat in 1987 when Nakasone removed the ceiling on defense expenditures. This move had been anticipated in China for several months. During this time, Foreign Minister Wu Xueqian voiced concern to LDP Secretary General Takeshita Noboru, expressing China's worry that Japan might become a major military power.[12] But Wu's remarks were of no avail. On January 24, 1987, Tokyo announced cabinet approval of military expenditures that amounted to 1.004 percent of GNP. Henceforth, the "Intermediate Plan for Improving Defense Strength, 1986–1990" would guide the budget, after which time the policy would be reviewed.

In China the defense expenditure ceiling had long been seen as a critical limit "to prevent Japan from becoming a military giant."[13] In June 1986, a former high official responsible for Asian affairs remarked to me privately that any change would be viewed most seriously.[14] Beijing's first major commentary on the Tokyo announcement came after a two-week delay, suggesting careful clearance at high levels. As such, it deserves quotation at length.

Zhou Bin, writing in *Renmin Ribao*, elliptically remarks, "For reasons known to all, this event evoked strong reactions inside and outside Japan."[15] Leaving Chinese views unmentioned, he cites "large numbers of reports and commentaries published by Japanese newspapers and magazines" that "clearly show that, apart from the United States, most countries still do not understand Japan's new policy and are upset by it." He further asserts, "According to historical experience and present conditions, Japan's defense strength should . . . be kept at a minimum level and must not exceed the limits of self-defense or grow out of control." Because "it is expected that Japan's GNP [in 1987] may reach $2,400 billion . . . 1 percent of its GNP is a huge amount . . . and is quite enough. . . . How could it be necessary to continue to increase . . . defense spending?"

Dismissing those who argue that the immediate increase is very slight, Zhou predicts, "Given the first 'break,' it is unavoidable that the second and the third 'breaks' and more 'breaks' will follow, and *the state of affairs will get out of control*" [italics added]. Expanding on this forecast, he warns, "The policy review in 1991 in light of the international situation and the domestic economic condition may very possibly lead to the complete rescission of all limits, thus freeing a small number of people who always try to push Japan back to the old road of being a 'military power.'"

Zhou then includes the prime minister in the "small number of people" by noting, "It could not have been an accidental event that the Nakasone cabinet made such a decision that met with widespread opposition in its last year." Two factors purportedly are at work. "First . . . to make Japan as soon as possible 'an international country' on an equal footing with other major powers so as to play 'a role commensurate with its economic strength,' in the eyes of some . . . it is necessary to increase . . . defense spending as much as possible." And "second, this measure was taken in order to meet the requirements of the United States and to strengthen Japan's alliance with the United States." By citing Nakasone's favorite phrases in inverted commas and by putting his goals before those of Washington as the primary cause of this development, Zhou carried the 1985 Yasukuni Shrine criticism to its logical conclusion. As the culmination of that controversy and taken together with the 1986 textbook dispute, the lifting of the twelve-year-old defense expenditure ceiling justified Chinese warnings of this eventuality, particularly after Nakasone's sweeping electoral victory in July 1986.

A specialist on Japan from the Shanghai Institute of International Studies analyzed Nakasone's victory as "not surprising" in view of "the emergence of an ever growing middle class" with a "national consciousness that is conservative and regressive." [16] He saw this social tendency producing the slogans popular in the

1980s, such as "great political power," "great aid power," "great cultural power," and "great creditor power," all of which taken together exemplified "great powerism." According to this analysis, the LDP reflects this basic domestic trend of thinking and furthers it with various policies. Thus, "the big electoral victory raises the possibility that the LDP will act more boldly on sensitive issues than in previous years, in particular on the extremely sensitive issue of defense."

Another analyst warned in early 1986, "Several previously existing principles have already been violated."[17] He cites "acquiescence in allowing U.S. ships with nuclear weapons to harbor in Japan" as being against the three nonnuclear principles. Weapons technology transfer to the United States violates the three principles against weapons exports. Escorting U.S. ships within one thousand miles of Japan transgresses the prohibition against collective defense, he claims. And without giving specifics, he further claims that defense expenditures in 1985 had already exceeded 1 percent of GNP.

This article cites JDA statements and strategic analyses as providing the framework within which these developments acquired a greater significance. It notes a shift of emphasis from war to "prewar preparation" and "preemptive attack." This in turn justifies a shift from "beachhead defense" to "sea-going annihilation" and from "in-shore warfare to deep-sea warfare." The regimentation and rapid mobilization of ground forces, underwater capabilities, and strengthened fighter and missile forces are all cited as evidence of a more aggressive posture. A unified command structure with improved command, control, communications, and intelligence "will pave the way for U.S.-Japan unified warfare."

The fullest public expression of concern followed the publication of the Japanese Defense White Paper in late August 1987. *Jiefangjun Bao* (Liberation Army Daily), the PLA newspaper, published two lengthy analyses of its contents. Curiously, the second was the more factual and less direct in its criticism. It summarizes a recent JDA report that detailed future maritime air defense plans and the commensurate weapons systems to be acquired.[18] It also notes the white paper's emphasis on "defending territories" and especially "the northern territories." Comparing these missions with those of the Outline Defense Plan, drawn up in 1976 and revised in 1985, the writer notes, "Obviously, it is imperative for Japan to revise the outline plan" further.

Yet after this factual presentation with its implied approval, the article asserts that "Japanese public opinion has pointed out that this year's Defense White Paper has caused concern among the people." Without citing any specific public opinion sources, it claims that concern arose because "it excessively stresses the existence and significance of military strength" and "in light of Japan's strong economic power, its continued arms expansion will inevitably result in a sense of threat to its neighbors." Tokyo also is accused of using "the pretext that foreign countries are strengthening and improving their military equipment and technological levels" to arrive at the conclusion that Japan "must develop its military strength in an unlimited manner."

This oblique attack, attributed to Japanese public opinion, was preceded two days earlier by a forthright critique by Cai Xiaohong. This authoritative commentary is bluntly entitled, "An Argument That Does Not Hold Water—Commenting on the Theory of 'Having No Choice' in Japan's 'Defense White Paper'." [19] Quoting the white paper to the effect that "because the nominal GNP remains at a relatively low level, we have no choice but to exceed one percent of the GNP," the author then proceeds to rebut this argument at length. He points out that with veterans' pensions outside the defense budget, actual defense expenditures, as calculated "in other countries," had already reached 1.5 percent. He notes that for the past five years, culture, education, and "other undertakings" had been cut while "only defense expenditure has constantly increased at an average progressive rate of seven percent annually."

Taking the new yen-dollar exchange rate into account, Cai claims that Japan's defense expenditures now rank "third in the world, second only to the United States and the Soviet Union," with $32.4 billion being spent. He rhetorically asks, "If this is a 'low level,' what is a 'high level'?" His recapitulation of weapons systems, acquired and planned, includes "super-visual radars which . . . can spy upon things *within Chinese* and Soviet territories" [italics added]. An unidentified "senior Pentagon official" is quoted to the effect that "by 1990 Japan will have the same number of crack fighter planes as the United States now has to defend its territory and the destroyers and anti-submarine aircraft owned by the

Japanese navy will be [respectively] three and five times what the United States has in its Seventh Fleet."

After flatly asserting that "viewed from Japan's defense requirements, the ceiling of one percent for defense expenditures is sufficient," Cai warns that this limit had been "a big obstacle to arms expansion." Now, "there will inevitably be a second, third, and innumerable obstacles which Japan will 'have no choice' but to 'break through.'" Although the white paper argued for military strength as a deterrence against enemy force, this showed "it can also be turned into political influence. Thus the outer cover of the 'exclusively defensive defense' strategy has been discarded." Because the "strategy of wiping out the enemy in the interior" had changed to a "strategy of wiping out the enemy in the sea," Tokyo had the choice of focusing on "Japan's territorial sea or at a great distance away." Cai concludes, "You can say it is defensive but you can also say that it is offensive because the operational radius of Japanese troops has gone beyond their territory. Can this change also be regarded as something Japan has to do 'because it has no choice'?" Cai ends his sharply worded commentary by citing a *Mainichi Shimbun* poll of February 1987 showing that 77 percent opposed lifting the GNP ceiling on defense expenditures on the grounds that this "violated the constitution's spirit of pacifism." He remarked, "This is precisely the voice of the Japanese people."

Despite this and other assurances of Japanese public opposition to rearmament, the thrust of these articles is to warn their readers to expect unchecked Japanese military growth. One unusual article went even further by making a low-key forecast that Tokyo would eventually acquire a nuclear capability. It begins by noting that "people often link nuclear wars with world war . . . while local wars will only be fought in the conventional way."[20] But the writers hold "that the threat of limited nuclear wars is an objective fact not to be overlooked." After contending that "microminiaturization and controllability of nuclear weapons" have "greatly raised the probability of their employment," they claim that "nuclear proliferation has enlarged the probability of employing nuclear weapons in local wars." Citing a recent report from "the Strategic Issues Research Center under the U.S. Army's Defense University," they identify "the nuclear club membership by the year 2010" as including "23 nations and regions, including Japan, Vietnam, and South

Korea. It is not unlikely that some of these nations and regions with an extremely strong adventurous inclination may push the nuclear button at a critical moment simply because 'they cannot help themselves' from doing so."

This was the most extreme scenario involving Japanese rearmament published in 1987 and it did not develop the reference beyond what has been quoted here. Rather, the subsequent paragraph only discusses "nuclear powers attacking nuclear-free nations" and "an attack by powers with nuclear superiority on nations with nuclear inferiority," neither case being applicable for China vis-à-vis Japan. Nevertheless, it revealed how far the image of potential threat had evolved in public discourse.

Against the preponderance of mainstream publications, an occasional dissenting view challenges this image of Japan's prospective military role in the Pacific region. An exceptionally long and closely argued analysis by Liu Jiangshui, "The Development of Japan's Foreign Strategy," takes explicit exception to mainstream emphases.[21] Appearing in the most prestigious scholarly journal on Japan, the article is prefaced by an unusual editorial note, denying that the journal endorses the argument but acknowledging that it deserves publication. This prompted one critic privately to dismiss it out of hand as "obviously wrong,"and not worth reading.[22] The editor probably agreed with Liu's analysis, but felt constrained to offer a disavowal for self-protection.

In an unusually direct opening, Liu asks, "Over the next five to ten years, in what kind of pattern, with what degree of evolution, and with what posture will Japan enter the world stage? This is a major question that directly relates to the political and economic situation in Asia and the world that will increasingly arouse people's close attention." He then contrasts the post–Meiji Restoration rise of military might with the post–World War II rise of Japanese economic productivity, which he argues achieved the same goals without the costs and catastrophe of war. He acknowledges that the capitalist system has remained the same throughout these periods, but notes that the structure and form of government has changed, as has the national strategy of development.

In the 1980s, a new strategy has emerged. Japan is moving away from a strategy emphasizing economic recovery as a means to national power toward a strategy emphasizing political power as a means to become a country of international influence. Liu diagnoses the new strategy in four parts. First, Japan wants to play a role on the world stage, "doing what the Soviet Union and the United States cannot do," while supporting the West's direction of international peace and free trade. Second, Japan's main means of exerting influence abroad is to back foreign relations with economic strength while at the same time gradually increasing defense capabilities. Third, while basically remaining "a member of the West" and allying with the United States, Japan does not seek to join with the superpowers in a tripartite confrontation on political and military matters. And fourth, although the global arena is important, Japan's main effort should be toward realizing goals in the Asian-Pacific region.

Making explicit what was implied in this four-part formulation, Liu emphasizes that these ends and means clearly differ from prewar militarism, the postwar concentration on economic power, and the vast military armaments that are the hallmark of the superpowers. Citing Nakasone's pledge "not to be a great military power," he notes that Japan has become the second-ranking Western country in the past forty years. This had not been possible in seventy years of prewar struggle.

Liu then directly addresses the alleged linkage between aspirations for great political power and the prospective revival of Japanese militarism. First, he notes that Japanese political power is "the product of the parliamentary monarchy and the peace constitution. It is the same as great economic power, with important reliance on economic power, and is not military power. Moreover, a 'great military powerism' cannot emerge directly from this political great power, but can only basically oppose the peaceful nature of political great power." Liu continues: "In recent years, the Japanese domestic demand for peace and disarmament has grown in volume and antinuclear momentum has greatly expanded. . . . The peace constitution and the parliamentary system are still obstacles in the gateway to the revival of militarism." In fact, "Japan cannot go very far to the extreme right or left in political power. . . . The main pattern of Japanese domestic and foreign policy cannot be easily changed."

Having stated his own views in absolute terms, Liu closes with reference to the orthodox worry about a worst-case scenario, most likely offered as a necessary concession to win publication. He notes that "seen in the medium- and long-term," Japan wants to gradually strengthen its military only enough for defense and not for expansionism, "but it is difficult to avoid an undesirable situation arising. As a well-known Japanese specialist on strategic problems said, 'If at some future time we become proud and arrogant and self-satisfied and take a course of action in violation of our word, that will greatly influence Japanese-Chinese relations.'" In addition to the danger of "emulating the intense American and Soviet arms race . . . if Japan intentionally falsified history through textbooks or other means, shirked responsibility for war crimes, and certain people hope through the whitewash of history to inspire so-called patriotic spirit and great power consciousness, then it will be like pouring oil on a fire."

Compared with the pages of closely and explicitly argued analysis to the contrary the brief attention that Liu gives to this negative scenario makes the author's intent clear. As such, the article reveals an important division among research analysts and perhaps at higher levels as well over the degree of confidence or concern with which to view Japan's intentions and ultimate power in the Asian-Pacific region.

JAPAN'S FUTURE ROLE: PRIVATE VIEWS

According to specialists in the field, there is no direct debate between the two main schools of thought on Japan's future role.[23] They do not confront one another in conferences or exchange papers. Instead they compete for influence at higher levels, in part through public dissemination of their articles, but principally by means of privately circulated papers and personal networks with highly placed officials, who in turn contend over policy.[24] These specialists note that the differences between the two groups are not wide, consisting mainly of disagreements over long-range projections. Both groups agree that there is no clear and present danger of the revival of Japanese militarism. Chinese historians tend to emphasize a possible return to past aggression; social scientists stress political and societal changes in Japan that make such a revival far less likely today. While public commentary tends toward the former position, these specialists see the latter, more confident analysis as dominating at the higher levels at which policy is made.

Historians aside, an overview of the Chinese who are professionally engaged in the analysis of contemporary Japan reveals three distinct generational groupings that differ in background, expertise, and outlook. The oldest specialists, semiretired or in top supervisory positions, hold a fairly well-informed view of Japan derived from living there as students in the 1920s, interacting with "friendship delegations" under Zhou Enlai's auspices in the 1950s, and negotiating the restoration of relations in the 1970s.

A second group, by far the largest in size and the most vocal in discussions, consists of working-level administrators and analysts of strategic problems in general and Japanese-Pacific problems specifically. These specialists, usually in their late thirties to late forties, acquired their positions immediately after the Cultural Revolution and had little experience in or contemporary knowledge of Japan. Although none had graduate education or social science training before starting research, they mobilize statistics and select facts to support analysis, projecting worst-case scenarios in the manner of Western think tanks.

A third group, small in size and influence, consists of younger men and women who have studied abroad in the past decade, usually in Japan or the United States. They occupy the lowest and least respected positions, are the last to speak, if they are given the opportunity to do so at all, and yet seem committed to Deng's aphorism "seek truth from facts." [25]

As might be expected, these groupings are neither airtight nor totally uniform in behavior. Individuals in the oldest generation may, depending on the occasion, tolerate or reiterate mainstream negative views for appearance while subtly indicating at some point their personal disagreements. Conversely, some in the youngest group will express strong anti-Japanese opinions, perhaps for self-protection or to curry favor with their immediate superiors or others at high levels.

These three groupings were generally all represented in my discussions. This did not lead, however, to the expression of different views within research institutes, as it did within university faculties and some, although not all, local academies of social science.

A certain degree of uniformity when outsiders are present probably results from the semiofficial nature of the institutes where any personal opinion could be misinterpreted as representing a governmental position or any disagreement might be seen as reflecting high-level debate. A more general problem, however, concerns the degree to which genuine differences of analysis are tolerated on the subject of foreign policy. In 1986, a nationwide campaign promoted the slogan "Let a hundred flowers bloom, let a hundred schools of thought contend." The campaign called attention to the thirtieth anniversary of the slogan's sponsorship in 1956 when the party had invited intellectuals to speak and debate freely without fear of retaliation. Unfortunately, in 1957 the Anti-Rightist Campaign attacked thousands of such intellectuals, stripped them of their positions, and assigned them to work in the countryside or worse.

Now Chinese intellectuals were once again being urged to "bloom and contend" with the additional assurance that this time no anti-rightist threat existed. Various academic sectors such as science and economics responded to the appeal with vigor. But foreign policy and international relations remained closed to debate, at least in public. Privately, specialists differed on how much freedom they enjoyed to challenge the official line, past or present. Several testified in detail on implied or expressed pressures to conform in written analysis and classified lectures. Others claimed that restricted, or *neibu*, journals invited different views on sensitive issues.

In October 1986, two members of the Shanghai Institute of International Studies wrote the first and only articles on this issue. They demanded independence in foreign policy research, an interdisciplinary approach far broader than political economy, and institute directors who were familiar with social science as well as with politics and administration.[26] Their complaints reflected conditions reported to be widespread by knowledgeable colleagues. These, however, were the only public attempts to "bloom and contend" in this area and they involved procedure, not substance.

This sense of constraint in foreign policy analysis does not mean that all those who participated in discussions necessarily held divergent opinions among themselves or that they differed from the official line. On the contrary, as became repetitively clear, a powerful consensus, especially among those in the second and largest group, viewed Japan with mistrust and suspicion. This view became more heatedly expressed the longer and more intensive the discussion or, alternatively, the more informal and alcoholic the ambience, suggesting that it genuinely reflected personal feelings.

Among the older generation, the official line coincided with their personal convictions that there is no present basis for a revival of Japanese militarism. But this reassuring analysis was invariably coupled with the cautionary assertion, "China does not fear Japan becoming a military power in the near future, but we must be on guard against a small group seeking to revive militarism in the future." At this point, discussion generally moved to the next younger age group, which elaborated, often with considerable emotion, on why vigilance is necessary.

Various analytic approaches emerged, depending on the particular orientation of the discussant. For example, one strategic specialist offered a simple syllogism, purportedly given by Henry Kissinger in a visiting lecture. "History shows that no nation can have political power without military power. Japan seeks political power. Therefore it will acquire military power by the next century and this will threaten all its neighbors." Another specialist warned me, "The United States encouraged Japan to strengthen itself economically without looking at the possible results. Today, Japan's economic power threatens you. Now you are making the same mistake, encouraging Japanese military expansion without looking ahead. One day Japan will not only threaten us, but will threaten the United States again. You have forgotten Pearl Harbor!"

A senior analyst reviewed Japanese military expenditures, calculating them to be the eighth largest worldwide with an annual increase of 7 percent. As the yen rose relative to the dollar, so would the expenditure, already reflected in the increase from $12 billion in 1984 to $25 billion in 1985. "Therefore," he concluded, "the Asian-Pacific countries feel very uneasy about Japanese military expenditures, although China is not as uneasy because China is a big country."

This latter theme, namely China speaking for the smaller Asian states rather than for itself, characterizes much of the private as well as public commentary. It appears, however, to be a shrewd tactical maneuver rather than a true reflection of views, given the degree of personal emotion attending this issue. As a tactic, it insinuates that China is a benign neighbor acting in the best interests of Asian countries against a possible Japanese threat. This helps to advance Beijing's influence at the expense of Tokyo, especially in Southeast Asia. At the same time, it permits the Chinese to reassure friendly Japanese counterparts that Beijing is only speaking for others, not itself. Finally, it reinforces China's self-assurance, that its basic superiority over Japan obviates any need for fear.

Another analyst emphasized the "strong social foundation" for revived militarism that makes the Japanese textbooks so important. As evidence he cites conversations in Japan with colleagues from the postwar generation. He claims that a new nationalism has prompted them to challenge the validity of the Tokyo War Crimes Trials and to ask why Americans were not tried for Korean and Vietnam war atrocities. Other specialists in the discussion supported his view. They emphasized the danger of Japanese youth remaining ignorant of history while their elders ask Asians to "understand" such matters as the Yasukuni Shrine without, however, trying to "understand" how others in Asia feel. Sweeping aside this marshaling of sociological and anecdotal evidence, one speaker heatedly attributed the threat to the aggressive Japanese "national character."

Older specialists weighed evidence of a peaceful present against their expressed anxiety over an uncertain future, remaining ambivalent about the likelihood of revived militarism in Japan. By contrast, the younger analysts displayed visible anger and distrust as they recited the record of Nakasone's statements and actions. They repeatedly moved from his emphasis on political and economic cooperation to Nakasone's military references and defense policies.

While the older specialists tended to offer evidence on both sides of the question, many in the younger group simply selected evidence that proved their point. As proof of popular support for revived militarism, one analyst cited the increased acceptance of the Self Defense Force that had been reflected in public opinion polls. When challenged to explain the strong opposition to increased defense expenditures recorded in these same polls, he admitted the duality of views without further response. This duality, however, can be explained by Japanese analysts. They see public acceptance of the Self Defense Force in its role in national disasters, for example, providing flood and earthquake relief, coexisting with public rejection of its military responsibilities.

Another line of Chinese argument stressed Japan's technological capacity, already evident in satellite launching and presumably able to produce nuclear weapons within a year or two if the decision were made to do so. In my discussions, no one countered this hypothesis by pointing to Japan's inability to survive a retaliatory attack from any of its nuclear neighbors, China, the Soviet Union, and the United States, given its unique concentration of government, population, and industry between Tokyo and Osaka. Instead, the term "the possibility exists" was used to justify worst-case projections with no attempt at estimating the probability that these scenarios would ever take place. The sheer fact that a particular development was theoretically possible at some time in the distant future was deemed to warrant serious concern now, including strong protests over any and all manifestations of an eventual military revival.

Two sources dissented from this emphasis on negative scenarios. Older specialists concluded, "We do not really fear Japan becoming aggressive again. We know the Japanese people suffered too much from the war to allow this to happen. We only want to make certain that the younger generation is properly taught the true lessons of history. That is why we must protest the textbooks and Yasukuni Shrine visits." The youngest experts who have recently studied in Japan privately refuted the assertion that Japanese youth exhibit "the social basis for militarism." On the contrary, these returned students saw no youthful tendency toward jingoism or militarism. Instead they claimed younger Japanese are hedonistic and are losing the work ethic that has propelled Japan's postwar economic growth.

One junior specialist bluntly accused his older colleagues of "mistakenly assuming that China and Japan are alike because of our common Confucian heritage and therefore we think we understand the Japanese." Instead, he asserted that "we should study Japan like any other foreign country and really learn how different it is." Perhaps with reference to the sense of constraints in such discussions, a retired scholar confidentially commented to me later, "That young man shows a lot of courage."

STRIKING A BALANCE

Within the constraints of analysis acknowledged at the outset of this chapter, two observations nonetheless seem borne out by the available evidence, public and private. First and foremost, in Chinese professional views, there is no basis of trust in Japan's future intentions sufficient to support any significant strategic or military collaboration. The suspicion of present Japanese motivations and concern over possible militarism is too strong at subelite levels to be overcome by official protestations of friendship and mutual interest. Moreover, this suspicion and concern is reinforced by developments in Japan, some of which are correctly understood, but many of which are misperceived because of an inadequate knowledge of how that system has evolved over the past forty years.

Second, Chinese views of Japan include contradictory aspects that coexist simultaneously, often within the same individual and organization. On the one hand, there is no fear of Japanese militarism at present and there is genuine confidence that the Japanese people will oppose a repetition of past aggression. On the other hand, "a small group," which included Nakasone while he was prime minister, is perceived to be capable of totally transforming public opinion over time through such indirect means as textbook revisions of history.

Similarly, the Japanese-American military relationship is seen as proper and necessary to offset growing Soviet strength in the Asian-Pacific region. Yet increases in Japanese military expenditure for armed forces, which are clearly inadequate to defend the islands much less project force elsewhere in Asia, are attacked as harbingers of hegemonic designs.

These contradictory sets of views carry their own contradictory consequences. On the one hand, they permit expressions of confidence or concern about Japan's future role to be given with equal conviction and sincerity, depending on the particular circumstances at any given time. On the other hand, they tend to give an incorrect public definition of the situation in responding to perceived or actual Japanese provocations because concern usually receives greater emphasis than does confidence. This in turn perpetuates older prejudices while generating new ones among younger audiences.

These contradictions have less consequence when the top leadership is strongly united in an agreed policy, but they can take on greater importance if debate, or worse, division occurs over relations with Japan. Intimations that this might be happening arose in early 1987, associated with Hu Yaobang's prominent role in promoting those relations. Such reports came secondhand through foreign journalists and focused more on the style than the substance of his actions in this area.[27] Reassurances from Deng Xiaoping, Zhao Ziyang, and other leaders attempted to convince Japanese officials and businessmen that Hu's decline would have no effect on the relationship. But regardless of Hu Yaobang's impact, positive or negative, the underlying Chinese sense of Japan's potential role in the Pacific is too ambivalent to warrant any expectation that these two powers will form a military entente in this century.

8

Fifty Years After

I think Deng has become a person above the clouds.
Vice Minister of Foreign Affairs, Yanagiya Kensuke,
June 4, 1987

Frankly speaking, the responsibility was never China's. Not
one of the past and present troubles was caused by China.
Deng Xiaoping to Japanese cabinet officials, June 28, 1987

July 7, 1987, marked the fiftieth anniversary of the Luguoqiao
(Marco Polo Bridge) clash, which Tokyo utilized to start war against
China. As luck would have it, 1987 also witnessed the most serious
tensions in Sino-Japanese relations in five years.

The exchange cited above[1] caused concern on both sides, but
particularly in Japan, because it followed a series of unsettling developments.[2] In January, Hu Yaobang's ouster as general secretary
of the Chinese Communist party coincided with Tokyo's lifting of
the 1 percent ceiling on defense expenditure. Both events cast a
shadow over the relationship. In February, a Japanese appeals
court sustained a lower court's decision to accept the Republic of
China as a legal party that could sue for the ownership of a Chinese
student dormitory in Kyoto.

Beijing's sharp response to the ruling prompted speculation in
Japan that the response was linked with Hu's fall, reported to have
been caused in part by his promotion of Sino-Japanese friendship.
Deng's unusually assertive remarks to the head of a Japanese opposition party in June prompted the vice minister's "off the record"
interview, at which point the public exchange rapidly escalated.
The vice minister's "voluntary retirement" ten days later did not
end the affair, as evidenced by Deng's adamant stand cited in the
quotation at the beginning of the chapter.

The timing of these developments could not have been worse. In
Japan, Nakasone's lame-duck status removed whatever leverage he

might otherwise have been able to apply after his party's over-whelming victory at the polls in 1986. In China, the commemoration of the anniversaries of the Japanese invasion in July and the Nanjing Massacre in December provided an inauspicious context in which to defuse the controversy and achieve a compromise.

Whatever the facts of the various issues, such as Tokyo's legal options in the court case or the precise words and meaning of various statements, the way in which they were subjectively perceived and publicized in the media on each side further complicated the relationship. For this reason, these seemingly minor matters deserve analysis in some detail. Aside from their impact at the time, they exemplify how issues of peripheral importance can become central to the Sino-Japanese relationship. On one side, Japan's pluralistic democratic system precludes the centralized control of all behavior. On the other side, China's priority for principle and the ritualistic reiteration of both past and present positions raises minor matters to major prominence and keeps them on the political agenda. This combination of characteristics proved particularly troublesome in 1987.

HU'S DISMISSAL

On January 16, an enlarged politburo meeting accepted Hu Yao-bang's "resignation" as head of the Chinese Communist party. Within days, Kyodo filed a "leaked" version of charges concerning Hu's mismanagement of Sino-Japanese relations.[3] Chinese press reports in Hong Kong included brief references to such charges at the time and in May authoritatively confirmed the initial stories.[4] The most complete and credible accounts, however, made clear that Hu was ousted primarily because of how he handled ideological issues and his personal style of operating without collective guidance. The Japan matter had been of lesser importance.

Kyodo's Beijing sources attacked Hu's "arbitrary" decision to invite three thousand Japanese youths to celebrate the thirty-fifth anniversary of the PRC in October 1984, claiming he did so without regard for the financial and hosting problems.[5] Moreover, Tokyo's reciprocal invitation in 1985 of only three hundred Chinese youths proved "unfair." In addition Hu's personal relations with Nakasone were criticized as "too close," particularly because he invited Nakasone and family to his official residence in March 1984.[6]

Ironically, in November 1986 Nakasone had visited Beijing on Hu's personal invitation to lay the cornerstone for a Sino-Japanese Youth Exchange Center, of which a "large part of the money" was "a gift from the Japanese Government through the prime minister."[7] Nakasone revealed that he had proposed the center during his 1984 visit and, moreover, that he was now ready "to invite 100 Chinese youths to visit Japan each year for the next five years."[8]

The cornerstone ceremony, attended by more than a thousand Chinese and Japanese youths, included the release of 3,000 pigeons and 1,500 colored balloons amid the sound of firecrackers, drums, and bugles.[9] These activities stood in marked contrast to the anti-Japanese university student demonstrations of the previous year, a point doubtless on the minds of observers as well as participants.

Both sides made the most of the opportunity to patch over the earlier acrimonious exchanges on textbook revision and Yasukuni Shrine visits, as well as the more recent provocation by Minister of Education Fujio.[10] Hu's initial speech included implicit criticism of the 1985 student demonstrations. He praised patriotism, but called for its integration with "a farsighted internationalist spirit of getting along harmoniously and cooperating amicably with people of other countries. If Chinese young people think merely of the well-being of their own country and . . . are indifferent to promoting unity, friendship, and cooperation for mutual benefit with young people of Japan and other countries, they are not sober-minded patriots."[11]

For his part, Nakasone acknowledged that "countless numbers of young people in your country have come forward and died one after another to free the country from the shackles of big powers," presumably an oblique reference to Japan.[12] On his second and last day he laid a wreath at the Monument to the People's Heroes in Tiananmen Square after being welcomed by a military band.[13] Following Hu's banquet address, which praised Nakasone's "enormous enthusiasm and efforts" on behalf of Sino-Japanese friendship as demonstrated by his "wise decisions . . . on some major issues," the Japanese prime minister modestly responded, "It is a statesman's mission to disregard the burden of bearing blame in order to sacrifice himself and to dare to deal with difficulties."[14]

Not all the notes sounded, however, were harmonious. Japanese businessmen called on Nakasone to press China for better living conditions for their families, specifically asking for new school and housing facilities.[15] Meanwhile, Zhao Ziyang expressed his "deepest concern" over the $2.3 billion trade deficit up to August 1986 and complained about Japanese investment levels.[16]

But no other untoward moments arose. Deng avoided making any critical comments, calling Sino-Japanese friendship "of vital and lasting importance" and the Commission for Friendship in the Twenty-first Century "a grand plan that should last 100 years, perhaps even lasting 1,000 years."[17] The visit ended with Hu and Nakasone giving each other "bear hugs" and making "a mutual promise to meet each other every two years," the latter at Nakasone's initiative.[18]

Hugs and promises notwithstanding, Hu's political vulnerability apparently included his prominence and procedures in promoting the relationship. His ouster obviously stemmed from far more serious causes in domestic politics, coming as it did only nine months before the scheduled Thirteenth CCP Congress in which he could have "retired" in a legitimately prescribed manner. But the immediate fallout surrounding Hu's ouster had a strong impact in Japan. One result was an increased tendency on the part of Japanese business to constrain investment until the apparent succession crisis in China was resolved.[19]

THE KYOTO DORMITORY CASE

The Kokaryō (Guanghua) Hostel in Kyoto has a complicated history within which lie the roots of the most serious political controversy for Sino-Japanese relations in 1987.[20] Built in 1931, the five-story, 1,000-square-meter building was purchased by the Republic of China in 1950 with funds derived from the sale of goods that had been taken from China during the war.[21] The dormitory was used for Chinese students and in 1962 was formally registered as being owned by the Taiwan regime. In August 1967, Taiwan appealed to the Kyoto District Court to evict eight Chinese students living there who had seized control as part of the radical student movement then sweeping through Japan as well as China. The issue dragged on and in 1974, after the normalization of relations between Beijing and Tokyo, the PRC began demanding that it be given ownership of the building.[22]

In 1977 the Kyoto District Court finally rejected the 1967 appeal on the basis that the PRC succeeded to ownership when the Republic of China lost Japanese recognition and thereupon also lost the capacity to pursue the suit. But in April 1982, the Osaka High Court overruled and ordered the Kyoto court to reexamine the case. On February 4, 1986, that court reversed its earlier decision, declaring in favor of the Taiwan authorities. At this point, the Union of Chinese Students in Japan appealed the case to the Osaka High Court on behalf of the fifty occupants and Beijing. Overseas Chinese associations in Kyoto, Osaka, Kobe, Tokyo, and Yokohama protested the Kyoto ruling, as did Beijing.

Finally on February 26, 1987, the Osaka High Court sustained the Kyoto decision in favor of Taiwan, ruling that the transfer of power from the Nationalists to the Communists was "incomplete," that property ownership does not move to a new government except where state representation or sovereignty exists, and that the dormitory did not constitute "diplomatic property."[23] The decision was promptly appealed to the Supreme Court where it rested for the following months.

Later that day a senior Japanese foreign ministry official rejected Beijing's "repeated requests" that the government exert influence in the pending appeal, noting that a court matter could not be interfered with.[24] That evening, in Beijing, the vice minister of foreign affairs summoned Ambassador Nakae Yosuke to receive a note of protest that termed the Osaka judgment "wrong both politically and legally" because it "reaffirms the argument . . . to openly create the 'two Chinas.'"[25] Furthermore, the note also said that "this is another illegal act of the Japanese authorities concerned that violates the Sino-Japanese Joint Statement [1972] and the Sino-Japanese Treaty of Peace and Friendship [1978]" over which "the Chinese Government expresses its deep regret." The note closed with a warning: "The Chinese Government earnestly requests the Japanese Government to deal with this issue, and adopt effective measures as soon as possible to reasonably and properly handle this case so as to prevent it from affecting the friendly relations between the two countries." These themes were reiterated the same day at press conferences called by the PRC political counselor in Tokyo and the PRC consul general in Osaka.[26]

Between the time of these court decisions in February 1986 and February 1987, the "two Chinas" question had become prominent in connection with private Japanese plans to celebrate the deceased Chiang Kai-shek's one hundredth birthday in September. Already in 1985, because of Chinese protests to various delegations visiting Beijing, most LDP officials had withdrawn from the planning committee, which was headed by former Prime Minister Kishi Nobusuke, together with Nadao Hirokichi, a former speaker of the lower house, and Satō Shinji, son of the late prime minister of 1964–72. Nevertheless, Foreign Minister Wu Xueqian had pressed the issue throughout his official Tokyo appearances in April 1986, adding it to his discussions of the Kyoto court case and the trade imbalance.[27]

Reportedly responding to warnings from the Japanese foreign ministry, no cabinet officers attended the public celebrations, although several went to dinner parties before and after the event.[28] Beijing had made six separate efforts to prompt Tokyo's cancellation of the memorial, including one by Ambassador Zhang Shu to Foreign Minister Kuranari Tadashi only two days before the event itself. Nonetheless, 130 members of parliament did participate, almost all of whom were from the 230 LDP members of parliament who belonged to the pro-Taiwan Japanese-Chinese Parliamentary Association. Xinhua sent two correspondents to the event who reported it as "tantamount to support for the creation of two Chinas."

Beijing's foreign ministry spokesman echoed this report, noting that such meetings were "not merely non-governmental actions but political ones, participated in by important persons from the political circles in Japan."[29] Terming this "detrimental to the healthy and smooth development of good neighborly and friendly relations between China and Japan," he declared, "The Chinese side has on many occasions reminded the Japanese to pay attention to the question and to take strict action to restrain those acts and to solve the matter properly." Hu Yaobang subsequently told a Japanese author that the Japanese who eulogized Chiang were doing their country wrong, just as the Japanese Imperial Army that invaded China fifty years ago had done.[30]

The following spring saw another "two China" criticism prompted by Tokyo's paying compensation to Taiwanese relatives of deceased soldiers that had been drafted in World War II.[31] Although Chinese sources conceded that the relatives were entitled to compensation, they criticized the fact that indemnity payments were being channeled through the Red Cross society in Taiwan as a dangerous step contributing to the "two China" trend.

Thus, the general issue of two Chinas had been high on Beijing's agenda while the Kyoto dormitory case was pending. Nevertheless, the degree to which Chinese media and officials focused on the case surprised and concerned observers in Japan.[32] A series of closely reasoned and juridically oriented essays in *Renmin Ribao* offered a running attack on the Osaka ruling.[33] Somewhat more polemical articles accused Tokyo of bad faith in using the "three branches of government" argument for refusing to change court rulings. As one *Beijing Review* author put it, this was a "sheer pretext" explained by a "lack of sincerity in living up to the treaties and agreements signed between the two countries."[34]

In contrast to their restrained handling of the textbook controversy in 1986, PRC officials vigorously protested the dormitory case, combining it with the issues of militarism and trade in a broad critique of Japanese policy. Deng personally launched a fresh attack on May 5 when he called the court decision "very serious" while meeting with a Japanese legislator.[35] According to Japanese reports, Deng surprisingly claimed the decision "is connected with the rise of Japanese militarism."[36] The next day the foreign ministry spokesman put Deng's position on the record, albeit without attribution, warning, "If the judicial organs in Japan cling to their present course and make an erroneous ruling, with the tacit connivance of the Japanese Government, the Chinese side will make a strong reaction."[37] Going further, the spokesman cited the issue as only one of several problems "prominent at present in Sino-Japanese relations." He claimed that in trade the Japanese side had talked much but done little to settle the imbalance. On militarism he repeated the standard charges and reiterated the need for continued concern. Speaking in general, the spokesman noted that the Japanese side had created difficult problems on many occasions that forced the Chinese side to react.

Tokyo's director general of the Ministry of Foreign Affairs (MFA)

Asian Affairs Bureau summoned Beijing's minister counselor, declaring Deng's remarks to be regrettable and harmful to bilateral relations.[38] In a separate interview, a "government source" emphasized to the press that there would be no interference in the decision by the Supreme Court and if Beijing did not "understand" by the end of the forthcoming visit by the head of Japan's Defense Agency and the joint Sino-Japanese ministers conference, "a temporary cooling of Sino-Japanese relations cannot be helped."[39]

On the same day that the MFA rebutted Deng's remarks, Beijing ordered a Kyodo correspondent to leave within ten days because he had allegedly stolen national intelligence data.[40] This situation had been brewing for some time, with demands from the Chinese foreign ministry that the reporter reveal his news sources.[41] This reporter was the third foreign correspondent to be ordered out of China in ten months, but the timing of his expulsion led many in Japan to believe that it was specifically linked with the current dispute.[42]

At this point the rapid escalation of exchanges stopped and both sides refrained from further steps while JDA Director General Kurihara Yūkō toured the People's Republic from May 29 to June 4. The highest JDA official ever to visit China, Kurihara inspected army, navy, and air force units for four days in addition to meeting with Defense Minister Zhang Aiping, Chief of Staff Yang Dezhi, and Vice Premier Wan Li. Wan said he was acting "on behalf of Zhao Ziyang"; Deng Xiaoping's failure to meet Kurihara was explained as owing to age.[43] The military side of Kurihara's visit included boarding a missile escort ship and a submarine at Qingdao, observing artillery practice near Beijing, and witnessing maneuvers by a "Qiang-5" fighter attack plane in Hangzhou.[44] Japanese press briefings emphasized the visit's "deterrent effect on the Soviet Union" and argued that it symbolized a Sino-Japanese-American alignment while stopping short of provoking Moscow by more substantial cooperation at this time. The Chinese were said to be "eager" for defense exchanges, "above all, technology associated with electronic equipment." The briefings also emphasized the "favorable" and "understanding" attitudes communicated by Chinese officials on all issues, including Japan's military expenditures.[45]

Despite this positive gloss, the only softening of Beijing's position came in Zhang's remarks that expressly supported the Japan-

U.S. security treaty and acknowledged "a better understanding" of Tokyo's defense plans after Kurihara's explanation.[46] Zhang's failure to raise the 1 percent of GNP issue was offset by the concern he expressed over signs of a reviving militarism in Japan, allegedly evident in textbook revisions and Yasukuni Shrine visits. He also raised the dormitory case.[47] Wan Li, noting that his remarks mirrored Deng's, stressed concern over those who advocate "a resurgence of Japan as a military power" because Japan had brought disaster to China and other countries during the 1930s and 1940s; "this should not happen again."[48] Kurihara apologized for the past and asked Wan to "trust us" in the present and future.

Wan reassured Kurihara that Hu Yaobang's resignation would have no long run effect on Sino-Japanese relations. Moreover, he added that the forthcoming July 7 commemoration of the 1937 Japanese invasion of China was designed "to have young Chinese generations learn a lesson from history" and was not intended to have any effect on the relationship.

DENG STRIKES AGAIN

On June 4, an authoritative "commentator" article in *Renmin Ribao* fired the opening salvo in what immediately became a high-level Chinese assault against the dormitory ruling in particular and the trend of Japan's China policy in general.[49] The ruling, the article claimed, was "not only politically erroneous and full of legal loopholes, but it also directly violates the legitimate rights of the Chinese Government and hurts the feelings of the Chinese people, and has thus naturally aroused strong dissatisfaction on the part of the Chinese Government and people." Adding insult to injury, Tokyo had also "spread extremely unfriendly comments such as China is making a mountain out of a molehill, 'interfering in Japan's internal affairs,' and so on."

After a lengthy recitation and rebuttal of Japanese positions, the commentary warned, "What this case reflects is a question of major political principle. Tolerating it means tolerating the creation of 'two Chinas' or 'one China and one Taiwan.'" It went on to add that "this is a major affair related to . . . whether or not the Sino-Japanese Joint Statement and the Sino-Japanese Treaty of Peace and Friendship can continue to be practiced and implemented."

Also on June 4, as Kurihara was leaving China, Deng Xiaoping received Yano Junya, head of Kōmeitō, the second largest opposition party. This was Deng's first meeting with a Japanese politician in almost a month. In view of his reported inability to meet with Kurihara because of "age," and given Yano's political status, the interview appeared to Japanese observers as a calculated affront. Its contents confirmed this impression, going beyond Deng's initial statements of May, which had triggered strong official as well as unofficial reactions.[50] Although Xinhua led with his assertion, "There is no reason for China and Japan not to live as friends, and in spite of any problems which may crop up, friendly relations will continue," it was the negative side that dominated the interview and that received the greatest attention abroad, especially in Japan.[51]

Deng raised the usual economic complaints over the import surplus and the blockage of Japanese markets. He also claimed that technology transfer was not up to European or North American levels in terms of sophistication. But he introduced a new line, at least for him, in arguing that Japan should help China's development more because it "has the biggest debt to China. In 1972 China did not ask for reparations. Frankly speaking, we harbor dissatisfaction over this point." This point won considerable press attention in Japan.[52]

In response to Yano's query concerning the abandoned limit for Japan's defense budget, Deng expressed "worry about a kind of tendency for a revival of militarism since the end of the war. The number who desire it is small but they have strong energy." Calculating defense expenditures using the yen at its newly established rates, he declared, "Japan's military expenditure exceeds France and West Germany. It is definitely not small. Why is it necessary to go through the one percent framework? If it is done once, there can be a second and third breakthrough . . . in accord with some segments of people who wish to make Japan a big military power." Deng concluded this section imperiously, "I want Japanese politicians to be more humble when considering these problems. I do not want them to take a high posture."

He then turned to the dormitory case, arguing that while "99% of the Japanese people desire friendship, a handful have never forgotten Taiwan. They never forget to interpret the constitution from a different angle and to cause friction between Japan and China.

This is very unfortunate." He expressed contempt for a current Japanese discussion of buying out the PRC claim for a million dollars, arguing that a principle was at stake, not economic interest. Deng then warned that if Tokyo did not respond properly, "the Japanese government will create a debt in history's account book of not faithfully abiding by the Peace and Friendship Treaty." He also addressed a new issue at this level, noting that "we have the wish that Japan will be more cautious when having contacts with Vietnam."

Deng's advocacy of "a more humble" attitude evoked just the opposite response. Yano briefed the Japanese press immediately after the interview and late that evening reporters in Tokyo heard "a senior official" respond "off the record" at his home, as quoted at the start of this chapter. The translated words, originally expressed as *kumo no ue*, could convey respect, as subsequently argued by Japanese officials, particularly since the phrase had been used to characterize the Japanese emperor's prewar status of being above politics and therefore unknowledgeable about administrative matters.[53] No such meaning, however, was given to these words in Japan or China in 1987, especially when an additional reference to Deng's being "hard in the head" or rigid implied that, at the very least, he did not understand the issues and, at worst, that he might be getting senile. Despite the anonymous attribution, the "senior official" was quickly identified as an MFA vice minister.

A complicated "billiard ball" communications pattern followed. *Renmin Ribao* informed its readers about Japanese newspaper coverage of Yano's next press conference in which he criticized the foreign ministry's "unfriendly remarks" on Deng's interview.[54] This approach permitted Beijing to publicize selected aspects without immediately staking out an official position. The paper also reported Japanese press stories on "malicious attacks" against Deng by "a high-ranking official of the Foreign Affairs Ministry." Xinhua relayed Japanese editorial criticism of the MFA official, including in its story Yano's claim that in his briefing at the ministry before he went to China, officials attributed China's tough stance to internal power struggles and an effort "to divert the attention of the Chinese people from their discontent."[55]

Fast and furious reactions followed on both sides. On Saturday evening, June 6, the Chinese foreign ministry summoned Minister

Yoshida Hiroyuki and delivered a strong protest, the gist of which was published three days later. It called Yanagiya's remarks "malicious attacks upon China's top leader" that "the Chinese Government and people cannot tolerate."[56] Moreover, the protest also stated that "the Chinese Government is gravely doubtful about the intention and aim of the Japanese side by making such remarks under the present situation." On June 7, Sun Pinghua, president of the China-Japan Friendship Association, told Japanese reporters traveling with Yano that the People's Republic had never supported Tokyo's lifting the 1 percent limit on defense spending and Kurihara was "incorrect" in thinking he had won China's approval during his recent visit.[57] Sun also attacked the "anonymous" official's criticism of Deng as impolite and arrogant.

The next day Chief Cabinet Secretary and Acting Foreign Minister Gotoda (Kuranari being with Nakasone at the Vienna summit conference) told a press conference that the MFA individual concerned had not spoken in his official capacity and that the government would elicit his "true intention" and, "depending on the circumstances," give an explanation to the Chinese side. Later that day, Asian Affairs Bureau Director Fujita Kimio informed Minister Counselor Xu Dunxin that because the interview had not been official and there was no record of it, the specifics could not be addressed.[58]

Fujita also said, however,

> In recent statements made by Chinese leaders and Chairman Deng, we can see that they are removed, sometimes, from the actual situation in Japan and our perception, and criticism against Japan has been openly voiced, based on this. It is also true that for this reason, not a few Japanese people harbor the feeling that this is strange and that this has been throwing cold water on the enthusiasm of persons who are seriously hoping for development of Japanese-Chinese relations. This situation is not desirable for the maintenance and development of long-range relations between Japan and China.

In effect Fujita defended the thrust of Yanagiya's remarks, albeit in more diplomatic language. He also reinterpreted the original interview to emphasize its positive intentions, praising Deng's role in developing friendly relations, and acknowledging, "It is regrettable if press reports on the remarks have caused China some disquiet."

On the same day, press interviews with Ambassador Nakae ap-

peared. He attempted to maintain common ground with his ministry while reducing tension between the two capitals, explaining
that "due to differences in their political structures, there are some
gaps in their perceptions and it is impossible for the two countries
to agree completely."[59] Ironically, the ambassador was in Tokyo to
attend the premiere performance by a Sino-Japanese ballet company of "Narrow Strip of Water Separating Two Countries, Rush-
ing in Great Sweep," which he had written and staged under a pen
name.[60] The ballet title embodied the cliché routinely advanced as
characterizing the closeness of the two countries in geographic
terms, which purportedly symbolizes cultural and political closeness as well.

The Ministry of Foreign Affairs promptly briefed reporters on
Fujita's representations to Xu, omitting any reference to Xu's position, after which the media claimed that Xu had made "no rebuttal." No sooner had this hit television and print releases than the
Chinese embassy telephoned the media to say that "Xu made rebuttal strictly." The ministry in turn explained this by saying that it
had specifically agreed not to release Xu's remarks made "as individual and friend," while the MFA had been speaking officially.[61] A
Xinhua commentary termed it "extremely odious" for the ministry
official to state Tokyo's view on Yanagiya's remarks "in a positive
way."[62] It charged that "obviously the Japanese side was shirking
its responsibility" in avoiding the specific interview "on the pretext
that the speech was not recorded and that no notes were taken."

On June 10, Beijing's foreign ministry spokesman struck back at
"malicious attacks" on Deng by a "leading member of the Japanese
Foreign Ministry."[63] In fact, "certain persons" in the ministry had
"made most unfriendly remarks on more than one occasion, which
will have no good effects on Sino-Japanese relations." Deng had
given "earnest and well-meaning advice." *Renmin Ribao* reported
Xu's "stern" rebuttal of Fujita's explanation. Xu called it "not satisfactory" and said that it "cannot be accepted by the Chinese
side."[64] In unusual wording, it said that "observers here [in Tokyo]
believe that the Japanese Foreign Ministry can hardly convince
others that it has cherished the hope of safeguarding and developing Sino-Japanese relations since it has repeatedly aired unfriendly
views and tried to muddle through some issues. . . . Such a practice . . . does not reflect sincerity."

This press "war" had reached its limits. On June 15, Yanagiya finally acknowledged that his statement "was an expression which was a breach of etiquette. . . . It was regrettable that it caused a sense of displeasure on the Chinese side."[65] Speaking at a press briefing from which foreign correspondents were excluded, he said that he had Nakasone's approval for the apology.[66] That evening Makita Kunihiko, director of the China and Mongolia Division in the Ministry of Foreign Affairs, repeated Yanagiya's statements to Counselor Lu Xi.[67] *Renmin Ribao* front-paged the apology on June 16. Both Nakasone and Gotoda voiced their "regret" even though they were still abroad.

Surface tensions immediately subsided as both sides moved to end the quarrel. On June 16, Beijing was ahead of Tokyo in announcing the fifth regular Sino-Japanese joint ministerial meeting, scheduled for June 27–28.[68] The next day Vice Minister Yanagiya "voluntarily" took "early retirement" at sixty-three, a step that the Ministry of Foreign Affairs said "has nothing to do" with his controversial interview, but that Xinhua attributed to the dispute.[69] Curiously, *Renmin Ribao* did not carry the story.

However, tensions remained under the surface. On the eve of the ministerial meeting, vandals splashed red paint over a monument in Kyoto that was inscribed with a poem by Zhou Enlai, chipped it with a hammer, and scattered eighty handbills criticizing China.[70] Later that day the Chinese foreign ministry asked Tokyo for a prompt investigation and serious handling of the matter.[71] Nakasone and Gotoda immediately expressed regret. Beijing's foreign ministry spokesmen said China took note of their remarks while denouncing the incident as "an outrageous act" that was deserving of anger.[72]

Further incidents followed through the summer. On July 14, an eight-meter-high stone monument in Nagoya, marking the 1980 establishment of a sister city relationship with Nanjing, was splashed with red paint and damaged with hammer blows.[73] A Japanese male claimed responsibility on behalf of a right-wing group, "Spirit of the Kantō Army," but was not apprehended until mid-September, at which time *Renmin Ribao* reported that his "small right-wing organization has only a few members."[74] Also in July, a young Chinese male smashed glass panes on a display case outside the Japanese embassy in Beijing and splashed red paint over the case in a professed retaliation for the June incident involving Zhou's memorial in Kyoto.[75] On September 2, Beijing's foreign ministry spokesman called on Japan to punish whoever had smeared red paint a few days before on the Sino-Japanese Friendship Monument in Gifu, a sister city to Hangzhou.[76]

The year 1987 ended with still another incident in which a statue was defaced, this one involving the "maiden statue of peace that China presented to Nagasaki in 1985 . . . at the request of the Municipal Government of Nagasaki."[77] These scattered occurrences were of little importance in themselves, but their unprecedented nature and their reporting in the press further fueled feelings of resentment and antagonism. The political exchanges and press war of the spring thus had repercussions well beyond the reach of officials on both sides.

Indeed, the officials themselves were not able to resolve any of the outstanding issues at the joint meeting, which was attended by Japan's ministers of foreign relations, finance, agriculture, forestry and fisheries, international trade and industry, and transport, together with the directors general of the Economic Planning Agency and the Science and Technology Agency. Their Chinese counterparts at the meeting included State Councillor Gu Mu and the ministers of foreign relations, the State Science and Technology Commission, foreign economic relations and trade, agriculture, animal husbandry and fisheries, and communications. Both sides joined in an effort to put the best face on relations while holding to their respective positions. Thus, as the second day began, Deng walked to where Finance Minister Miyazawa Kiichi was seated to shake his hand.[78] Miyazawa, a candidate for Nakasone's position, had helped solve the 1982 textbook dispute and was regarded by the Chinese as the minister least enthusiastic about military expansion. Deng also surprised Kuranari by opening his remarks with a somewhat jocular, if unwelcome, reference to Yanagiya's remarks: "The high official who said I was old and muddle-headed was partly right. I am old but I'm not muddle-headed."[79]

Having started lightly, Deng then moved to reassert his original position, noting that what he had said to Yano "was not words spoken rashly . . . [or] because I am muddled." In a shift of emphasis from the earlier interview, Deng said he had stressed the enduring nature of Sino-Japanese friendship because "there were surmises that this policy may change because of the resignation of Comrade Hu Yaobang, but this grand policy was established in the days when Mao Zedong and Zhou Enlai were still living." His next words went beyond any previously known utterances in asserting China's innocence and Japan's guilt for past and present problems. The gist of his remarks as printed in the Japanese press bear extended quotation as the public—and, therefore, the perceived— position of Beijing, regardless of whatever inaccuracies may have developed in their notation and translation.

> If unpleasant matters between the two countries are disposed of in a proper way, it will bring about benefits to the two great nations and peoples. It is not that just one side is responsible for ill-feelings. Frankly speaking, however, I do not think that the responsibility for the vexatious feelings between China and Japan lies with China. Care should be taken not to bring up difficult problems under a new situation and create new ill-feelings. None of the stiffness between China and Japan are difficult problems raised by the Chinese side, and the Chinese side takes an attitude of self-restraint in the case of the appearing of difficult problems. It takes an attitude of self-restraint, including persuasion toward the people. In regard to China-Japan relations, reactions among youths, especially students, are strong. If difficult problems were to appear still further, it will become impossible to explain them to the people. It will become impossible to control them. I want you to understand this position which we are in.

In sum, Deng conceded nothing, alluding instead to the 1985 anti-Japanese student demonstrations as evidence of Beijing's inability to control public opinion in the event of further "problems" arising in Japan. He next cited the dormitory ruling as a specific instance of "causing trouble" and brought up the vandalization of the Zhou memorial, saying, "This kind of problem becomes more disadvantageous, if protracted. It is not that the Japanese Government is unable to do anything, is it?" He pointed to "the textbook problem" as an instance in which Tokyo had proven helpful in the settlement, but he added, "Of course, we were not completely satisfied over this problem." Deng then reiterated the well-established line linking the dormitory case to "the one-China, one-Taiwan problem," and called on Kuranari to report to Nakasone and to "tackle the problem earnestly." He also brought up economic matters, where "it is not that we are greatly satisfied." Deng argued that "we want to obtain many things from Japan, but if we look at the future, 30, 50, or 100 years from now, will not China come to have many things to give to Japan? I think that the politicians of China and Japan must look at the problem from a high and broad perspective."

As might be expected, aside from a modest agreement to expand bilateral trade, the meeting accomplished nothing except to record the fixed positions of both sides, which remained irreconcilable, especially on the dormitory issue. Xinhua described "a candid exchange" on the dormitory issue between Wu and Kuranari and Kyodo claimed they "clashed."[80] But Wu went beyond the current agenda, adding the earlier controversy over Japanese textbook treatment of the war. He said that China "has always adopted a look-ahead attitude toward the history of Japanese militarists' aggression against China, but that does not mean a handful of people who distort history and reverse the verdict on the aggression will be tolerated."[81] He asserted that "to relax vigilance against such a tendency and let it run rampant" would "endanger Sino-Japanese friendship." Wu repeated the saying, "Past experience, if not forgotten, is a guide for the future."

The Chinese foreign minister also charged that there had been "repeated instances" in which Tokyo had violated the Sino-Japanese agreement that Japan would maintain only nongovernmental and local contacts with Taiwan and claimed that "Japan-Taiwan relations have grown greatly instead of being restricted." He also cited trade deficits with Japan of $5.22 billion in 1985 and $5.13 billion in 1986 as constituting 90 percent of China's total foreign trade imbalance in these years and called on Japan to open its market, lower its tariffs, relax its quotas, and abolish its "unreasonable restrictions." Wu expressed hope that Tokyo "will adopt a positive attitude to encourage and support private enterprises to invest in and transfer technology to China." He said that the Chinese and Japanese peoples "are all indignant" over the defacing of Zhou Enlai's poem in Kyoto, but took note of Tokyo's remarks on the matter.

In summing up, Wu pledged China's effort to continue working for good relations. He used standard formulations, but did not make reference to the "four points" attributed to Hu Yaobang, which had been a ritualistic part of earlier meetings. For his part, Kuranari responded to Wu's agenda with the usual reassurance on militarism, an explanation of Japan's three-branch governmental system, a reaffirmation of the one-China policy, and an apology for the monument incident. He also invited Zhao Ziyang to visit Japan in 1988 for the commemoration of the tenth anniversary of the Treaty of Peace and Friendship. Zhao reportedly responded favorably, but he did so informally, and the invitation was not mentioned in the Chinese press.[82]

Zhao struck a strong stance, arguing that "we should not ignore the existing problems, both political and economic, between the two countries just because their relationship is in the main good."[83] He developed this further by warning, "If the political problems are not handled correctly, they will do greater harm to Sino-Japanese relations than economic problems may do. If some Japanese friends hold that once economic problems are resolved, what should be said on political matters can be saved, then they will make a very erroneous judgement."

Zhao then declared that Deng's remarks to Yano were totally in the interest of Sino-Japanese friendship, that he made them on behalf of the Chinese government and people, and that they had the warm support of the entire nation. He pointedly remarked, "We hope that Japanese friends have a correct judgment of the situation in China and Sino-Japanese relations. Any incorrect understanding based on incorrect judgment will bring harm to Sino-Japanese relations."

Although Wu and Kuranari publicly agreed that the conference had been "successful," press releases and briefings spelled out the wide divergence in positions and focused attention on the assertive statements of Deng, Wu, and Zhao. This reopened the earlier media war that had been waged so intensively following Deng's remarks to Yano.[84] That war had escalated in a rapid action-reaction sequence, with little if any time left between statements and media coverage for careful deliberation at high levels. Positions adopted at the ministerial conference, on the contrary, represented fully considered views advanced with a presumed foreknowledge of their consequences, both inside and outside the meeting. As such, the exchanges constituted the lowest point in official relations since 1982. Nakasone in effect acknowledged this on June 29 when he told newsmen his government was in "anguish" over the dormitory issue.[85]

The dormitory issue remained a publicly festering sore in relations throughout the summer. Tokyo officials reiterated their inability and refusal to influence the deliberations of the Supreme Court unless requested to do so by the court.[86] Speaking as the highest PRC governmental official, Li Xiannian met with Japanese reporters in late July to restate Beijing's position and termed the court ruling as "obviously in violation of the joint communique and the Peace and Friendship Treaty" and added that it "also runs counter to international law."[87]

Li's expansion on Deng's "we're always right, you're wrong" position carried more long-term implications for the relationship than did the dormitory issue as such. In Li's words,

> We only say and do things which are conducive to friendship between China and Japan and will not say and do things which may harm this friendship. We hope that the Japanese side will do the same. Please stop saying and doing things which are harmful to friendship between China and Japan. We have not done a single thing which may do disservice to the Japanese Government and people. We bear no responsibility for what has happened.

Whatever Li's intent, the impact of this high posture in Japan could only harden nationalistic sentiments against compromise with Beijing on this or any other matter.

The polarization of positions associated with the dormitory issue prompted a Hong Kong report in early July by *Cheng Ming*, a usually well-informed journal, alleging that Deng Xiaoping had said China should consider reprisals if Tokyo did not interfere on China's behalf with the dormitory ruling.[88] He reportedly had ordered the State Council to consider economic and technical cooperation as areas for action and this happened after Deng had already asked it to broaden China's economic ties so as to reduce reliance on Japan. Another Hong Kong magazine simultaneously claimed that Beijing was considering the cancellation of large industrial imports from Japan or suspending the Sino-Japanese Bohai Bay oil project.[89]

These articles, the indirect corroboration for which will be treated in the next section, suggested that popular sentiment, as manifested in isolated acts of vandalism in both countries, responded to provocative statements at high levels. But popular sentiment also reflected increasingly intransigent postures at high levels. This was the context in which China commemorated the fiftieth anniversary of Luguoqiao on July 7, 1987.

FIFTY YEARS AFTER

As might be expected, the spate of speeches, articles, and television films that focused on the Sino-Japanese war went beyond the inevitable recapitulation of its history and its horrors. Folded into this recounting of the past was the current Chinese agenda of problems in the relationship, all of which allegedly arose on the Japanese side. However, in addition to the standard litany of textbook revisions, Yasukuni Shrine visits, dormitory decisions, and reviving militarism, Taiwan won increased attention, not only because it was taken by Japan in 1895, but also because it was another point of present-day protest. A countervailing theme exonerated "the Japanese people" from this indictment, although it was asserted their numerical preponderance did not assure that "a small handful" might not prevail in reviving militarism. Last but not least among the recurring themes and worthy of note for its broader implications was reference to patriotism, or *aiguo zhuyi*. The July 7 commemoration not only aimed at "teaching youth about the past" so as "to guard against repetition in the future," but also specifically called on the nation to work hard, make sacrifices, and be proud of China's achievements as exemplified by the victory over Japan.

Not all of the materials had a strident anti-Japanese tone. One example is the PLA newspaper's editorial on the subject entitled "Do Not Forget History While Reinvigorating China."[90] Victory in the war "showed that once the Chinese nation was awakened and the Chinese people were united, they formed a great strength that could topple the mountains and overturn the seas, and could smash all attempts to invade and enslave China." Commemorating Luguoqiao "will help us better understand and adhere to the four cardinal principles." No other purpose for commemoration was given than this reference to the ideological matrix of modernization. The mobilization call was clear, "History repeatedly teaches people this lesson: those who are backward will certainly be bullied and attacked; those who are in a split condition will certainly suffer disasters. Only when we are united and make joint efforts to invigorate our country can we have a bright future and make progress." Although the editorial made no effort to arouse anti-Japanese emotions, neither did it make more than a passing reference to friendship with Japan.

In contrast, *Renmin Ribao* followed its account of the war, wherein "military and civilian casualties totalled 21 million people while property losses and costs of the war reached approximately U.S. $100 billion" with an extended tribute to the friendship between the two peoples that had been achieved over the past fifteen years.[91] The *Renmin Ribao* editorial, however, then turned to the negative themes. Vigilance was necessary against "a handful of people in Japan . . . [who] though few in number are quite capable of maneuvering and acting against the tide of history." Although "in general Sino-Japanese relations are good, nevertheless in recent years the Japanese side has created one difficult problem after another, thus obstructing the development of friendship between the two countries." In contrast, the editorial claimed that "we have always been faithful to the statement and the treaty and never have we created trouble detrimental to the friendly relations between the two countries." The final message, like the PLA editorial, was one of mobilization and unity: "We must remain sober-minded and realize that although the momentum for peace is continuously strengthening, a danger of war still exists. China's economic and cultural standards are still not so high, its people are not rich, and . . . the great cause of the reunification of the motherland has not yet been completed." Therefore, eliminating "arrogance, the love of luxury, laziness, being content with things as they are" will

> rapidly increase China's strength, improve the life of its people, enhance its defense capabilities, realize the peaceful unification of the motherland and ward off any possible aggressor. Only in this way will it be possible for us to firmly rank among the world nations, stand erect [*yi li*] in the East, and offer our contribution to world peace and development.[92]

The editorial concluded,

> We should always keep in mind our old teaching to "be vigilant in peacetime," and carry forward the spirit of national solidarity and willing to make sacrifice . . . maintain our higher degree of national respect and self-confidence, work harder than ever before, and vigorously forge ahead along the path of socialist modernization.

The absence of anti-Japanese rhetoric was most striking at inauguration of the Memorial Hall of the Chinese People's Anti-Japanese War, located near Luguoqiao. General Yang Shangkun, vice chairman of the Central Military Commission, called on "historians, theorists, and propaganda workers" to use the wartime materials for "educating the masses of people, young people in particular, and . . . upholding the four cardinal principles and patriotism and repudiating the fallacies that distort the nature of aggressive war." [93] This significantly widened the purpose of recalling the past from that which previously had made it a "guide for the future."

Perhaps because of high-level disagreement over its contents, the museum had not been completed as scheduled by July 7, 1987; only 5,400 of its planned 20,000 square meters were ready for the inaugural ceremonies. [94] Another small but suggestive change in plans found two officials from the Japanese embassy present at the ceremonies, contradicting an earlier press interview by Beijing's mayor, who said no Japanese would be in attendance. [95]

Atrocities committed in the course of Japanese aggression appeared prominently in the memorial hall's display of photographs and won attention in the media treatment of the war. Television featured grim footage of the Nanjing Massacre. [96] *Renmin Ribao* recounted the fate of 41,760 persons who had been shipped from prison camps in China for "slave labor" in Japan. [97] The prisoners included civilians as well as soldiers, "eleven-year-old children as well as the aged in their seventies." In one mining area, physical conditions and brutality were reported to have killed off 418 of the 986 Chinese working there between August 1944 and August 1945. Two weeks before the war ended, a rebellion broke out but was ruthlessly suppressed. In 1948 a war crimes tribunal imposed either death sentences or twenty-year terms of imprisonment on four supervisors of the mine and two policemen, but all were subsequently released. The reporter's comment noted,

> The Japanese authorities concerned and the Kajimu Corporation that had direct responsibility for the crimes of maltreating and brutally slaughtering the laborers, have, to date, failed to openly express their apology regarding this historical fact . . . that they had violated international law in committing the crimes of mistreating and slaughtering war prisoners.

Here as elsewhere, "the Japanese people" won praise for their attitude. Thus, an "elegaic couplet written in 1950 for the first public memorial ceremony" held in Tokyo read, "Their lofty aspirations unfulfilled, they sacrificed their lives in Hanaoka, an irredeemable regret; when will their blood be atoned? Here we attend the public memorial ceremony for the death of tens of thousands of martyrs."

The report also described how on June 30, 1987, the Odate city government held the forty-second memorial service before the "Monument in Memory of the Chinese Martyrs," which was attended by prominent Japanese "friends" and Geng Chun, the original commander of the 1945 rebellion.

Similarly, an account of the "more than 400,000 Chinese and foreigners" who had visited the Nanjing Massacre museum since its opening in 1985 emphasized that of the 4,000 foreigners from sixteen countries, the majority were Japanese.[98] "Tears were often seen in their eyes," according to a museum official while "the first group of Japanese visitors brought a 1.6-meter-tall bell engraved with words of condolence and best wishes for Japan-China friendship."

To a far greater degree than in 1985, when the fortieth anniversary of the war's ending had been commemorated, *Renmin Ribao* featured Japanese attention to and atonement for the war in general and the Nanjing Massacre in particular. It reported a special exhibition in a provincial capital that informed viewers that "in December 1937 during the first ten days of occupation in Nanjing the Japanese troops cruelly slaughtered Chinese ordinary civilians, including women and children. Edgar Snow reported that 300,000 Chinese were killed."[99] One veteran recalled, "My superiors ordered us not to let one Chinese alive. Therefore we committed arson, murder, and rape, like beasts. There is nothing evil I haven't done." Some 56,000 reportedly saw the exhibition during the week it was open, according to the sponsors who said they chose the summer vacation time so that young people who know nothing about the war could appreciate peace and not allow Japan to go to war again. These admissions of guilt and expressions of regret touched an important element in Chinese culture and, over time, could significantly reduce the anger and resentment toward Japan. In this regard, another story covered a meeting cosponsored by the Japan-China Veterans Friendship Association and the Returners from China Association in which a former Japanese officer claimed he had cut off the heads of more than thirty Chinese with his sabre.[100] In his speech, which was reportedly choked with sobs, he said "we carry out our introspection and engage in peace and the anti-war movement. We owe the Chinese too much to be able to return their kindness." One of the veterans told of meeting two female students at the University of Tokyo who knew nothing about

Japan's invasion of China but only about the war with the United States and the atomic bombings of Hiroshima and Nagasaki. He commented, "This situation makes me worry. Therefore a gathering such as today's is significant."

The reports from Japan were not uniformly positive. One meeting sponsored by the Japan-China Friendship Association was disrupted by right-wingers when a university professor spoke on "Looking into the Japanese War of Invasion in China Through the Examination of Textbooks." [101] Arriving in cars equipped with loudspeakers, the agitators shouted "To say 'massacre' is lying!" in response to statements about the Nanjing Massacre, and broke up the meeting. They also seized newsmen's cameras and beat up some of the audience, prompting one woman to remark, "It worries me and reminds me of prewar militarism."

On balance, the dominant tone of the commemorative articles and statements in China served to reinforce anti-Japanese sentiment by linking the historical record with recent and present disputes. Thus, Sun Pinghua, president of the China-Japan Friendship Association, told a Japanese delegation in Beijing for the Third Conference on Sino-Japanese Friendly Exchange that there were "some problems that grossly contravene the principles embodied in the 1972 Sino-Japanese Joint Declaration and the 1978 Treaty on Sino-Japanese Friendship." [102] After citing textbook revisions and Yasukuni Shrine visits as examples, Sun charged that "a handful of people in Japan today—including some influential people—still refuse to admit the aggressive nature of the war." He then dwelt at length on the dormitory issue, warning "those in Japan who want to create 'two Chinas' or 'one China, one Taiwan,' to stop harboring evil designs on Taiwan which is part of China's sacred territory."

Two major articles that received widespread distribution came down heavily against Japan as a reliable "friend." He Fang, head of the Institute for Japanese Studies in the Chinese Academy of Social Sciences, devotes the first half of his essay to the positive side in the relationship. [103] He asserts that "economically there are not fundamental conflicts between China and Japan; on the contrary economic relations are actually mutually demanding and mutually complementary." He also goes well beyond earlier oblique references to strategic interests, arguing that "as long as China and

Japan maintain friendly relations and carry out friendly cooperation with each other, no full-scale wars will break out in this region."

In the second half of the article, however, He itemizes the "problems and negative factors," omitting nothing, past or present.
Thus, "some people in Japan . . . have tried to reverse the verdict
on Japan's aggressive war and the verdict on Japanese war criminals, spread fallacies, distort history . . . [and have] also refused to
admit to the 'Nanjing Massacre,' [and] denounced the 'Tokyo trial'
as illegal." Moreover, he adds that "this handful of people has an
enormous capacity to maneuver and have exerted a very bad influence on Japanese society. They often stir up opinion, cheat the
masses, poison the minds of Japanese youths, stir up chauvinism,
and frequently stir up troubles to hurt the national feelings of the
Chinese people." He sums this up as the "tendency of trying to
revive the spirit of Japanese militarism and of making new efforts
to realize the fond illusion of the 'East Asia co-prosperity sphere.'"

He then suggests that "perhaps these few people have also fixed
their eyes on China's Taiwan Province and used various methods,
such as political parties, diplomacy, and so on, to repeatedly upgrade . . . relations between Taiwan and Japan." His reference to
"methods" includes official government actions as well as those of
a "handful of people." This is then made explicit by reference to
Tokyo's having sent "a special plane and officials from its Ministry
of Foreign Affairs" to escort some defecting North Korean seamen
to Taiwan from which they traveled on to South Korea. The dormitory case is then mentioned, together with Zhao Ziyang's earlier
assertion that political issues are more important than economic
ones. Deng's assertion is expanded on to the effect that "all the
problems since the restoration of relations, such as revising textbooks, Japanese officials paying official respects to the Yasukuni
Shrine, the case of the Guanghua dormitory, and so on, have been
caused by the Japanese side."

Moving to economic relations, He says, "the Japanese side has
not been keen on solving" the trade imbalance, and "in terms of
technological transfer and funds cooperation, Japan has obviously
discriminated against and imposed restrictions on China." In a
somewhat unexpected concession, He adds, "Compared with the
above-mentioned political problems, although the Japanese side
should mainly be held responsible for the economic problems . . .

the Chinese side should also be held responsible for them in a certain manner." However, he does not elaborate on this point. In this connection, He hints at China's ability to pursue economic modernization without Japan's involvement if necessary. Anticipating a concurrent statement by Li Xiannian, He claims, "At present the major obstacles lie in [the fact] that some people in Japan think that China and Japan do not have a mutually demanding and mutually complementary economic relationship, [that] China needs the support of Japan, and [that] China's 'four modernizations' will not possibly be realized without the support of Japan. . . . Although these views do not naturally conform with reality, they have had an impact on . . . economic cooperation and friendly relations."

He then returns to his earlier theme, claiming that "since World War II there have always been a handful of remnant militarists . . . [but] what is particularly noteworthy is that in recent years there has been a tendency of great-nation chauvinism among some Japanese . . . not only trying to make Japan a political power but also actually trying to make Japan a military power." He expands on "great nation chauvinism," a term that had not been authoritatively used previously, noting, "There has been more talk on the superiority of the Japanese nation and narrow nationalism in Japan. Some Japanese think that their country is a big power, so they are very 'proud of the wealth of their country' and look down on other countries. . . . Pride and prejudice have made these Japanese unwilling to know historical common sense."

He ends on an upbeat note in contrast to his earlier statements, claiming that even though this "handful of people . . . will probably be able to temporarily cheat some people and cause certain troubles, their entire aim will never be realized." Provided that both sides "do all they can" to strengthen relations and avoid "things which will hurt the feelings of both peoples," handle problems "through friendly consultations," and "resolutely struggle against remarks and behavior which are harmful to friendship . . . especially activities which are aimed at creating 'two Chinas' and reviving Japanese militarism," all will be well.

His essay was almost evenly divided in space between the positive and the negative aspects of Sino-Japanese relations; his opening and closing sections stressed "friendship" exclusively. But the weight of his indictment of Tokyo's behavior clearly made this the dominant message for Japanese as well as Chinese audiences. In particular, his allusion to the alleged misperceptions of Japan's necessary role in China's economic modernization raised the faint shadow of economic sanctions on Beijing's part should Tokyo not respond to its demands on various political issues.

Concurrent with the publication of He's article, President Li Xiannian attended the Sino-Japanese Friendly Exchanges conference, where he attacked the dormitory case in standard terms but went beyond this issue to declare that a few Japanese had the wrong idea that Japan was indispensable to China.[104] Li added that "China bases its opening to the outside world on equality and mutual benefit and opposes any acts aimed at achieving political ends through economic pressure." Kyodo reported Li's words in stronger terms than did Xinhua, claiming he explicitly threatened to "decline Japan's economic assistance" if it were used to pressure China for political ends.[105]

The longest and most assertive article, however, came from politburo member Hu Qiaomu. Hu was prominent in the coterie of conservative party elders who were associated with the fall of Hu Yaobang and attacks on "bourgeois liberalization" following the December 1986 student demonstrations for "freedom and democracy." Unlike other commemorative essays and speeches, Hu begins with the 1894–95 war and its "treaty of national betrayal and humiliation according to which Taiwan and some nearby islands were ceded to Japan."[106] He emphasizes that "Japan was not the first imperialist country to invade China but we should particularly notice that Japan occupied our sacred territory—Taiwan— for as long as half a century. . . . Some people in Japan at present still spread the opinion that 'the ownership of Taiwan has not been finally determined' and try to create 'one China, one Taiwan' or 'two Chinas' in various forms."

A rather detailed summary of events follows leading to the May 4, 1919, "anti-Japanese patriotic movement." In this and other sections, Hu's negative depiction of American policy and behavior introduces a new theme joined to the parallel, but more negative, treatment of Japan. Thus, he claims that "Japan in fact did not participate in the war [World War I] and its position was similar to that of the United States," a historical distortion made more explicit in the subsequent *Beijing Review* version.[107]

Hu recounts how "U.S. President Wilson proposed that the German privileges [in China] be temporarily taken over by the peace conference, and then he proposed that they be put under the joint control of the United States, Britain, France, Italy, and Japan." The subsequent student opposition spread rapidly in China and "scored greater achievements than the 1911 Revolution. The struggle dealt a heavy blow to the arrogant Japanese imperialists and the pro-Japanese traitors in China." Hu justifies this historical recapitulation "because we want to show that the Chinese people's new democratic revolution began precisely with a national struggle against Japan's aggression."

Likewise, the May Thirtieth movement in 1925 "resulted from the killing of . . . a worker representative of a textile mill in Shanghai by the Japanese capitalists and this movement marked the beginning of the great revolution from 1925 to 1927." Hu then claims,

> The Japanese imperialists formulated their plan to carry out aggression against China as early as in the same year Chiang Kai-shek betrayed the revolution. In July 1927, Japanese Prime Minister Giichi Tanaka said in an official report to the Japanese Emperor that "In order to conquer China, we must first conquer Manchuria and Mongolia; in order to conquer the world, we must first conquer China." In fact, Japan actually acted step by step according to this plan.

Hu's resurrection of the spurious Tanaka Memorial compresses the history and domestic politics of Japan in the following decade to the point of distortion, as did his next statement that "Britain and the United States simply looked on unconcerned until Japan raided Pearl Harbor in December 1941." A long recitation of the Communist party's struggle against Chiang's passivity and Japan's aggression followed with swipes at the United States among others. Thus, he rhetorically asks whether "socialist New China" could expect the "vigorous support" in economic development rendered by the United States and Japan to Taiwan after 1945, sardonically concluding, "No miracle has ever appeared or will appear." Hu also notes that although victory came after America dropped two atomic bombs on Japan, "It is known to all that we have always been opposed to this method of warfare," ignoring the fact that, until the bombs were dropped, the Communist party had not addressed the question because it did not exist.

Hu's reprise of the relationship's postwar evolution toward normalization and friendship omits all references to Hu Yaobang's role, giving Mao, Zhou, and Deng full credit. His recitation of postwar "controversial events" juxtaposes unnamed "Japanese statesmen and businessmen of insight [who] are not content with current conditions" in the relationship against similarly unidentified "Japanese authorities [who] still just pay lip service to . . . the principles" in the joint statement and treaty "on a series of major issues."

Hu Qiaomu's final paragraph stands in marked contrast to Hu Yaobang's admonitions to youth the previous November. Hu Yaobang had cautioned the students to temper patriotism with "a far-sighted internationalist spirit . . . promoting unity, friendship, and cooperation for mutual benefit with young people of Japan." But Hu Qiaomu declares,

> We ardently hope that all Chinese soldiers and people, especially young people, will seriously review this section of revolutionary history which is full of tears and blood that lasted over a half century, will pay close attention to the occurrences in Sino-Japanese relations, and will make joint efforts with the majority of the Japanese people

to improve and develop relations on the basis of the joint statement and treaty. The shift of emphasis from November 1986 to July 1987 is underlined by the inclusion of Deng's provocative statement that had put all the blame on Japan. Hu then asserts, "He is completely correct in making these remarks, which represent the voice of the one billion Chinese people!" After stating the necessity to settle outstanding problems "properly as soon as possible," Hu closes this lengthy essay with an atypical allusion, "As Confucius said: 'Today, when we observe other people, we should not only listen to what they say but should also see what they do.' We will see what actions the Japanese Government will take in the future."[108]

An interesting addition to the version of Hu's article that was distributed worldwide through *Beijing Review*'s various linguistic editions, including Japanese, strengthened the depiction of China's power relative to that of Japan. Thus, "any serious-minded Japanese politician . . . must consider the existence of an independent and unyielding power on the other side of the sea, a power . . .

whose international position becomes increasingly important with each passing day. Japan gives China the cold shoulder, China will not accept it quietly. It is Japan that will suffer in the end." [109]

The length and content of Hu Qiaomu's essay, its authoritative ranking, its widespread dissemination, and his well-established opposition to Hu Yaobang, all served to support speculation in Japan and elsewhere that the worsening of relations during the first half of 1987 could not be wholly divorced from the inner party struggle that was occurring in anticipation of the forthcoming CCP congress. The spillover effects in the mass media, however, provoked public responses that gained a life of their own, in turn exacerbating relations at higher levels, which further sharpened internal divisions in Tokyo as well as in Beijing.

Symptomatic of this dynamic interaction was the surrounding of the Chinese embassy on July 7 by "right-wingers who gathered . . . to shout anti-Chinese slogans and insult the Chinese flag." [110] Adding this incident to earlier ones, a *Renmin Ribao* reporter warned,

> The occurrence of these incidents one after another shows that the spirit of militarism still exists in today's Japan. . . . Such activities . . . are carried out by only a small number of people; however, they represent a dangerous movement. If they are not immediately exposed and checked, and if they are allowed to continue to grow, they will unavoidably affect the overall friendly relations between China and Japan.

A postscript to the July 7 commemorative ceremonies and statements came with the annual Yasukuni Shrine service on August 15 marking the anniversary of the end of World War II. Beijing's foreign ministry spokesman remarked, "We have noticed that Prime Minister Nakasone did not worship at the Yasukuni Shrine at this time. . . . Some Japanese Government officials' worshiping . . . while holding public offices has objectively blurred the nature of that war, hurt the feelings of the victimized people of many countries, and also fanned up the arrogance of a very small number of people who attempt to restore militarism. We express regret for this." Thus, although Nakasone was absent, the fact that sixteen of his colleagues attended, six in their official capacity, rubbed more salt in the wound as far as the Chinese were concerned. [111]

Two days later, the PLA Anti-Chemical Corps Department released its tabulation of Chinese chemical warfare casualties. [112] In rebuttal to "a small number of Japanese militarists [who] have denied the fact," the report claimed that "the Japanese troops used toxic chemicals on Chinese soldiers and civilians on 1,600 occasions, killing and wounding 50,417 people." This occurred "in 81 counties, towns, and regions in thirteen provinces . . . [and] included tear gas, sneezing gas, choking gas, vesicant agents, and blood poisoning agents." In all, compared with chemical warfare elsewhere in World War II, "the Japanese aggressor troops in China registered the highest record in terms of the length of time used, the number of times used, types of chemicals used, and number of regions involved."

These mid-August 1987 press notes captured the dour mood of Sino-Japanese relations fifty years after the Luguoqiao incident.

THE FIFTEENTH ANNIVERSARY OF THE NORMALIZATION OF RELATIONS

By happy coincidence, another event was commemorated in 1987, namely the fifteenth anniversary of the restoration of diplomatic relations between Tokyo and Beijing. The Diet passed a resolution noting the event and calling on the Japanese government to increase its efforts toward friendly relations.[113] Celebratory meetings in Japan were featured in *Renmin Ribao* stories with warm reminiscences by prominent figures of how they worked with Zhou Enlai to bring the two countries together. Nakasone attended the main banquet, giving a "friendly and enthusiastic speech" that acknowledged that "since the two countries have different systems, it is unavoidable that some problems happen but through consultation, any problem can be solved."[114]

Subsequent meetings in Beijing, however, held by the Commission for Friendship in the Twenty-first Century sounded a more cautious note. Zhao Ziyang, now CCP general secretary, described the dormitory dispute as a negative element in an otherwise favorable relationship; Acting Premier Li Peng told the Japanese visitors that the government was "extremely concerned" over the issue.[115] He added that the trade imbalance and the damage suffered as a result of Japan's banning sensitive exports to communist countries were further problems, concluding that if matters involved important principles, principles must be followed. "Otherwise it will be no good for the China-Japan relations, but harmful." [116]

Renmin Ribao's account quoted the commission's Chinese chairman, Wang Zhaoguo, at length, on how to "not use any excuse to make trouble" and

> look into our problems squarely and solve them on time, learn lessons from past problems, find out the source of the problems, and prevent them. . . . If we pretend that we don't see the problems that have already happened, passively avoid them, let them develop, or handle them wrongly, the problems are not going to be solved. Moreover, they are going to harm the overall situation of relations between the two countries. [117]

He emphasized, "What should be pointed out in particular are political problems. They are more important and sensitive." Wang then referred to the dormitory issue as a political problem. The Japanese side failed to make any reference to it, according to the Chinese account, but Kyodo claimed it "dominated the three-day meeting" at the end of which both sides acknowledged its importance and "pledged to resolve the issue as soon as possible." [118]

9

Problems and Prospects

The People's Republic of China has drastically changed its public postures and policies toward the Soviet Union and the United States during its first forty years. For the most part, these changes have been motivated by changing domestic priorities. The imperatives of military defense and economic development produced the Sino-Soviet alliance in 1950. But by 1960, Mao Zedong's political and ideological goals placed military and economic development secondary to self-reliance and his personal vision of communism, provoking Khrushchev to withdraw all Soviet aid. The alliance dissolved even though it remained in effect on paper until it was renounced by Beijing in 1979.

Conversely, China's avowed political opposition to "U.S. imperialism" from 1950 to 1970 gave way to the priorities of military defense and economic development, initially under a perceived Soviet threat, subsequently because the "four modernizations" of agriculture, industry, science and technology, and defense became the new domestic goal. This had the effect of aligning Beijing with Washington, in tacit opposition to Moscow. Beijing and Washington both agreed on the policy of making China strong and stable. Then in the 1980s, China proclaimed an independent foreign policy not aligned with any superpower, reflecting a more balanced approach that included detente with Moscow as Beijing devoted its entire effort to economic development while decreasing investment in the military.

In view of these changes and their varying motivations, what are the likely prospects for Sino-Japanese relations over the next decade? The mutually avowed goal of friendship in the twenty-first century reflects rhetoric, not reality, at the level of state-to-state interaction. Governments pursue national interests as they perceive them, free of those bonds and obligations inherent in personal friendships. In the East Asian context, however, individuals may be viewed as "friends" by a regime on the basis of a proven relationship attested to by past behavior that engenders trust in word as well as deed. Beyond the manipulative use of the term friend to beguile a foreigner into serving the regime instrumentally, the concept genuinely reflects feelings and attributes evident on the part of Chinese and Japanese officials as they identify individuals who have advanced mutual interests in the relationship, such as Zhou Enlai and Tanaka Kakuei. The public interaction of Hu Yaobang and Nakasone Yasuhiro gave evidence of such a relationship on a personal level, which both men tried to elevate to the governmental level.

As is clear from the study of international relations, however, friendship is not necessary to the pursuit of common interests through trade and diplomacy. For governments and organizations to negotiate with confidence in the good faith of the other side, it is sufficient that they trust in contracts and commitments of future performance. Admittedly, such trust and confidence does not come easily, especially between past enemies. Therefore the question arises: as China's bitter wartime experience becomes more distant, will positive economic interaction build a strong mutuality of interests that results in increased understanding and accommodation on both sides? Or will negative political interactions prevail and strain pragmatic ties, keeping the relationship unstable and acrimonious?

Thus far we have examined various aspects of the relationship as they developed in the period, 1982–87. At this point we must distill from the detailed account those political, economic, and perceptual factors that bear positively or negatively on the interaction between Beijing and Tokyo. In addition to the historical record, I will also draw on my personal interviews with Chinese and Japanese scholars, diplomats, journalists, and business persons as subjective evidence of how the relationship was perceived on both sides in these years. This recapitulation will then permit us to assess the impact of key variables as they are likely to evolve in the foreseeable future and strike a balance on the relationship's probable course to the year 2000.

POLITICAL FACTORS

"If the political problems are not handled correctly, they will do greater harm to Sino-Japanese relations than economic problems."[1]

By putting politics ahead of economics, Zhao Ziyang correctly characterized the escalation of tensions from the anti-Japanese student demonstrations of 1985 to the high level exchange of charges and countercharges, some ad hominem, in 1987. Although economic problems worsened during this time, political issues triggered the heaviest attacks by government and media on both sides. Among the factors contributing to these attacks were the attributes of individual personalities, the differences in political systems, inadequate levels of information, and traditional behavior.

Tactically and in fact, Zhao erred in only targeting "some Japanese friends" for his admonition and not conceding that the Chinese might also handle political problems incorrectly. Granting this possibility for both sides might have assuaged feelings both in his audience and, probably, in Japan as well. But Zhao could not make this concession, even if he had wanted to, because Deng Xiaoping had already blamed all problems on Tokyo, excusing Beijing from any responsibility. Deng's remarks and their impact in Japan demonstrated the potential importance of personalities as a political factor. We have noted how Hu and Nakasone promoted the image of Sino-Japanese friendship in both countries. Within the Beijing leadership, Hu was not alone in this endeavor, but his association with the cause far exceeded that of any of his associates, as was also true for Nakasone in Japan. Hu personally invited the Japanese prime minister to China, entertaining him and his family informally at home, an event that was covered on national television. Nakasone in turn accommodated Chinese protests over his visit to the Yasukuni Shrine and to some extent over textbook revision as well. Hu publicly reproached Chinese youth for not putting friendship with Japan on par with patriotism, and Nakasone accepted individual responsibility for difficulties arising more generally on the Japanese side.

Ironically, both leaders contributed to the problem that they endeavored to ameliorate. Hu's personal style proved inimical to the course he was pursuing. His impromptu invitation for three thousand Japanese youths to visit China aroused widespread resentment, particularly among younger Chinese, and antagonized his party cohorts who had not been consulted in advance. Hu's informal handling of the Nakasone relationship caused criticism as being improper, if not impolitic. In the name of Sino-Japanese friendship, Hu went too far, too fast for the climate of China at the time.

Nakasone's negative contribution was more substantive. He sought to raise Japanese self-confidence through a renewed sense of nationalism so that Japan could assume a higher international posture, both politically and economically. But this reawakened deep-seated antagonism and suspicion in China. He broadened Japan's military role in the American alliance and his constant pressure, finally successful, removed the ceiling on defense expenditures. These actions intensified Beijing's warnings against revived militarism. Meanwhile, Nakasone's concessions to Chinese attacks on shrine visits and revisionist textbooks aroused resentment among right-wing Japanese, whose activities enlarged on the new nationalism that he nurtured. In the final analysis, Nakasone came to personify Chinese worst-case fears.

Hu Yaobang did not fall from power because of his Japan policy alone. On the contrary, his primary problems were domestic, including collegial relations, ideological liberalization, and personal style. Nevertheless, Chinese criticisms of the way in which he conducted relations with Japan surfaced in reports "leaked" to foreign correspondents after his fall, foreign policy being too sensitive a topic to discuss openly. These reports echoed the privately voiced views of Hu that I encountered earlier in 1986. About that same time, Chinese suspicions of Nakasone were obliquely insinuated in public remarks and freely vented in private interviews. For example, one specialist at the Institute of Japanese Studies lamented the sweeping victory of Nakasone and the LDP that July as portending an "even worse problem with his nationalist and militarist tendencies." Repeated questioning of Nakasone's "true motives" and his "sincerity" came from various groups, especially among younger persons. In contrast to official speeches, no one praised him as China's "friend" in private.

Far more important than passing personalities as political factors are fundamental systemic and behavioral characteristics. As has become true in general for Chinese policy, the previously postulated ideological incompatibility of communism and capitalism no longer obstructs Sino-Japanese relations. In contrast to most of the Maoist era, virtually no Marxist stereotypes or categories appear in Chinese references to Japan. Rather, the basic obstacle to better Sino-Japanese relations lies in the gap between an authoritarian system that grants party and government a directing role over all public aspects of society and a pluralistic, democratic system in which public diversity within both government and society is necessary and proper. As a result, the Chinese expect and demand that Tokyo will behave as Beijing does, inducing conformity in compliance with professed policies.

This systemic problem is aggravated by behavioral aspects of the relationship. Any manifestations of rising nationalism in Japan evoke Chinese protests against any and all actions that challenge the Chinese formulation of what accords with the Sino-Japanese agreements of 1972 and 1978. These protests, publicly reiterated ad infinitum at all levels, in turn irritate and exacerbate rising nationalistic sentiments in Japan, creating an action-reaction syndrome as exemplified by developments in 1987. In the course of those developments, Ambassador Nakae addressed this phenomenon with unusual candor: "Due to differences in their political structures, there are some gaps in their perceptions and it is impossible for the two countries to agree completely."[2]

Another behavioral difference that plagues the politics between the two capitals was noted by *Mainichi*'s Beijing correspondent, who observed that although Japan always tackles problems case by case, the Chinese "grasp these problems as one trend in history."[3] For Tokyo, an issue may lie wholly outside of governmental authority, as with the celebration of Chiang Kai-shek's birthday. It may lie beyond the reach of the executive, as with the dormitory judgment. It may be separable as private activity, as with shrine visits, or it may be subject to limited influence, as with textbook revision. In any event, Japan addresses each situation on its own terms. For Beijing, all of these activities are aggregated under the rubric of a "tendency" for which Japanese officials are responsible and therefore for which they can be held accountable, whether as evidence of rising militarism or a "two Chinas" plot. This behavioral difference causes the two sides to talk past each other, most notably when Chinese protests over statements or actions by private Japanese groups or the Japanese courts are answered with explanations of the Japanese system of government and constitution.

During 1982–87, this behavioral aspect of the relationship became worse because of misinformation on the Chinese side. Sel-

dom did the public analysis in the Chinese media offer a full account of the factual situation that the two governments confronted
on any particular issue. Thus, little attempt was made to educate
readers on the true dimensions of a problem. In one exceptional
instance, *Renmin Ribao* belatedly explained that no single textbook,
if officially approved, would thereby be required for all Japanese in
a particular grade. The level and weight of attention given to this
issue, however, had implied just the opposite. As late as mid-1986,
a highly placed official in the Academy of Social Sciences believed
that universal mandatory adoption followed approval by Tokyo's
Ministry of Education.

Factual misunderstandings are inevitable in international relations and cross-cultural contact. Their initial appearance in Sino-
Japanese relations was understandable in view of the 1937–45 war,
the absence of diplomatic relations and normal intercourse from
1949 to 1972, the rigid Marxist frame of reference on the Chinese
side through 1978, and, in particular, the extremist isolation of the
Cultural Revolution. The cumulative impact of these factors im-
poverished the knowledge of entire generations, especially those
under the age of fifty-five who recently entered positions as analysts and publicists.

It might be expected, however, that the significance of this relationship for China would engender the same effort toward factual
understanding among those who must address it as emerged with
respect to the United States after 1972 and, more markedly, after
Mao's death. The very costly war in Korea from 1950 to 1953, the
total economic as well as political estrangement from 1950 to 1972,
the intensity of attack against "U.S. imperialism" down to 1972,
and the continuing U.S. support for Taiwan all obstructed a well-
informed view of American policy and society. Yet despite occasional distortions, as illustrated by Hu Qiaomu's July 7 essay, an
impressive body of Chinese literature, both scholarly and popular,
educates the government and the public about various aspects of
Washington's politics and policies with considerable accuracy and
objectivity.[4]

By comparison, only in professional economic and military articles is the general level of Chinese writing on Japan factually informative, at least as of mid-1987. Political analysis rarely rose to
this level. When an unusually objective essay in the journal of the

Institute of Japanese Studies, *Riben Wenti*, delineated the societal and political factors that mitigate against militarism, an introductory editorial note implied disapproval.[5] This prompted one local director of Japanese studies to reject the article out of hand in discussion.

At some point in many books and articles on Japan, the reader is reminded of Japan's potential threat by the ritualistic incantation, "Past experience, if not forgotten, is a guide for the future" (*Qianshi buwang, houshi zhishi*). This admonition to recall the past, characteristic of Chinese behavior, stands in contrast to the professed proclivity of the Japanese to live in the present with little interest in the past, particularly if it reflects unfavorably on the nation. The resulting reluctance to deal with the guilt of aggression and atrocities in China while dwelling on the Hiroshima and Nagasaki atomic casualties both frustrates and infuriates the Chinese, who believe apology and atonement are mandatory for any injury, personal or societal.[6] The annual antinuclear ceremonies in Japan, with international attendance, are seen by the Chinese as creating sympathy for the aggressor while ignoring what the Chinese assert to be a disaster of comparable degree: the Nanjing Massacre. In my interviews, many Chinese juxtaposed this aspect of Japanese behavior unfavorably with the West German willingness to admit the monstrous consequences of Nazism, including the Holocaust, a comparison explicitly raised in He Fang's July 7 essay.[7]

This cultural difference in dealing with the past distorts perceptions and explanations of behavior on each side. The Chinese see the Japanese desire to avoid discussion of their aggressive record as a deliberate effort to justify behavior that can one day be repeated more successfully. At best, it is unconscionable; at worst, it is intolerable. The Japanese in turn see Chinese attempts to rake up the past as either a tactic to extract unilateral concessions or simply as an irrational obsession with what is no longer relevant to current business. At best, it is for the purposes of bargaining; at worst, it constitutes interference in domestic affairs. The net result is conflict and intransigence on both sides.

Another behavioral aspect that increases misinformation is the authoritarian "top-down" pattern of the Chinese bureaucracy, both traditional and communist. This inhibits any correction from below of misunderstandings from above. For example, lengthy legal articles argued the Chinese position on the dormitory case, basing their argument in part on Tokyo's alleged obligation under international law to override domestic court rulings in cases involving a foreign state. However, Beijing had previously agreed to accept American domestic court jurisdiction in settling a suit brought against the People's Republic of China for the payment of railroad bonds that had been issued by the Qing dynasty earlier in this century.[8] Presumably legal writers knew about the bond case, which Beijing ultimately won, but did not dare to raise it in public as a precedent because it countered official policy.

Similar inhibitions and pressures can also operate privately. For example, in one of my interviews, two retired senior diplomats erroneously claimed that the ceiling on Japanese defense expenditures was mandated both by the constitution and by the security treaty with the United States. After repeating this claim a second time, I corrected them, at which point the interpreter interjected, "Yes, it was done under [prime minister] Miki, wasn't it?" although she had not intervened earlier.[9]

Younger scholars in research institutes and instructional academies told of being unable to write internal papers or give lectures that challenged the public line on Japan. A senior official characterized an assistant professor as having shown "courage" when the assistant professor declared in a group meeting, "We think that we understand Japan because of our common cultural heritage. But that is wrong. We must study Japan like any other foreign country." This assertion that Chinese knowledge was inadequate carried special weight coming from an individual who had done graduate work in Tokyo, yet it clearly astonished the official by its forthrightness.

As previously noted, these interviews occurred during the peak of intellectual excitement over the revival of the policy of "blooming and contending," which enjoined authors, artists, academics, and journalists to express themselves freely without regard for strict Marxist orthodoxy or official views. Contrary to these official injunctions, the behavior I found in private group discussions on Sino-Japanese relations was exemplified by the Chinese aphorism, "One voice, one room." This combined with low levels of information to produce a highly uniform but often inaccurate point of view. After the head of the group, usually the oldest person present and invariably a man, had held forth, everyone else echoed or expanded his remarks. Despite my assurances that all remarks were off the record and would never be attributed to specific individuals, dissent rarely occurred and then only when the first speaker specifically called for it.

In lengthy expositions of Japan's potential military threat, speakers would frequently deny having any immediate concern but nonetheless insist that unless China worked to counter "a small handful of persons," the threat would eventually materialize. Their argument drew on the standard litany of incidents publicized in the Chinese media. No contrary evidence from public opinion polls or societal behavior entered the discussion. Only a vague rhetorical reference to "the Japanese people," who were said to oppose militarism, balanced the presentation.

Just as no scenario spelled out how "a small handful of people" might reverse majority opinion, so too the future threat was left unspecified in terms of strategy, weaponry, and objectives. Instead, this threat was defined in general terms as being directed against China, against other Asian countries, and at times even against the United States. No one questioned this, much less explained how Japan's exceptional geographical and demographic vulnerability to nuclear retaliation would permit it to attack any of its three huge nuclear neighbors. Alternative targets in Asia were never specified, perhaps because they lacked credibility as being worth the effort. Instead, the overall line of argument leapt from premise to conclusion, with an occasional syllogism along the way.

Because this reasoning emerged from such a wide variety of individuals in terms of age, profession, and location, it warrants brief recapitulation as a general framework for Chinese perceptions of this relationship and its potential hazards. Successive steps in the argument are numbered, with parenthetical comment to highlight each step's limitations.

1. Projecting ahead from the well-known past, one future possibility posits Japan returning to militarism and aggression. (No probability estimates were ever offered, the concept being wholly alien to the discussants.)

2. The consequences of this possibility becoming reality would be so serious that it cannot be ignored. Therefore, China must respond to any and all early indicators of this possibility in Japan

or they will grow more prominent. (No cost-benefit estimates were made of the actual effects in Japan of repeated Chinese protests.)

3. A recent trend involving such indicators is said to exist and there is a strong social basis for the revival of militarism among Japanese youth. (No trend analysis based on a time-series analysis of public opinion polls and editorials was offered and no data was presented on Japanese youth.)

4. Japan wants to become a great political power now that it is a great economic power, but this will require military power; therefore, Japan will become strong militarily. (No definition of "political" demonstrated a necessary linkage with military power.)

5. China must therefore remain vigilant and fight against the revival of Japanese militarism. (No consideration was given to the possibility that excessive vigilance might give rise to misperceptions.)

I will return to this line of argument when I examine the images at the media and the mass levels.

ECONOMIC FACTORS

Objective conditions in the recent past and immediate future complicate the economic complementarity that has made Japan so important in China's modernization program. Structural differences cause trade to be imbalanced to China's disadvantage, a point freely acknowledged by economists but rarely by other Chinese, whether in public or in private. The importation of machinery, technology, and consumer products in exchange for natural resources, agricultural products, and light industrial goods creates an unequal relationship. This structural imbalance was worsened by the rapid appreciation of the yen in 1985–87, together with the fall in the price of oil, a major export to Japan. The higher yen raised the costs of imports for China and proportionately lowered the value of its exports to Japan.

The actual level of the imbalance depends on several factors, including Chinese export capabilities for meeting Japanese market conditions, the accessibility of the Japanese market, and the amount of Chinese imports. Beijing's complaints against marketing obstacles parallel those of other capitals, but privately Chinese economists admit that these complaints exaggerate the degree to which Tokyo's facilitating Chinese exports would correct the imbalance.

It was not only the objective factors, however, that made the trade imbalance a continuing point of dispute. Beijing also argued that the imbalance was a measure of what Japanese investment in China should have been. The Chinese made this argument on the subjective premise that the two items should correlate to some degree. The Chinese also pointed to the investment levels of other countries that had far smaller trade surpluses than Japan, such as the United States and West Germany. Both arguments failed to move Japanese firms looking for profits and security, neither of which were as yet seen to be of sufficient promise to warrant large amounts of capital for long-term ventures. The trade balance was simply irrelevant to such calculations as far as the Japanese were concerned. As for comparison with the United States, much American investment was in off-shore oil exploration, inevitably costly, necessarily high risk, and an area in which Japanese technology was not competitive.

A similar problem arose with Beijing's new assertion that because China had not demanded reparations in 1972 to cover wartime damage, Japanese investment was due as a "debt." Aside from the fact that Chiang Kai-shek had renounced reparations immediately after World War II, thus leaving little choice for Mao and Zhou, who wanted Tokyo to transfer recognition from Taipei to Beijing, war losses could not be made the responsibility of private entrepreneurs several generations later. Also, demanding investment as a debt owed to China had even less chance of persuading the Japanese in 1987 because they had seen political instability in the form of student demonstrations followed by the ouster of Hu Yaobang. Once again both sides were talking past each other.

Technology transfer was a recurring bone of contention, in part because Japan abided by COCOM regulations on trade with communist countries. Although exceptions for China had been enacted, certain limitations inevitably remained. In 1987, investigation revealed that a Toshiba subsidiary, without the head firm's knowledge, had surreptitiously sold highly sensitive technology to the Soviet Union. This raised a storm of protest in Washington, prompting Tokyo to tighten export controls. This in turn evoked protests from Beijing. Nakasone gave vague assurances that China had no need for concern. The incident illustrated the difficulty of separating the People's Republic of China from the Soviet Union in such matters. It also showed how resistant Beijing remained to any limits on technology transfer.

As with trade, not all of Beijing's complaints were invalid. Japanese specialists privately admitted to the fear that technology transfer agreements might not be adhered to, with the Chinese recipient passing technical data or hardware to other users. Alternatively, some firms held back on information or components for fear that Chinese competition in domestic or foreign markets might grow in the future. The net result of these objective and subjective factors on both sides was to make technology transfer a recurrent issue on Beijing's agenda.

Certain wholly subjective aspects on the Chinese side exacerbated economic relations. As He Fang's essay showed, it was a matter of conviction that Japan's economic need for China's resources and markets matches China's need for Japan's technology and capital.[10] Outside of economic circles, this argument rested on a total ignorance of Japan's overall trade patterns and options. Thus, a specialist in international relations confidently asserted, "If we threatened to cut off all trade with Japan tomorrow, they would change their ways." That "some people in Japan," as He Fang puts it, saw the situation in reverse aroused Chinese resentment, but did not cause the situation to be reconsidered.

Underlying this attitude is a discernible frustration, perceived and acknowledged by the Japanese, over China being the student and Japan the teacher. This reversal of their historical roles was difficult enough to accept in the last century and was made worse by subsequent conflicts. Moreover, as of 1987, China remained dependent on Japan for one-fifth of its total trade, for the largest source of its foreign aid, and for a major share of its loans. A subjective sense of being exploited by the former enemy underlay some of the vigor and vehemence of Chinese economic complaints.

Japanese behavior often heightened this problem. In my interviews, Chinese women told of humiliating treatment as inferiors by Japanese business managers, treatment that was underscored by the aloof and formal style of the Japanese managers. The solicitation of prostitutes caused further criticism. An alleged "national characteristic to think only of the wallet" explained the epithet, "economic animals." Informed sources in Tokyo admitted that "the behavior of our businessmen causes difficulties" while lamenting that not much could be done to change it. The particular circumstances are not unique to Sino-Japanese relations and arise elsewhere in Asia, with similar criticisms and reactions. But given the preceding history and the current context, they acquire somewhat greater significance in China.

These subjective aspects joined with objective factors to make economic problems more difficult than might otherwise have been anticipated. As such, they highlight the importance of images and perceptions in which rationality is often mistakenly assumed to prevail.

IMAGES AND PERCEPTIONS

As we have seen, positive and negative images of Japan and the Japanese coexist in official Chinese statements and media. These contradictory inputs to public consciousness complicate the task of assessing their impact. An additional barrier to assessment is the impossibility of verifying any hypothesis through polls or systematic interviews. Such an assessment is nevertheless necessary as part of the framework within which to project potential developments in the relationship.

Prior to 1971, no such contradiction between positive and negative images existed; all images portrayed Japan in essentially negative terms. Films, plays, novels, and children's picture booklets depicted the Japanese soldier as a lustful and brutal being. Japan epitomized the rapacious imperialist world that had preyed on China's weakness. After World War II, Japanese monopoly capitalism joined with American imperialism to threaten Asia in general and China in particular. Except for those "friends" in the Japanese business world and political circles who were willing to deal with China on its own terms, no positive images of the nearby neighbor existed.

Beginning in 1971–72, as Sino-Japanese detente led to diplomatic relations between Beijing and Tokyo, Chinese audiences gradually witnessed a softening of these images. Although war-time imagery returned briefly a decade later during the first text-book dispute, it otherwise remained muted or disappeared alto-gether. Children's booklets rarely focused on the war. Those that did depicted Japanese soldiers as comical or cowardly, but not as bestial.[11] Instead, Japan became a model for study and, in some instances, emulation. Economists saw its phoenixlike rise from the ashes of World War II to preeminence in the industrial world as a possible guide for China's modernization. The youth journal, *Zhongguo Qingnian,* showed Japanese and their society favorably, with only infrequent references to societal problems. Some writers suggested that the Japan of today foreshadowed the China of to-morrow, particularly in technological aspects.

These positive images of Japan were not passively transmitted through the media. A constant flow of delegations moved between the two countries, complete with welcoming and departing cere-monies, sister city relationships, friendship groups, and tours that involved local hospitality and receptions. By 1984, more than 900 Japanese exchange students were in China with another 1,600 in short-term language classes; by 1985, some 2,500 Chinese exchange students were in Japan.[12] In that year, 237,500 Japanese visited China and more than 100,000 Chinese went to Japan. The prolifera-tion of "Japanese taught here" signs in the alleyways of major Chi-nese cities testified to the increased level of personal contact be-tween the two countries.[13]

In July 1987, a special symposium was organized by Chinese students in Japan commemorating the fiftieth anniversary of Luguoqiao and the fifteenth anniversary of the restoration of Sino-Japanese diplomatic relations.[14] More than a hundred Ph.D. stu-dents met with Japanese senior scholars and young specialists to examine "China and Japan, modern and contemporary, and per-spectives on the twenty-first century." The largest and broadest such assemblage to that time, it examined past hostility and con-trasted it with present friendship. The Japanese participants al-leged that the assertion "Japan and China will not fight each other" was "the oath of the Japanese people."

Thus, the cumulative effect of wider interactions engendered many favorable impressions of Japan. It is no coincidence that in my personal conversations during 1986 I found that the most positive and accurate analysis of contemporary Japan came from young scholars who had lived there in graduate school. Only after the anti-Japanese student demonstrations in China did one Chinese sense any hostility among his colleagues at Keio University, and that soon disappeared.

Yet against these trends in official statements, mass media, and people-to-people exchanges was the contrary image of a ruthless aggressor whose rape and plunder of China must not be forgotten and whose potential return to this role is allegedly promoted by the Japanese in official as well as private circles. The emotional content of this latter image offset the favorable images and, under the circumstances of 1985–87, became dominant in certain sectors, particularly among Chinese university students.

The relative weight of the contradictory images was suggested by random reactions to two television series that won nationwide attention. The first, "Four Generations Under One Roof," appeared in 1985 and depicted in grim detail the suffering one family endured as a result of Japanese aggression and occupation. The second, "Ah Xin," was shown in 1986. Made in Japan, it traced the suffering of a Japanese family during the war, followed by the postwar regeneration.

Many Chinese agreed that the first film aroused powerful emotions that probably contributed to anti-Japanese student demonstrations that fall. Older viewers expressed sympathy with the second film, many for the first time seeing that their counterparts in Japan were also victims of the war. Their intense interest, sustained over many weeks, reflected the potential impact of the medium for challenging stereotypes. Younger Chinese, however, were less avid viewers, finding the series slow and beyond their ken. Moreover, neither group appeared to change its basic image of Japan as a result of the film.

Not surprisingly, my discussions in mid-1986 with educated urban Chinese found many with dual images of Japan. They expressed little or no fear of Japan in the short run, but displayed genuine concern that the past will be repeated in the future. They considered Japanese technology as the best in most cases, but believed that Japan sold shoddy goods to China and did not make its advanced technology available to the Chinese. They saw the Japanese-American alliance as countering Soviet expansionism, but opposed lifting the limit on Japanese defense expenditures. They believed that the Japanese people were basically peaceful, but thought this could change under the influence of revised textbooks and revived nationalism. Alleged indicators of reviving militarism were coupled with a recitation of past aggression and seen as a cause for concern. In sum, there was no trust in Japanese motives, goals, and growth in power. Instead Japanese behavior was repeatedly characterized as "arrogant" and "cunning." This duality of thought about Japan was a direct reflection of the signals sent by government and media.

I have focused on Chinese images and perceptions because the Chinese side has expressed more complaints about the relationship. Japanese images and perceptions, however, are clearly relevant, especially as they react to Chinese criticisms. In this regard a public opinion survey conducted annually by the prime minister's office revealed a sharp decline in favorable attitudes toward China between June 1985 and October 1986.[15] This followed a steady improvement in attitude from May 1981 to June 1985, suggesting the negative change was a reaction to the anti-Japanese student demonstrations and Beijing's various criticisms of Japanese behavior. Thus, in response to the question, "Do you feel friendly toward China?" 75.4 percent responded affirmatively in 1985 as against only 68.6 percent fourteen months later. Negative responses rose correspondingly from 17.8 percent to 24.8 percent. This outcome reverted to the May 1981 level, when 68.4 percent expressed friendly feelings. It did not, however, betoken a sense of crisis, as shown by the response to the question, "Are Sino-Japanese relations good?" in which 76.1 percent responded positively, with 20.3 percent saying "good" and 55.8 percent "more or less." But it did show how the action-reaction syndrome can affect the relationship.

FUTURE PROSPECTS

To the extent that Chinese images and perceptions of Japan are a result of the signals sent by government and media, then the prospect for change in the present duality of images depends on the mix of signals that emerges in coming years. Past changes in this regard are illustrative and include the reversal of the official posture toward Japan in 1972, toward the United States in 1971, and toward the Soviet Union in 1981. The main difference in the Japanese case, as we have noted, is the historical heritage that burdens Chinese memories of the past and prejudices perceptions of the present.

But images and perceptions of foreign relations are not solely the product of domestic signals. They obviously result to some extent from external statements and actions as well. The Chinese are not hermetically sealed off from the outside world and subject only to their own media transmissions. Millions listen to the Voice of America and the British Broadcasting Corporation overseas services, hearing about what is happening abroad while learning Engish. At least ten million Chinese have access to *Cankao Xiaoxi* (Reference News), a selected compilation of translated reports culled from foreign news services and newspapers. This source is issued by Beijing for restricted groups and individuals who are presumed to need this information for study and work. A more restricted compilation, *Cankao Ziliao* (Reference Materials), is issued for higher-level personnel. Foreign business persons and tourists move freely throughout the major cities, conveying additional information on world affairs.

For these reasons, what the Japanese say and do will be known to some extent in China independently of what the local media report. Debates and decisions over defense spending, anti-Chinese acts of vandalism, and textbook controversies become common knowledge within a relatively short time after their occurrence. Like the annual commemoration of atomic bombings and Yasukuni Shrine visits, these phenomena will arouse reactions at the mass level whether or not they are protested by Chinese officials and publicized by the Chinese media.

These challenges to friendship as defined in Beijing are likely to increase in frequency and expand in nature as Japanese nationalism develops in coming years. The Nakasone era marked a passage in time for Japan. The withdrawn or hesitant approach to regional and world affairs that characterized Tokyo's previous posture is evolving toward an assertive involvement in political and military matters, not only in East Asia but in the Middle East and elsewhere. Japan's military capabilities will grow, qualitatively and quantitatively, both as a function of American encouragement and as a spur to economic and technological development should the civilian economy fail to sustain its three decades of postwar prosperity. In addition, there will be a continuing diversity of political groups, statements, and behavior, including extreme right-wing manifestations of nationalism. World War II will fade even further from Japanese consciousness as death removes its participants.

How Beijing responds to these developments will depend on two key factors, neither of which can be forecast with confidence. The first and foremost factor will be the stability and orientation of politics at the highest level. Sino-Japanese relations were strained before the fall of Hu Yaobang and his fall did not result from his role in promoting the Commission for Friendship in the Twenty-first Century. Nevertheless, the increase in Chinese assertiveness and acerbity after Hu's political demise suggests the possibility that this relationship will be affected by domestic politics, if not in actuality, at least in the perceptions of Japanese. Will the future leadership be both united and determined to manage the relationship in a way that minimizes friction? Disunity invites a faction to exploit any available issue on which the current leaders are vulnerable. Japan will be a tempting target of opportunity in this regard.

The second factor concerns the success of economic modernization, especially in those areas in which Japanese trade, technology transfer, and investment play a visible role. Shortfalls and failures are easy to blame on the foreigner, at least in the initial instance, and the Japanese provide an inviting scapegoat. In addition, Chinese accusations that the Japanese create marketing obstacles, restrict technology transfer, and provide inadequate investment will continue, with considerable justification given the likely course of the two economies in the near future. None of these patterns will change quickly and some will not change at all.

In sum, much will depend on the degree of provocation that the Chinese perceive in Japanese behavior and the extent to which political actors in China choose to accent the positive as opposed to the negative aspects in the relationship. On balance, however, certain limits and options appear probable.

First, no significant strategic or military cooperation between China and Japan will emerge in this century. Wholly apart from the issue that Tokyo's avowed policies prohibit such cooperation, there is too much opposition and distrust in China to permit it in the next decade. The conventional cliché about a "love-hate relationship" does not apply here. There is no "love" on the Chinese side; at best, there is a grudging admiration for Japanese economic growth and technological modernization. Chinese suspicions and criticisms of Japan's growing military capability will increase commensurately with that growth. Moreover, this situation will continue regardless of the future Soviet military presence in Asia. Beijing will base its security on indigenous forces, mainly nuclear, together with a tacit reliance on the American ability to maintain a sufficient balance of power to deter Soviet aggression. Japan's contribution to that balance will be accepted, but not applauded, as its share increases.

Second, Japan is likely to play a proportionately smaller part in economic modernization in the future, at least to the extent that Beijing can manage this reduction. Already in 1987 a major journal warned that "the worst policy China could make would be carelessly to let strategic necessities, whether for defense or for economic construction, be controlled by Japanese business."[16] Noting that in 1986 trade with Japan surpassed China's total trade with the United States, West Germany, and the United Kingdom, the article called for greater flexibility in sources. By coincidence it cited Toshiba machinery as an example of something that could be replaced by American or German equipment, which would "enable China not only to strengthen her leverage in trade negotiations, but also free China to bargain or withdraw at any time."

This quantitative and qualitative reduction in dependence on Japan had already been stimulated by the appreciation of the yen, but it will be further encouraged by the type of thinking expressed in this article. Reduced dependence, in turn, will encourage continued, perhaps greater, Chinese pressure on Tokyo to curb perceived provocations lest "friendship" be further jeopardized.

China's growing ability to compete with Japan in third world markets, although still small, is likely to be accompanied by expressed concern over Japanese ambitions, political as well as economic, in the Asian-Pacific region. This concern, feeding on other Asian apprehensions and prejudices, will be benignly cast in terms of their interests. Basically, however, it will mask an underlying Sino-Japanese rivalry for influence in the area. This in effect rules out any genuine Pacific basin cooperation insofar as that depends on the two countries working together.

None of these tendencies, either singly or combined, threatens the relationship with rupture. Its mutually positive economic attributes, supplemented by its parallel political and military interests vis-à-vis Moscow and Washington, can contain the strains engendered by politics in both countries and their circular interaction. The only serious challenge to a limited but continuing relationship lies in conflicting claims to the continental shelf, symbolized by the nascent dispute over the Senkaku Islands, or Diaoyutai. Until the area is proven to have significant reserves of offshore oil, these claims will remain quiescent. Even should such reserves be proven, it is probable that a compromise involving joint exploitation will avoid an open break. But on balance, the Commission for Sino-Japanese Friendship in the Twenty-first Century may be well-named in a somewhat ironic sense. Insofar as that friendship requires mutual trust, it is unlikely to be realized in this century.

As a postscript to this study, in April 1988 another Japanese cabinet official outraged Beijing by using the occasion of a Yasukuni Shrine ceremony to deny that Japan was the aggressor prior to and during the Pacific war, declaring that Japan had fought to protect itself after the white race had turned Asia into a colony. Okuno Seisuke, director general of the National Land Agency, added insult to injury by declaring it was a "crying shame" that Deng Xiaoping's admonitions should have such repercussions throughout Japan. After three weeks of increasing pressure from China, the two Koreas, and both ruling and opposition figures alike in Japan, Okuno finally resigned, by which time the damage had been done. Prime Minister Takeshita Noboru's failure to take stronger and more immediate action provided an inauspicious start to his handling of Japan's delicate position with East Asian countries, including first and foremost the People's Republic of China.

Thus, the historical heritage of 1894–1945 continued to weigh heavily, casting a shadow over prospects for the 1990s. Contention will coexist with cooperation, leaving the two neighbors separated by more than the proverbial "narrow strip of water." Although this is a qualitative improvement over the earlier half century of recurring conflict, it does not provide a sound basis for Sino-Japanese alignment or alliance. In the final analysis it will be Beijing, not Tokyo, that defines the course of the relationship, although the larger context of East Asian relations—specifically, the relative power and postures of the Soviet Union and the United States—will set the parameters of the relationship.

In sum, as China eyes Japan, what it perceives will determine how it reacts. The interactions of 1982–87 caution against extrapolating from economics alone. Thus, even though Sino-Japanese trade neared balance in 1987–88, as Zhao Ziyang warned, it is the political problems that will carry greater weight over time. The solution to these problems will remain vulnerable to the nationalistic images on both sides that stand in opposition to the pragmatic dictates of practical interests. Whether nationalism or pragmatic intervals will prevail in the relationship may ultimately depend on how the two leaderships balance domestic and international politics. In this regard, although the greater power will remain in Tokyo, the greater uncertainty will lie in Beijing.

Notes

CHAPTER 1

1. Chae-jin Lee, *China and Japan: New Economic Diplomacy* (Stanford: Hoover Institution Press, 1984), 147. Professor Lee's first book on this subject, *Japan Faces China* (Baltimore: Johns Hopkins Press, 1976) stimulated my own interest, which is reflected in the way I emulated his title.

2. Chalmers Johnson, "How China and Japan See Each Other," *Foreign Affairs* 50, no. 4 (July 1972): 711, 717.

3. Lee, *New Economic Diplomacy*, 144.

4. Han-sheng Lin, "A New Look at Chinese Nationalist 'Appeasers,'" in *China and Japan: A Search for Balance Since World War I*, ed. Alvin D. Coox and Hilary Conroy (Santa Barbara: ABC-Clio, 1978), 217–18.

5. Marius B. Jansen, *Japan and China: From War to Peace, 1894–1972* (Chicago: Rand McNally, 1975), 369.

6. Bunzo Hashikawa, "Japanese Perspectives on Asia: From Dissociation to Coprosperity," in *The Chinese and the Japanese: Essays in Political and Cultural Interactions*, ed. Akira Iriye (Princeton: Princeton University Press, 1980), 347.

CHAPTER 2

1. The epigraphs are from the Li Hungzhang memorial, December 10, 1874, as translated in Ssu-yu Teng and John K. Fairbank, *China's Response to the West: A Documentary Survey, 1839–1923* (Cambridge: Harvard University Press, 1979), 119, and Li's conversation with Itō of March 20, 1895, ibid., 126.

2. Liu Huiwu and Liu Xuezhao, eds., *Riben Diguojuyi Qinhua Shilue* [A brief history of Japanese imperialist aggression against China] (Beijing: Huadong Shifan Daxue, 1984), 202.

3. Conversation of September 1898 as translated in Teng and Fairbank, *China's Response*, 180.

4. Marius B. Jansen, *Japan and China: From War to Peace, 1894–1972* (Chicago: Rand McNally, 1975), 137.

5. Ibid., 150.

6. Ibid., 150–51.

7. Ibid., 156.

8. Chou, Jen-hwa, *China and Japan* (Singapore: Chapman Enterprises, 1975), 71.

9. Jansen, *Japan and China*, 157.

10. Ibid., 212.

11. Y. L. Ting, "Nanjing Massacre: A Dark Page in History," *Beijing Review*, September 2, 1985, 15–21.

12. Yoshida Soeya, "Japan's Postwar Economic Diplomacy with China: Three Decades of Non-Governmental Experiences" (Ph.D. diss., University of Michigan, 1987), 57.

CHAPTER 3

1. Wu Jingsheng, "Reassessing The War In China," *Beijing Review*, August 12, 1985, 22.
2. Interview with author, June 19, 1986.
3. Interview with author, June 19, 1986.
4. The editor of *Zhongguo Qingnian Bao*, interview with author, July 1986.
5. *Zhong Ri Guanxishi Lunwenji* [Collected papers on the history of Sino-Japanese relations] (Harbin: Heilongjiang Renmin Zhubanshi, 1984).
6. Wang Jinlin and Zhao Jianmin, "Shilun gudai Zhong Ri zhijian de sanci zhanzheng" [A preliminary discussion on the three wars between China and Japan in ancient times], in *Zhong Ri Guanxishi Lunwenji* (Heilongjiang Renmin Zhubanshi, 1984), 16.
7. Gao Pin, "Quzhe de daolu, kanke de licheng—zhanhou Zhong Ri maoyi sanshi nian" [Twists in the road, bumps in the way—thirty years of postwar Sino-Japanese trade], in *Zhong Ri Guanxishi Lunwenji* (Heilongjiang Renmin Zhubanshi, 1984), 361.
8. Liu Huiwu and Liu Xuezhao, eds., *Riben Diguojuyi Qinhua Shilue* [A brief history of Japanese imperialist aggression against China] (Beijing: Huadong Shifan Daxue, 1984).
9. Ibid., 2.
10. Ibid., 3.
11. Ibid., 205.
12. *Riben Diguozhuyi Duiwai Qinlue Shiliao Xuanbian* [Selected compilation of historical materials on Japanese imperialist foreign aggression], 2nd ed. (Shanghai: compiled by the History Department of Fudan University, 1983).
13. On September 7, the conservative daily *Sankei Shimbun* retracted the charge, acknowledging it had erroneously reported "draft changes" where none had occurred. The story had resulted from a single reporter's mistake that had been repeated by all his colleagues, who failed to check his facts.
14. PRC official, interview with author, August 1985.
15. The weekly timing of developments suggests a planned campaign. For similar patterns on other occasions, see Allen S. Whiting, *The Chinese Calculus of Deterrence* (Ann Arbor: University of Michigan Press, 1975), 212–16.
16. Xinhua in English, July 3, 1985, in United States Foreign Broadcast Information Service, *Daily Report: China* (Washington, D.C.: Government Printing Office) (hereafter referred to as FBIS), July 5, 1985, D1.
17. Xinhua in English, May 11, 1985, in FBIS, May 13, 1985, D2.
18. The museum's architecture is quietly impressive as is the entire display. The texts accompanying the visual exhibits are not polemical or hortatory, allowing the materials shown to speak for themselves. Photographs of visitors include Japanese friendship delegations. Apparently, however, no high officials from Tokyo had been there as of August 1986.

19. *Qinhua Rijun Nanjing Datusha Shiliao* [Source materials on the horrible massacre committed by Japanese troops in Nanjing] (Nanjing: Jiangsu Guji Chubanshi, July 1, 1985).

20. *Riben Qinhua Baoxing—Nanjing Datusha* [The Japanese army's outrageous atrocities in their invasion of China—The horrible Nanjing Massacre] (Shanghai: Riben Chubanshi, August 1, 1985).

21. Xinhua in English, September 3, 1985, in FBIS, September 3, 1985, A1–2.

22. This account is based on investigative reporting in *Mainichi*, October 15, 1968. It should be noted that Japanese war criminals were divided into three classes: class–A, those who plotted and waged the war; class–B, those who actually violated the laws and customs of war; and class–C, those who ordered or did not stop crimes against humanity. See Philip R. Piccigallo, *The Japanese on Trial* (Austin: University of Texas, 1979), xiv, 32–33.

23. Xinhua in English, September 19, 1985, in FBIS, September 20, 1985, D1.

24. *Zhongguo Xinwen She*, August 13, 1985, in FBIS, August 14, 1985, D1.

25. *Jingji Ribao*, August 1, 1985, in FBIS, August 14, 1985, G1.

26. My interviews with academic and media specialists subsequently acknowledged this linkage.

27. *Far Eastern Economic Review*, April 10, 1986, 22–23.

28. Japanese official, interview with author, June 19, 1986.

29. Ibid.

30. Rong Sheng, "What Is the Japanese 'Textbook Issue' All About?", *Renmin Ribao*, June 22, 1986, in FBIS, June 26, 1986, D3, quoting from the "publisher's statement" of a textbook submitted for approval in 1985.

31. This reconstruction of the textbook's review is based on my interviews in Tokyo, June 1986, and Japanese newspaper accounts.

32. Xinhua in English, June 4, 1986, in FBIS, June 5, 1986, D1.

33. Xinhua in English, June 9, 1986, in FBIS, June 11, 1986, D1; also *Renmin Ribao*, June 10, 1986.

34. Interviews with author, Beijing and Shanghai, June-July 1986.

35. Rong, "Japanese 'Textbook Issue.'"

36. *Japan Times*, June 20, 1986.

37. Japanese official, interview with author, June 19, 1986.

38. Commentator, "Take a Correct View of History, Attain Friendship for Generations to Come," *Renmin Ribao*, July 7, 1986, in FBIS, July 9, 1986, D1–2.

39. Xinhua in English, July 10, 1986, in FBIS, July 11, 1986, D6–7.

40. Xinhua in English, July 16, 1986, in FBIS, July 16, 1986, A2.

41. This was especially evident in Tokyo from firsthand observation. For a detailed comparison of the various versions on selected points, see "Japanese History, New Edition," *Asahi*, July 8, 1986, in *Daily Summary of the Japanese Press* (Tokyo: U.S. Embassy) (hereafter referred to as DSJP), July 16, 1986, 11–12.

42. Kyodo in English, July 28, 1986, in FBIS, July 29, 1986, D1.

43. Kyodo in English, July 30, 1986, in FBIS, July 30, 1986, A1.

44. *Tokyo Shimbun*, April 12, 1986, in DSJP, April 22, 1986, 9.

45. *Sankei Shimbun*, in DSJP, April 29–30, 1986, 1.

46. *Nihon Keizai*, April 14, 1986, in DSJP, April 22, 1986, 11.

47. Kyodo in English, April 22, 1986, in FBIS, April 22, 1986, C1.
48. *Japan Times,* June 20, 1986.
49. Interviews with author, Tokyo, June 18–19, 1986.
50. Xinhua in English, August 14, 1986, in FBIS, August 15, 1986, D1.
51. Kyodo in English, August 15, 1986, in United States Foreign Broadcast Information Service, *Daily Report: Asia and Pacific* (Washington, D.C.: G.P.O.) (hereafter referred to as FBIS *Asia*), August 15, 1986, C3.
52. Xinhua in English, September 6, 1986, in FBIS *Asia,* September 8, 1986, D2.
53. Xinhua in English, August 15, 1986, in FBIS *Asia,* August 18, 1986, D5.
54. *Far Eastern Economic Review,* August 21, 1986.
55. Kyodo in English, August 26, 1986, in FBIS *Asia,* August 27, 1986, C5.
56. Xinhua in English, September 6, 1986, in FBIS *Asia,* September 8, 1986, D2. This dispatch combines quotes with paraphrase and, as received, is at least one translation removed from the original Japanese text. However, what is reported to Chinese audiences pertains more to our inquiry than what Fujio may actually have said.
57. Kyodo in English, September 8, 1986, in FBIS *Asia,* September 8, 1986, C2.
58. Kyodo in English, September 8, 1986, in FBIS *Asia,* September 9, 1986, C3.
59. For instance, the morning after Nakasone's overwhelming reelection victory, a senior specialist in a major research institute said that this was "very bad" because "Nakasone will be much worse now." The possibility that this freed Nakasone from right-wing pressures on such matters as visiting the Yasukuni Shrine did not enter his discussion.
60. Fujio had belonged to the Seirankai, a Young Turk LDP group formed in 1973, which attacked the government from a right-wing position throughout the 1970s. I learned that Fujio belonged to the Abe faction in my interviews in Tokyo, October 16–17, 1986; see also *Far Eastern Economic Review,* August 21, 1986, 26.
61. Wen Jierao, "Yingpan 'Dongjing Shenpan' Ji Qita" [The film "Tokyo Trial" and others], *Riben Wenti,* 3 (1986): 48–53. This journal is published by the Institute of Japanese Studies in the Chinese Academy of Social Science.
62. Visit of July 21, 1986. The museum is more than a thirty-minute drive from Harbin and occupies a deserted school house. An unkempt briefer excused his appearance and that of the museum, explaining it was "closed for repairs," but claimed that forty thousand Chinese had visited it in 1985, 40 percent of whom were from Heilongjiang province. In addition, five hundred foreigners had come of whom 85 percent were Japanese. Unlike the Nanjing exhibition, there were no gruesome photos and only one gruesome magazine-type illustration. A simple two-page pamphlet explained the laboratory's history.

CHAPTER 4

1. For a careful examination of this period in the larger context of Chinese politics in the preceding fifty years, see Andrew Nathan, *Chinese Democracy* (New York: Columbia University Press, 1985).

2. This account is drawn from the *New York Times*, September 19, 1985, and Agence France Press (hereafter AFP) Hong Kong in English, same date, in FBIS, same date, D1. It is supplemented here and elsewhere with my interviews in Beijing during June and July 1986, especially with John Woodruff of the *Baltimore Sun*.

3. Xinhua in English, September 18, 1985, in FBIS, September 19, 1985, D1.

4. AFP Hong Kong in English, September 18, 1985, in FBIS, October 4, 1985, D1.

5. Kyodo in English, November 14, 1985, in FBIS, November 15, 1985, D1; also my interviews with informed sources.

6. The information in this paragraph was gathered in my interviews in Beijing, Harbin, and Wuhan in June-August 1986.

7. Kuo Chin, "'Anti-Japanese' Murder Case in Xian," *Cheng Ming*, November 1, 1985, in FBIS, November 5, 1985, W2.

8. Author's observation in Tokyo at the time.

9. Interview with author, Beijing, October 1986.

10. The most informative contemporary account is Luo Ping, "'Campus Upheaval' That Shocks Zhongnanshi," *Cheng Ming*, November 1, 1985, in FBIS, November 6, 1985, W1–6.

11. Author's interview with British visitor to Beijing University campus, May 18, 1986. The visit was September 17, 1985.

12. Interview with author, Beijing, October 1986.

13. Summarized in *Zhongguo Xinwen She*, October 26, 1985, in FBIS, October 28, 1985, K10–11.

14. Sun Pinghua and Liu Deyou, "Cherish Sino-Japanese Friendly Relations Forged with Such Arduous Effort," *Renmin Ribao*, October 27, 1985, in FBIS, October 29, 1985, D1–14.

15. *New York Times*, October 10, 1985.

16. Kyodo in English, October 10 and 11, 1985, in FBIS, October 11, 1985, D1, D3.

17. Kyodo in English, October 30, 1985, in FBIS, October 31, 1985, C1.

18. Xinhua in English, October 30, 1985, in FBIS, October 31, 1985, D1.

19. Kyodo, November 5, 1985, in FBIS, November 6, 1985, C1.

20. Kyodo in English, November 9, 1985, in FBIS, November 12, 1985, C1.

21. Kyodo in English, November 20, 1985, in FBIS, November 21, 1985, D1.

22. Kyodo in English, October 30, 1985, in FBIS, October 31, 1985, D1.

23. Copy acquired by author, December 1985.

24. *Beijing Review*, December 30, 1985, 15. Diplomatic sources claimed that more than one hundred students were rounded up with twenty-three held for interrogation. *Far Eastern Economic Review*, January 9, 1986.

25. *Cheng Ming*, December 1, 1985, in FBIS, December 13, 1985, W1–3.

26. *New York Times*, December 11, 1985.

27. Xinhua, Domestic Service, December 8, 1985, in FBIS, December 9, 1985, K2–4.

28. *Renmin Ribao*, overseas edition, December 9, 1985, in FBIS, December 9, 1985, K8–10.

29. Interview with author, July 31, 1986.

30. Based on my interviews at Beijing University, 1986.

31. My interviews during 1986 with newspaper and magazine editors elicited near uniform agreement on this point.

32. The material in this section was gathered during July-August 1986.

33. When reminded of Red Guard atrocities during the Cultural Revolution, this young woman reflected and then agreed that "bestiality" is omnipresent in the human animal and is not characteristic of any particular people.

34. My interviews in Japan and China elicited no positive, but many critical, comments concerning this venture.

35. It is impossible to verify the details of an event two years past that was not fully reported in the press at the time. However, the concurrence between Japanese and Chinese on most points is striking. Moreover, it is Chinese memory and belief, accurate or not, that counts politically.

36. *Cheng Ming,* January 1, 1986, in FBIS, January 6, 1986, W3–8.

37. Ibid.

CHAPTER 5

1. Chen Tiansheng, "School for Plucking up One's Courage and Self-confidence," *Zhongguo Qingnian,* no. 1 (1985).

2. Wang Wei, "Japanese Young People's Social Contacts," *Zhongguo Qingnian,* no. 2 (1985).

3. *Shijie Zhishi,* no. 5 (1985): 30.

4. Gao Zengjie, "Education in Japan," *Shijie Zhishi,* no. 9 (1984).

5. *Renmin Ribao,* January 6, 1985, 5.

6. *Renmin Ribao,* January 25, 1985, 7.

7. *Renmin Ribao,* December 13, 1984, 5.

8. Zhang Leizhi, "Beijing Youth Study and Work in Japan," *Zhongguo Qingnian,* no. 2 (1984).

9. Zhang Jin, "Japanese Youth Make People Worry," *Shijie Zhishi,* no. 4 (1985).

10. Feng Shaokui, "Inside and Outside the Campus," *Shijie Zhishi,* no. 5 (1984).

11. Xin Jin, "The Secret of How the Japanese are Growing Taller," *Luxing Jia,* no. 2 (1985).

12. *Renmin Ribao,* December 8, 1984, 7.

13. Liu Qinchun, "The Public Libraries I've Seen in Japan," *Shijie Zhishi,* no. 21 (1983).

14. *Renmin Ribao,* December 8, 1984, 7.

15. "Friends of Our Daily Life" column, *Shijie Zhishi,* no. 3 (1985).

16. *Renmin Ribao,* January 28, 1985, 4.

17. Li Nanyou, "After Reading 'Knowing Japan Through Travel,'" *Shijie Zhishi,* no. 17 (1983): 17.

18. *Renmin Ribao,* February 11, 1985, 6.

19. Dang Deng, "Japanese Psychological Pressure," *Shijie Zhishi,* no. 12 (1986): 16–17.

20. Kong Fanjing, *Riben Jingji Fazhan Zhanlüe* (Beijing: Zhongguo Shihui Kexue Chubanshe, 1983): 169.

21. Feng Shaokui, "Resource Poor Country's Pressure and Vitality," *Xiandaihua,* no. 1 (1985).

22. Wu Baogong, "Japanese Superiority in Competition," *Xiandaihua,* no. 2 (1985).

23. Ma Chengsan, "Japanese Government Provides Information to Enterprises," *Shijie Zhishi*, no. 22 (1984).

24. *Renmin Ribao*, January 12, 1985, 7.

25. *Renmin Ribao*, December 16, 1984, 6.

26. Sun Zhizhong, "Japanese Government's Measures in Encouraging Individual Consumption During the Period of Rapid Economic Development," *Shijie Jingji*, no. 1 (1985).

27. Li Zhong, "Japanese Career Training in the 1980's," *Shijie Zhishi*, no. 4 (1985).

28. Peng Jizhang, "Japan's Information Automation," *Shijie Zhishi*, no. 11 (1984).

29. *Renmin Ribao*, January 14, 1985, 6.

30. *Renmin Ribao*, February 3–5, 1985.

31. Wang Chuanbi, "Japan—A Robot's Kingdom," *Shijie Zhishi*, no. 5 (1985).

32. Li Yuan, "Knowledge Is Strength," *Zhishi Jianshi Lilian*, no. 3 (1985).

33. Kong, *Riben Jingji*, 3.

34. He He et al., *Riben Zhengzhi Gaikuang* (Beijing: Zhongguo Shihui Kexue Chubanshe, 1984). Although the introduction is signed September 1982, the first printing did not occur until August 1, 1984.

35. For a thorough examination of this phenomenon, see David Leigh Shambaugh, *China's America Watchers' Images of the United States, 1972–1986* (Ph.D. diss., University of Michigan, 1988).

CHAPTER 6

1. *Far Eastern Economic Review*, April 24, 1986, 73.

2. Chae-jin Lee, *China and Japan: New Economic Diplomacy* (Stanford: Hoover Institution Press, 1984), 146.

3. Hong N. Kim and Richard K. Nanto, "Emerging Patterns of Sino-Japanese Economic Cooperation," *Journal of Northeast Asian Studies* 4, no. 3 (Fall 1985): 46.

4. Unless otherwise noted, the bulk of this section draws on Lee, *New Economic Diplomacy*; also Yoshihide Soeya, "Japan's Postwar Economic Diplomacy with China: Three Decades of Non-Governmental Experiences" (Ph.D. diss., University of Michigan, 1987).

5. For a succinct summary of this period, see Kim and Nanto, "Emerging Patterns," 29–47.

6. This portion draws on Ryosei Kokubun, "The Politics of Foreign Economic Policy-making in China: The Case of Plant Cancellations with Japan," *The China Quarterly*, no. 105 (March 1986): 19–43.

7. Ibid., 34.

8. This portion is based on "Japan-China Trade in 1985," *China Newsletter*, no. 61 (March-April 1986): 17–24.

9. *Asahi*, June 6, 1986, in *Daily Summary of the Japanese Press* (Tokyo: U.S. Embassy) (hereafter DSJP) June 21–23, 1986.

10. "Japan-China Trade in 1986," *China Newsletter*, no. 67 (March-April 1987), 20.

11. This proved to be one of the more sensitive issues I encountered during my interviews in Japan and while its general contours were confirmed, it was impossible to evaluate its operational impact.

12. "Japan-China Trade in 1986," 20. Trade figures differ considerably, both between Japanese and Chinese data as well as between the PRC Ministry of Foreign Economic Relations and Trade (MOFERT) and the PRC State Statistical Bureau (SSB). These differences stem mainly from different accounting procedures, mainly concerning customs statistics. SSB data are disseminated annually in comprehensive compilations covering the entire economy and therefore are utilized by most Chinese writers. SSB data will be used throughout this study except when it is noted that Japanese data are being utilized.

13. Shigeru Ishikawa, "Sino-Japanese Economic Cooperation," *The China Quarterly*, no. 109 (March 1987): 3, n. 7.

14. Devendra Prakash, "On Special Economic Zones in China," *China Report* (July-September 1986): 349–71.

15. This point in particular is acknowledged by Chinese economists who privately admit that "some imbalance is inevitable for at least five years, perhaps [an imbalance] of one to two billion dollars." Such observations, however, rarely if ever appear in public commentary.

16. Jin Yan, "Remove Obstacles, Achieve a Balance in Sino-Japanese Trade," *Guoji Shangbao*, May 26, 1986, in FBIS, June 13, 1986, D1.

17. Interview with author, July 16, 1986.

18. These frank and informed observations were echoed by other economists, but rarely published in Chinese journals and never in the mass media.

19. Author's interviews with informed Japanese specialists in June 1986.

20. Satoshi Imai, "How the Japanese Market Views Chinese Goods," *China Newsletter*, no. 62 (May-June 1986): 12–14. This is abstracted from a report delivered in Beijing in December 1985 to a joint research committee formed by the Japan External Trade Organization (JETRO) and the PRC State Economic Commission.

21. "Up-And-Coming Chinese Products," *China Newsletter*, no. 62 (May-June 1986): 15. This is written by the China Section, JETRO.

22. Interview with author, August 1986.

23. "Up-And-Coming Chinese Products."

24. Imai, "Japanese Market Views Chinese Goods," offers a detailed exposition of this point.

25. Author's interviews in July-August 1986.

26. The candor and credibility of these interviews were enhanced by the fact that they included China specialists in some of the biggest trading companies in Tokyo. All questions were answered in considerable detail over many hours of discussion, both in groups and in individual conversations.

27. The Hainan operation became a national scandal when it was discovered that it involved more than 100,000 vehicles that were sold illegally at high markups.

28. Private interviews with author, July-August 1986.

29. Kyodo in English, February 27, 1987, in FBIS *Asia*, February 27, 1987, C2.

30. "China's Sweeter," *The Economist*, October 15, 1986.

31. Interview with author, June 1986.

32. "Toward Stable Growth in Sino-Japanese Trade: Shifting the Content of Chinese Exports to Japan," *China Newsletter*, no. 62 (May-June,

1986): 16–17. This article summarized three papers presented in Tokyo in March 1986 by the previously mentioned joint research committee. The three papers were authored by Ma Chengsan, assistant director, Japan Research Section, Research Institute of International Trade, MOFERT, Guo Li, assistant director, Japan Section, Second Bureau, MOFERT, and Yu Hui, assistant director, Electronics and Machinery Export Office, State Council.

33. Ibid.

34. "Japan-China Trade in 1986," 20.

35. Although this was not reported in the Chinese media, it was confirmed by participants on both sides in private interviews.

36. "Toward Stable Growth in Sino-Japanese Trade," 16–17.

37. Takashi Uehara, "Changes in China's Policy Regarding the Introduction of Foreign Capital," *China Newsletter*, no. 66 (January-February 1987): 13.

38. *Asian Wall Street Journal*, July 18–19, 1986. *China Daily*, January 24, 1987, in FBIS, January 28, 1987, K15, claimed that $6.3 billion had been contracted in 1985.

39. *China Daily*, January 24, 1987, in FBIS, January 28, 1987, K15.

40. Ibid., 15.

41. For a case study of this phenomenon, see "The Price of Patriotism," *Far Eastern Economic Review*, May 28, 1987, 74.

42. Ma Chengsan, "New Developments in China's Policy of Introducing Foreign Capital," *China Newsletter*, no. 67 (March-April 1987): 4.

43. Ibid.

44. Sun Guanhua, "We Must Attach Importance to the Summing up of Experience Acquired from Joint Ventures—An Investigation of the Fujian-Hitachi Television Company Ltd.," *Jingji Guanli*, no. 3 (1984) in Washington, D.C., Joint Publications Research Service: G.P.O., CEA-84-017, 40–48.

45. Li Lin, "Problems in the Introduction of Foreign Capital," *China Newsletter*, no. 62 (May-June 1986): 3.

46. Author's interview with informed source, June 13, 1986; see also *South China Morning Post*, August 26, 1986, in FBIS, August 27, 1986, 1–2.

47. A similar crisis prompted the American Motors Jeep venture to shut down production at the same time. The attendant publicity abroad, however, prompted sudden Chinese concessions that were sufficient to resume operations amid mutual pledges of confidence. See the *New York Times*, April 11, 1986, and Uehara, "Changes in China's Policy."

48. *Far Eastern Economic Review*, August 14, 1986, 103. The survey was conducted by Professor Nigel Campbell, University of Manchester.

49. Xinhua in English, September 5, 1986, in FBIS, September 8, 1986, D1.

50. *Asian Wall Street Journal*, July 18–19, 1986. This portion draws heavily on this article, but was reinforced by my interviews in Japan, China, and Hong Kong in 1986.

51. For a typical rundown of such problems, see Tomozo Morino, "Running an Office in China—Costs," *China Newsletter*, no. 64 (September-October 1986): 15–16.

52. My interviews in Japan and Hong Kong provided first-hand accounts of these activities, although Japanese apparently are more willing to accommodate them than are Americans.

53. *Asian Wall Street Journal*, June 6–7, 1986, and my interviews in Japan shortly thereafter.

54. Interview with author, June 20, 1986. As mentioned earlier, oil from China's northeast region is heavy, that is, it has a high paraffin content that requires special refining.

55. Both quotations may be found in the *Asian Wall Street Journal*, June 6–7, 1986.

56. For extracts and summary, see *China Newsletter*, no. 66 (January-February 1987): 19–21.

57. Uehara, "Changes in China's Policy," 18.

58. For a case study involving a Sino-American joint venture parts company in Hubei, see ibid., 17.

59. Richard Conroy, "China's Technology Import Policy" (Contemporary China Centre, Research School of Pacific Studies, Australian National University, August 1984).

60. Kim Woodard, "Technology Transfer and China's Energy Industries," in *Energy Technology Transfer to China* (Office of Technology Assessment, Washington, D.C.: G.P.O. September 1985).

61. After the Sino-Soviet split gradually gave way to detente in the mid-1980s, Chinese media acknowledged that without Moscow's help the PRC atomic and hydrogen weapons programs could not have advanced so rapidly; similar credit was given to Soviet assistance in the aircraft industry.

62. Kim and Nanto, "Emerging Patterns," 34. All of the data in this paragraph come from this source.

63. Masaki Yabuuchi, "Technology Transfer and Technological Reform of Existing Enterprises in China," *China Newsletter*, no. 64 (September-October, 1986): 7–10. Unless otherwise noted, the following paragraphs draw on this article.

64. This was uniformly expressed during my interviews in June-August 1986, except by economic specialists and persons directly associated with Japanese technology transfer.

65. I am indebted to Martha Caldwell Harris, United States Office of Technology Assessment, for much of the information in this section.

66. Ibid. The following views emerged in a joint conference held in June 1986.

67. Information from interview with author, October 1986.

68. Author's interview with an informed source, July 1985.

69. *Japan Economic Journal*, April 12, 1986.

70. Ibid., March 22, 1986.

71. Xinhua in English, August 2, 1986, in FBIS, August 5, 1986, D2. The joint venture between the Xian Electric Cable Factory and Furukawa Electric Company, Ltd. expected to produce 20,000 kilometers of optical fiber and 2,400 kilometers of optical cable annually.

72. Author's interviews with American embassy officials and specialists in Washington and also Japanese specialists, June-October 1986.

73. *New York Times*, March 30, 1987.

74. Chao Yang, "An Active Move," *Renmin Ribao*, October 18, 1987, in FBIS, October 26, 1987, 2.

75. Zhao Yang, "Bitter Fruit," *Renmin Ribao*, November 21, 1987, in FBIS, November 27, 1987, 7.

76. Kyodo in English, December 9, 1987, in FBIS, December 9, 1987, 6.

77. Akira Furuhashi, "China's Plastics Industry," ibid., 11–14.

78. Ibid., 12.

79. One exception is the Tianjin Otsuka Pharmaceutical corporation where 2.5 million plastic containers or 40 percent of production is sold in Japan; author's interview with factory manager, July 30, 1986.

80. Masaki Yabuuchi, "Japanese Technology Transfer and China's Technological Reform," *China Newsletter*, no. 65 (November-December 1986): 10–12.

81. Takaaki Yokota, "Joint Ventures and Technology Transfer to China— The Realities," *China Newsletter*, no. 71 (November-December 1987): 9–12. The following paragraphs draw mainly on this article.

82. *China Daily*, August 19, 1986, in FBIS, August 19, 1986, A1. The total figure was given by Luo Qing, vice director of the External Finance Department of the Ministry of Finance.

83. Unless otherwise noted, the following section draws largely from Kim and Nanto, "Emerging Patterns."

84. Xinhua in Chinese, February 17, 1987, in FBIS, February 19, 1987, D1–2. This report places the loan at 330.9 billion yen. Various amounts are given in different sources, ranging from $1.33 billion to $1.7 billion, depending on what exchange rate is used.

85. Interview with author, August 18, 1986; the banker had spent fifteen years managing a major foreign bank, speaks Chinese fluently, and has traveled frequently and extensively throughout China.

86. Author's interviews of June-July 1986, including a senior professor at Beijing University and a major exporter in Wuhan, mid-thirties in age.

87. *Asian Wall Street Journal*, June 26, 1986.

88. *Far Eastern Economic Review*, May 10, 1986, 140.

89. Kyodo in English, September 28, 1987, in United States Foreign Broadcast Information Service, *Daily Report: East Asia* (Washington, D.C.: G.P.O.) (hereafter referred to as FBIS *East Asia*), October 2, 1987.

90. Xinhua in English, August 18, 1986, in FBIS, August 19, 1986, D1.

91. *Beijing Review*, January 12, 1987.

92. *Japan Economic Journal*, February 21, 1985, and Xinhua in English, June 15, 1985, in FBIS, June 18, 1985, D3.

93. Liu Yongxiang, "China, Japan Extend Cooperative Ties," *Beijing Review*, March 3, 1986), 16.

94. *Japan Economic Review*, April 15, 1985.

95. *Japan Economic Review*, January 22, 1985.

96. *Japan Economic Review*, August 6, 1985.

97. Professor Shinkichi Eto, interview with author, June 16, 1986.

98. Interview with author, June 20, 1986. The scholar is a leading specialist on China.

99. *Asahi Shimbun*, February 11, 1985; informal translation provided by an American official. The survey was conducted from September 26 to November 20, 1984.

100. Lin Xi, "Stern Challenge, Great Hope—First Installment of Sidelights on the Second Sino-Japanese Economic Seminar," *Renmin Ribao*, November 17, 1986, in FBIS, November 20, 1986, D2–5.

101. Charles Smith, "The Ties That Bind," *Far Eastern Economic Review*, April 24, 1986, 73.

CHAPTER 7

1. David L. Shambaugh, "China's National Security Research Bureaucracy," *The China Quarterly*, no. 110 (June 1987): 276–303. This provides

the fullest account in English of the Chinese organizational structure and activities associated with international relations research. For a well-informed account of the policy process at the highest level circa 1984, see A. Doak Barnett, *The Making of Foreign Policy in China: Structure and Process* (Boulder, Colo.: Westview Press, 1985).

2. Over several hours of intense discussion in mid-June 1986, various analysts spoke at length, with considerable force, and in apparent agreement on such matters as Japanese military and strategic goals, political reliability, economic behavior, and national character.

3. Interview in *Time,* February 5, 1979.

4. Conversation with Nakasone Yasuhiro, leading an LDP delegation to Beijing, April 19, 1980, excerpted in *Asahi Shimbun,* May 16, 1980, and quoted in Jonathan D. Pollack, *The Lessons of Coalition Politics: Sino-American Security Relations* (Santa Monica: The Rand Corporation, R-3133-AF, February 1984), 57. Even though the conversation is reported secondhand and has gone through three translations, its general thrust is credible.

5. Conversation with junior diplomat in Soviet Embassy, Tokyo, May 1975.

6. Joseph Y. S. Cheng, "China's Japan Policy in the 1980s," *International Affairs* (1985): 91–107, citing *Newsweek,* April 2, 1984.

7. Fang Xiong, "Sino-Japanese Relations and Security and Development in Asia," *Riben Wenti,* 2 (1986): 2; also Qian He, "Sino-Japanese Relations and the Security of Asia," *Journal of Northeast Asian Studies* 3, no. 1 (Spring 1984): 76.

8. Joachim Glaubitz, "Japan," in *Chinese Defense Policy,* ed. Gerald Segal and William Tow (Urbana: University of Illinois Press, 1984), 227–32.

9. *Sankei Shimbun,* May 21, 1986, in *Daily Summary of the Japanese Press* (Tokyo: U.S. Embassy) (hereafter DSJP), May 30, 1986.

10. Ibid.

11. Ibid.

12. Kyodo in English, January 12, 1987, in FBIS *Asia,* January 12, 1987, C4.

13. Song Yimin, "A Brief on Japanese Politics—Retrospect and Prospect," *Riben Wenti,* 1 (1986): 12–13.

14. Both he and another high but retired diplomat mistakenly believed that the defense ceiling had been written into the Japanese constitution and the U.S.-Japanese security treaty. Not knowing that it was only a prime ministerial decision of 1975, voluntarily subscribed to by successive prime ministers, their sense of alarm at the prospect that it might be lifted is readily understood.

15. Zhou Bin, "The Key Point Is the 'Break'—A Brief Discussion on Japan's Defense Spending Limits," *Renmin Ribao,* February 11, 1987, in FBIS, February 12, 1987, D1–2.

16. Qian Xueming, "The Trend of Japanese Social and Political Thinking After the Big Election Outcome," *Shijie Jingji Daobao,* July 28, 1986.

17. Chou Chihua, "A Preliminary Exploration of the Japanese Strategy and 'General Security Guarantee,'" *Riben Wenti* 2 (1986): 117–21.

18. Xi Zhihao, "Japan's Defense White Paper Causes Concern," *Jiefangjun Bao,* September 21, 1987, in FBIS, October 1, 1987, 5.

19. Cao Xiaohong, "An Argument That Does Not Hold Water—Commenting on the Theory of 'Having No Choice' in Japan's 'Defense White Paper,'" *Jiefangjun Bao,* September 19, 1987, in FBIS, September 30, 1987, 5.

20. Zhai Zhigang and Guo Yuqian, "We Should Not Overlook the Threat of Limited Nuclear Wars," *Jiefangjun Bao*, September 11, 1987, in FBIS, September 25, 1987, 22.

21. Liu Jiangshui, "The Development of Japan's Foreign Strategy," *Riben Wenti*, 1 (1986): 6–11.

22. The individual, who specializes in Japanese history, refused to consider the article on its merits. This suggests a large political gulf dividing scholars on this subject.

23. The following section draws on verbatim notes covering my discussions with research scholars, editors, journalists, and university faculty. Full anonymity and nonattribution were assured. In addition to group discussions, many additional exchanges occurred in private.

24. Shambaugh, "National Security Research Bureaucracy," discusses these networks, known as relationships or *guanxi;* for a fuller analysis in the broader political context see Lucian Pye, *The Dynamics of Chinese Politics* (Cambridge, Mass.: Oelgeschlager and Gunn and Hain, 1981).

25. This pattern of discrimination against youth and women was broken on rare occasions, always at the initiative of the senior official present and always with rewarding results in terms of thoughtful and informed views. Typically, women remained silent unless questions were directly addressed to them; the younger men patiently awaited their turn after one or two hours of monologue or discourse by older analysts.

26. Zu Jianlong, "The Research Methods of International Relations Need to Be Improved," *Shijie Jingji Daobao*, October 6, 1986, and Yong Qimang, "International Studies and Foreign Policy Making," *Shijie Jingji Daobao*, October 13, 1986. This journal, which was regarded as being on the cutting edge of new thinking and reforms, underwent a wholesale change of editorial staff in January 1987, following the student demonstrations of the previous month, and reportedly came under conservative control.

27. See for instance Kyodo in English, January 22, 1987, in FBIS, January 22, 1987, D1, concerning alleged "arbitrary" decisions in inviting Japanese youth in 1983 and in having Nakasone and his family to Hu's official residence in 1984. A less detailed but parallel criticism was reported in *Ming Pao*, January 26, 1987, in FBIS, January 27, 1987, K5. On May 8, 1987, a Kyodo correspondent was officially expelled for having allegedly divulged "internal secrets to confuse the public and debase China's reputation," specifically including CCP Central Committee documents on Hu's resignation; see Xinhua in English, May 12, 1987, in FBIS, May 13, 1987, D1.

CHAPTER 8

1. Yanagiya's quotation is from *Asahi*, June 8, 1987, in *Daily Summary of the Japanese Press* (Tokyo: U.S. Embassy) (hereafter referred to as DSJP) June 13–15, 1987. Yanagiya was not identified by name until subsequent articles, but his identity was known because his comment was made at an "off the record" press conference in his home. Deng's quotation is from Xinhua in English, June 28, 1987, in FBIS, June 30, 1987. *Renmin Ribao*, June 29, 1987, frontpaged the account. For a parallel but fuller version, see *Asahi*, June 29, 1987, in DSJP, July 7, 1987, "gist" of Deng's remarks at

the Fifth Japan-China Periodic Ministerial Conference, June 28, 1987. Excerpts, including this quote, are in *Beijing Review,* July 6, 1987.

2. See, for instance, editorials in *Sankei Shimbun,* June 30, 1987, and *Tokyo Shimbun,* July 2, 1987, in DSJP, July 9 and July 11–13, 1987.

3. Kyodo in English, January 22, 1987, in FBIS, January 22, 1987, D1. Unless otherwise indicated the following summary is drawn from this account.

4. See *Ming Bao,* January 26, 1987, and January 31, 1987, in FBIS, January 27, 1987, K5 and February 2, 1987, K2; *Cheng Ming,* May 1, 1987, in FBIS, April 30, 1987, K1–2, summarizes a classified document allegedly distributed to the PLA.

5. I was given a similar account by an informed source in Beijing in June 1986, well before Hu's ouster.

6. An overseas Chinese traveling in China at the time heard widespread criticism of television coverage of Hu's reception for Nakasone; interview with author, August 1985.

7. Xinhua in Chinese, November 8, 1986, in FBIS, November 10, 1986, D3–4, reporting Hu Yaobang's speech at the cornerstone laying ceremony.

8. Ibid., reporting Nakasone's speech at the ceremony.

9. Xinhua in English, November 8, 1986, in FBIS, January 10, 1986, B1.

10. Although the ceremony had been planned long in advance, Japanese officials privately expressed relief at the opportunity it provided to repair relations and hoped that it would dampen further controversy; interviews with author, Tokyo, June and October, 1986.

11. See note 7.

12. See note 8.

13. Kyodo in English, November 9, 1986, in FBIS, November 10, 1986.

14. Both remarks are from Xinhua in Chinese, November 8, 1986, in FBIS, November 10, 1986, D7–8.

15. Kyodo in English, November 8, 1986, in FBIS, November 10, 1986, D4–5.

16. Kyodo in English, November 9, 1986, in FBIS, November 10, 1986, D13–14.

17. The first reference is from Beijing Domestic Service, November 9, 1986, and the second from Kyodo in English, November 9, 1986, both in FBIS, November 10, 1986, D10–11.

18. Kyodo in English, November 9, 1986, in FBIS, November 10, 1986, D16.

19. This tendency was conceded by Ambassador Nakae Yosuke in subsequent interviews; see *Mainichi,* June 8, 1987, and *Asahi,* June 6, 1987, in DSJP, June 13–15 and June 16, 1987.

20. Unless otherwise indicated, the following account is from *Liaowang Overseas Edition* (in Chinese), no. 16, April 20, 1986, in FBIS, April 28, 1986, D3.

21. *China Daily,* November 16, 1987, in FBIS, November 17, 1987, 5.

22. Commentator, "What Is the Essence of the Kokaryo Dormitory Case?", *Renmin Ribao,* June 4, 1987, in FBIS, June 10, 1987, 2–4.

23. Kyodo in English, February 26, 1987, in FBIS, February 26, 1987, C1.

24. Kyodo in English, February 26, 1987, in FBIS, February 26, 1987, C2.

25. Xinhua Domestic Service, February 26, 1987, in FBIS, February 27, 1987, D1.

26. Xinhua in English, February 26, 1987, in FBIS, February 27, 1987, D1–2.

27. *Tokyo Shimbun*, April 12, 1986, in DSJP, April 22, 1986, 9.

28. Unless otherwise noted, the following account draws on the *Far Eastern Economic Review*, September 25, 1986.

29. Agence France Press in English, September 9, 1986, in FBIS, September 10, 1986, D6–7.

30. Kyodo in English, October 23, 1986, in FBIS, October 24, 1986, D1.

31. Kyodo in English, April 6, 1987, in FBIS, April 7, 1987, D1–2.

32. *Mainichi Shimbun*, May 13, 1987, called on Beijing to recognize the independence of Japan's judiciary and noted that threats by Deng Xiaoping and accusations by Foreign Ministry Spokesman Ma Yuzhen "might discourage the Japanese people's wish to promote friendship." Summarized by Kyodo in English, May 13, 1987, in FBIS *Asia*, C2.

33. See, for instance, Fu Zhu, "On the Question of Recognition in the Guanghua Dormitory Case," *Renmin Ribao*, March 23, 1987, in FBIS, April 1, 1987, D1–3; Jia Qian, "The Ruling on the Kokaryo Case by Japan's Osaka Higher Court Is Wrong," *Renmin Ribao*, June 16, 1987, in FBIS, June 17, 1987, D1–2; Fu Zhu, "Japanese Court's Recognition of Right to Sue by the So-called 'Republic of China' Is a Serious Violation of International Law," *Renmin Ribao*, July 11, 1987; and Xiao Ohou, "The Question of Determining the Nature of the Domain of the Kokaryo Dormitory," *Renmin Ribao*, July 25, 1987, in FBIS, July 30, 1987, D2–8. See also Tang Tianri, "The True Nature of the Kokario Issue," *Liaowang*, no. 22, June 1, 1987, summarized by Xinhua Hong Kong Service in Chinese, May 30, 1987, in FBIS, June 2, 1987, D2–3.

34. Zhang Huanli, "Creating 'Two Chinas' in Kokario Case," *Beijing Review*, no. 22, June 1, 1987.

35. Kyodo in English, May 11, 1987, in FBIS, May 12, 1987, C1.

36. *Tōkyō Shimbun*, May 16, 1987, in DSJP, May 20, 1987.

37. Xinhua in English, May 6, 1987, in FBIS, May 7, 1987, A1. The following summary is from this dispatch; for more direct quotes less authoritatively transmitted, see Kyodo in English, May 6, 1987, in FBIS, May 7, 1987, D1.

38. Kyodo in English, May 11, 1987, in FBIS *Asia*, May 12, 1987, C1.

39. See note 34.

40. Kyodo in English, May 11, 1987, in FBIS *Asia*, May 12, 1987, C1–2.

41. Kyodo officials claimed that the Chinese demanded to know the source for exclusive stories filed in February concerning CCP documents, apparently associated with Hu's ouster; Kyodo in English, May 12, 1987, in FBIS *Asia*, May 13, 1987, C6. No specific charges were filed when the ouster finally occurred, the Chinese telling Japanese embassy officials to ask the reporter what he had done.

42. *Far Eastern Economic Review*, June 25, 1987.

43. Kyodo in English, May 30, 1987, in FBIS, June 1, 1987, D3–4.

44. *Yomiuri*, June 4, 1987, in DSJP, June 11, 1987.

45. See, for instance, note 42; also *Tōkyō Shimbun*, June 4, 1987, in DSJP, June 11, 1987; and *Asahi Shimbun*, May 31, 1987, in DSJP, June 11, 1987. *Tōkyō Shimbun* headlined its story, "Added Momentum to Japan-China Defense Exchange" while *Yomiuri* said "Chinese Side Shows Enthusiasm."

46. Xinhua in English, May 29, 1987, in FBIS, June 1, 1987, D1.

47. Kyodo in English, May 29, 1987, in FBIS, June 1, 1987, D1–2.

48. Kyodo in English, May 30, 1987, in FBIS, June 1, 1987, D3–4.

49. Commentator, "What Is the Essence of the Kokario Dormitory Case?" *Renmin Ribao*, June 4, 1987, in FBIS, June 10, 1987, D1–3.

50. Unless otherwise indicated, the following section comes from the "gist" of Deng's remarks provided in *Mainichi*, June 5, 1987, in DSJP, June 12, 1987. For a parallel account confirming the general tone of the "gist," but without as much detail, see Kyodo in English, June 4, 1987, in FBIS, June 5, 1987, D1–2. See also *Far Eastern Economic Review*, June 25, 1987, 19.

51. Xinhua Domestic Service in Chinese, June 4, 1987, in FBIS, June 4, 1987, D1–2.

52. See the interviews with Ambassador Nakae in *Mainichi*, June 8, 1987, and *Asahi*, June 8, 1987, in DSJP, June 13–15 and June 16, 1987 respectively. Nakae confirmed that Deng had never raised the reparations as "debt" question before.

53. I am indebted to Gail Bernstein for this information.

54. *Renmin Ribao*, June 7, 1987, in FBIS, June 8, 1987, D1–2.

55. Xinhua in English, June 7, 1987, in FBIS, June 8, 1987, D2–3.

56. Liu Wenyu, "Round-up: A Futile Quibble," Xinhua in English, June 9, 1987, in FBIS, June 11, 1987, D1–2.

57. Kyodo in English, June 7, 1987, in FBIS, June 8, 1987, D3–4.

58. *Asahi*, June 9, 1987, in DSJP, June 16, 1987, gives a full "gist" from which the following section draws; for a shorter but corresponding version, see Kyodo in English, June 8, 1987, in FBIS, June 9, 1987, A1–2.

59. *Mainichi*, June 8, 1987, in DSJP, June 13–15, 1987.

60. *Asahi*, June 8, 1987, in DSJP, June 16, 1987.

61. See note 57 for *Asahi* reference.

62. See note 54.

63. Xinhua in English, June 10, 1987, in FBIS, June 10, 1987, A1–2.

64. *Renmin Ribao*, June 10, 1987, in FBIS, June 12, 1987, D2–3.

65. *Sankei Shimbun*, June 17, 1987, in DSJP, July 1, 1987.

66. Xinhua in English, June 15, 1987, in FBIS, June 16, 1987, D1.

67. Kyodo in English, June 15, 1987, in FBIS, June 16, 1987, A2–3.

68. Kyodo in English, June 17, 1987, in FBIS, June 18, 1987, A2. The report as reprinted erroneously dated the meeting June 26–28.

69. Xinhua in English, June 19, 1987, in FBIS, June 22, 1987, D1. The headline read "Japanese Vice Foreign Minister Resigns Over Remarks About Chinese Leader."

70. Kyodo in English, June 25, 1987, in FBIS *East Asia*, June 26, 1987, A1.

71. Xinhua in English, June 26, 1987, in FBIS, June 29, 1987, D7.

72. Kyodo in English, June 16, 1987, in FBIS, June 26, 1987, A2; see also note 70.

73. Xinhua in English, July 16, 1987, in FBIS, July 17, 1987, D2.

74. *Renmin Ribao*, September 20, 1987.

75. Kyodo in English, July 24, 1987, in FBIS, July 27, 1987, D3.

76. *Zhongguo Xinwen She*, September 2, 1987, in FBIS, September 2, 1987, 2.

77. Xinhua in English, December 12, 1987, in FBIS, December 14, 1987, 7.

78. *Far Eastern Economic Review*, July 9, 1987.

79. Ibid. A "gist" of Deng's June 28 remarks appeared in *Asahi,* June 19, 1987, in DSJP, July 7, 1987, and is the basis for the following section. According to this "gist," Deng said, "I was called 'a man above the clouds.' It seems to mean an aged person suffering from senile dementia. One-third of *lao hutu* [old muddlehead] (which is the Chinese equivalent to this expression) is correct. That is the 'old' part. It is not that there is no criticism against me. There are people both within and outside the country who criticize me. There is no perfect person. However, 'hutu' does not apply to me now, although it may be applicable three or five years from now." No Chinese version of these remarks was published, although other portions were paraphrased or quoted directly by Xinhua.

80. Xinhua in English, June 27, 1987, in FBIS, June 30, 1987, D3–4; Kyodo in English, June 27, 1987, in FBIS, June 29, 1987, D3–4.

81. Xinhua in English, June 27, 1987, in FBIS, June 30, 1987, D1–3.

82. *Far Eastern Economic Review,* July 9, 1987, 12.

83. Xinhua Domestic Service in Chinese, June 27, 1987, in FBIS, June 30, 1987, D4–5.

84. *Tōkyō Shimbun* noted the "strong tone" of the conference exchanges and compared it with the "cooler" handling of issues in 1986. It speculated that the change resulted from Hu's ouster and called on the "two countries to understand differences;" editorial of July 2, 1987, in DSJP, July 11–13, 1987. The more conservative *Sankei Shimbun* rephrased its earlier editorial of June 17 when it stated, "It is difficult for us to understand where the true intention of Deng lies. At least we want the Chinese side to use care, so that this kind of thing will not be repeated in the future, for the healthy development of Japanese-Chinese relations." See DSJP, July 1, 1987. On June 30, *Sankei* said, "We request the Chinese side to understand and respect the differences between its social system and Japan's." See DSJP, July 9, 1987.

85. Kyodo in English, June 29, 1987, in FBIS *East Asia,* June 29, 1987, A4–5.

86. On July 7, Nakasone said the government would express its one-China recognition policy to the court if so requested, but later that day a senior official said no such request was likely; Kyodo in English, July 8, 1987, in FBIS *East Asia,* July 8, 1987, 4. Nakasone restated his position for a Diet committee on July 16, see Kyodo in English, July 16, 1987, in FBIS *East Asia,* July 17, 1987, A2–3.

87. Beijing Domestic Service, July 29, 1987, in FBIS, July 30, 1987, D1.

88. Kyodo in English, July 1, 1987, citing the Hong Kong magazine *Cheng Ming,* FBIS, July 2, 1987, D1.

89. Ibid., citing the Hong Kong magazine *The Nineties.*

90. *Jiefangjun Bao,* July 7, 1987, in FBIS, July 15, 1987, D1–3.

91. *Renmin Ribao,* July 7, 1987, in FBIS, July 8, 1987, D1–3.

92. FBIS translates *yi li* as "stand like a giant." This is the initial equivalent in *The Pinyin Chinese-English Dictionary* (Hong Kong: Commercial Press, 1981) with the Monument to the People's Heroes in Tiananmen Square cited as an example of the usage. I have chosen the second equivalent offered because the connotation of "giant" is so much more far-reaching in its international implications, particularly for Sino-Japanese relations. It would be interesting however, to know the writer's intent as well as the average reader's interpretation.

93. Xinhua Domestic Service, July 6, 1987, in FBIS, July 8, 1987, D3–5.

94. *Beijing Review,* July 13, 1987. No explanation was offered for the delay in completion.

95. Agence France Press, July 2, 1987, in FBIS, July 2, 1987, D3, quotes Beijing Vice Mayor Chen Haosu: "Some Japanese friends in Beijing will attend the ceremony of July 7th but no one has been invited from the Japanese Embassy."

96. *Washington Times,* July 21, 1987.

97. *Renmin Ribao,* July 4, 1987, in FBIS, July 8, 1987, D8–10.

98. Xinhua in English, July 3, 1987, in FBIS, July 8, 1987, D10.

99. *Renmin Ribao,* July 30, 1987, 6, report by Wang Dajun from Tokyo, July 29, 1987.

100. *Renmin Ribao,* July 13, 1987, report by Wang Dajun from Tokyo, July 11, 1987.

101. *Renmin Ribao,* July 10, 1987, 6.

102. *China Daily,* July 6, 1987, in FBIS, July 8, 1987, D11.

103. He Fang, "Remember the Lessons from History, Develop Sino-Japanese Friendship: Commemorating the 50th Anniversary of the Luguoqiao Incident," *Renmin Ribao,* July 6, 1987, in FBIS, July 16, 1987, D1–6; the piece originally appeared in *Shijie Zhishi.*

104. Xinhua in English, July 7, 1987, in FBIS, July 9, 1987, D3–4.

105. Kyodo in English, July 6, 1987, in FBIS, July 9, 1987, D4.

106. *Renmin Ribao,* overseas edition, July 8, 1987, in FBIS, July 21, 1987, D1–9; also *Renmin Ribao,* domestic edition, July 8, 1987. A nearly identical version appeared in *Beijing Review,* July 20, 1987, in which "the author made revisions during the translation."

107. There it was relegated to an extended footnote, which included the parenthetical observation, "Japan, like the United States, did not really take part in the war."

108. The *Beijing Review* version truncated the Confucius quote, "Now my way is to hear their words, and look at their conduct," followed by, "We await the Japanese government's next move."

109. Ibid., 22. This was not the first time that this journal carried a tougher line than what appeared in domestic media. In a special interview with the journal, Hu Sheng, president of the China Academy of Social Science, gave the Nanjing Massacre toll as "400,000–500,000," a figure not found in any other source. He also claimed that "300 people were found dead every day in Beiping (Beijing) in 1943" from unspecified causes; see "Past Experience—Guide for the Future," *Beijing Review,* July 6, 1987.

110. Chao Yang, "Trends Worth Vigilance," *Renmin Ribao,* July 18, 1987, in FBIS, July 27, 1987, D1–2. According to a Hong Kong account, the flag was pulled down and trampled, see *Ching Pao,* August 10, 1987, in FBIS, August 10, 1987, D1.

111. *Renmin Ribao,* August 16, 1987, report by Yao Li from Tokyo, August 15, 1987, 6.

112. Hong Kong *Zhongguo Xinwen She,* August 17, 1987, in FBIS, August 18, 1987, D1.

113. *Renmin Ribao,* September 21, 1987, 6.

114. *Renmin Ribao,* September 29, 1987, report by Sun Dongmin from Tokyo, September 18, 1987, 6.

115. Kyodo in English, December 3, 1987, in FBIS, December 3, 1987, 3.

116. Direct quote from Xinhua in English, December 3, 1987, ibid.

117. *Renmin Ribao*, December 1, 1987, 1.

118. Kyodo in English, December 2, 1987, in FBIS, December 2, 1987, 6–7.

CHAPTER 9

1. Zhao Ziyang, speech to joint meeting of Japanese and Chinese cabinet officials, Xinhua Domestic Service, June 27, 1987, in FBIS, June 30, 1987, D4–5.

2. *Asahi*, June 9, 1987, in *Daily Summary of the Japanese Press* (Tokyo: U.S. Embassy) (hereafter referred to as DSJP), June 16, 1987.

3. *Mainichi*, June 5, 1987, in DSJP, June 12, 1987.

4. I am indebted to David Shambaugh on this point, which he has researched over several years for a doctoral dissertation at the University of Michigan.

5. Liu Jiangshui, "The Development of Japan's Foreign Strategy," *Riben Wenti* 1 (1986): 6–11.

6. I am indebted to Juyen Teng for this point.

7. He Fang, "Remember the Lessons from History, Develop Sino-Japanese Friendship: Commemorating the 50th Anniversary of the Luguoqiao Incident," *Renmin Ribao*, July 6, 1987, in FBIS, July 16, 1987, D1–6.

8. I am indebted to Samuel Kim for information on this point.

9. It might be objected that no interpreter would dare to challenge an official's remarks. In October 1975, however, the author observed Tang Wenshen correct Deng Xiaoping when Deng addressed a U.S. World Affairs delegation. Deng accepted the factual correction at the time, whatever may have been her private feelings. Tang's subsequent fall from favor resulted from her participation in the anti-Deng demonstrations of January 1976 and not from this incident.

10. See note 7.

11. The author acquired more than two dozen such booklets, all published in the mid-1980s, of which only one depicted an atrocity. My random sampling of bookstores in 1986 found few war-oriented booklets available.

12. The data in this section are from former Foreign Minister Okita Saburō, "China-Japan Relations," address delivered at Cornell University, Ithaca, New York, May 5, 1986.

13. I am indebted to Paul Kreisberg for this observation.

14. *Shijie Jingji Daobao*, July 13, 1987; the sponsor was the Overseas Chinese Students Social Science Association.

15. *Public Opinion Survey on Diplomacy by Prime Minister's Office, March 1987*, Foreign Press Center, Tokyo, Japan, July 1987, S–87–12, 6.

16. *Shijie Jingji Daobao*, June 15, 1987.

Index

DATE DUE			

Whiting   226140